Jeffery P. Dennis

Queering Teen Culture
All-American Boys and Same-Sex Desire in Film and Television

*Pre-publication
REVIEWS,
COMMENTARIES,
EVALUATIONS . . .*

"This is an important book that bravely tackles what may be two key questions in modern mass culture: What is the place of the gay teen? How do we understand the social institutions that continue to marginalize modern conversations of youth same-sex attraction and desire? The strength of this book is its balanced examination of popular media and entertainment, with theoretical and analytical explanations. It draws us closer to understanding the importance of locating and openly recognizing teen homosexuality in America today."

Melanie A. Hulbert, PhD
*Assistant Professor of Sociology,
George Fox University*

"Jeffery P. Dennis has crafted a wonderfully readable book that is an important addition to the growing body of literature on queer desire. *Queering Teen Culture* will forever change how we view the staples of teenage boy imagery in popular culture. From Andy Hardy to Ricky Nelson to Dobie Gillis and beyond, the author's reading of the same-sex erotic subtext in some of the most popular films and television shows forces us to reconsider the presumed heteronormativity of the male teenager—and the male teen idol. The book is a veritable joy for students of popular culture as well as old movie and television buffs. Using a queer lens and a queer gaze, Dennis takes his readers down a teenaged pop culture memory lane, complete with teen heartthrobs, brooding adolescents, and erotic bonds of friendship. *Queering Teen Culture* will be a welcome text for those interested in queer studies, gender studies, and cultural studies."

Ann Marie Nicolosi, PhD
*Associate Professor of Woman's
and Gender Studies/History,
The College of New Jersey*

Queering Teen Culture

*All-American Boys
and Same-Sex Desire
in Film and Television*

HARRINGTON PARK PRESS®
New, recent, and forthcoming titles of related interest

Queering Teen Culture
All-American Boys and Same-Sex Desire in Film and Television

Jeffery P. Dennis

HPP

Harrington Park Press®
An Imprint of The Haworth Press, Inc.
New York • London • Oxford

For more information on this book or to order, visit
http://www.haworthpress.com/store/product.asp?sku=5484

or call 1-800-HAWORTH (800-429-6784) in the United States and Canada
or (607) 722-5857 outside the United States and Canada

or contact orders@HaworthPress.com

Published by

Harrington Park Press®, an imprint of The Haworth Press, Inc., 10 Alice Street, Binghamton, NY 13904-1580.

PUBLISHER'S NOTE
The development, preparation, and publication of this work has been undertaken with great care. However, the Publisher, employees, editors, and agents of The Haworth Press are not responsible for any errors contained herein or for consequences that may ensue from use of materials or information contained in this work. The Haworth Press is committed to the dissemination of ideas and information according to the highest standards of intellectual freedom and the free exchange of ideas. Statements made and opinions expressed in this publication do not necessarily reflect the views of the Publisher, Directors, management, or staff of The Haworth Press, Inc., or an endorsement by them.

Cover design by Jennifer M. Gaska.

Library of Congress Cataloging-in-Publication Data

Dennis, Jeffery P.
     Queering teen culture : all-American boys and same-sex desire in film and television / Jeffery P. Dennis.
          p. cm.
     Includes bibliographical references and index.
     ISBN-13: 978-1-56023-348-0 (hard : alk. paper)
     ISBN-10: 1-56023-348-6 (hard : alk. paper)
     ISBN-13: 978-1-56023-349-7 (soft : alk. paper)
     ISBN-10: 1-56023-349-4 (soft : alk. paper)
     1. Teenage boys in motion pictures. 2. Teenage boys on television. 3. Homosexuality and motion pictures. 4. Homosexuality and television. I. Title.

PN1995.9.Y6D45 2006
791.43'6353—dc22
                                                                                    2005024407

CONTENTS

Preface

To "queer" a culture means to find for evidence of same-sex desire, romantic interactions, or identities in books, movies, television programs, popular songs, and other mass-media texts where, according to the dominant ideology, they do not and cannot exist. Since teenagers are adult in form and features and able to make their own decisions about mass-media consumption, yet under the direct supervision of parents, guardians, teachers, and counselors, they are subject to more heteronormative policing than any other age group. More than adults, and certainly more than children, from morning to night, teenagers are overwhelmed by Top 40 songs, articles in teen magazines, teen-oriented soap operas, sitcoms, and movies, all repeating the same litany: teenage boys are by nature obsessed with girls, and teenage girls are by nature obsessed with boys. Teenagers are defined by their pubescent "discovery" of the other sex, universally and without exception. Adults may occasionally fail to express heterosexual desire, but never a single teenager in the history of the world. To queer teen culture, we must look beyond the litany to determine when adults began to be so insistent about universal teenage desire, and why. Then we can demonstrate how same-sex desire will not be silenced, how it informs the plotlines of the most doggedly boy-meets-girl teen-idol ballad, and waits quietly in the background of the most tenaciously girl- and boy-crazy sitcom characters.

Within a hermeneutic model, meanings emerge from the interplay between the text and the reader. "What the producer/director/author/actor intended" is a meaningless statement; as Foucault tells us, texts establish endless possibilities of signification. Our job is to "imagine the general condition of each text, the conditions of both the space in which it is dispersed and the time in which it unfolds."[1] Unfortunately, many postmodern readings result in a revelation that there is nothing to reveal, that the signifier signifies nothing, or

doi:10.1300/5484_a

conversely, as DiStefano cautions, in an ideological adulteration in which the text is "massaged, or deconstructed, or otherwise manipulated to meet the avowed and explicit interests of the critic."[2] Furthermore, Epstein disputes the applicability of textual criticism altogether, since it devalues "crucial questions of social-structural political organization and historical context."[3] Cultures are not merely an intersubjective web, a series of texts to be interpreted by discursive communities. As Rosemary Hennesey reminds us, the social articulation of such supposedly "indeterminant" binaries as heterosexual/homosexual can have profound and tragic effects on human lives.[4]

To avoid these problems, we must interrogate the producers along with the text, evoking the physicality of Frankie Avalon in the hot Malibu sun, pressed into an exuberant mass with his beach buddies. In other words, we must restore the body to the theory. Turner contends that the social sciences have deliberately excluded the body in order to distance themselves from biological determinism.[5] The self, therefore, became an entity devoid of physicality, a sort of intellectual/social ghost that never felt hunger, thirst, fatigue, or sexual stirrings. We must make the body, with its "sedimented history of sexual hierarchy and sexual erasures,"[6] visible again.

Next, we must identify the ways in which the texts evoke or fail to evoke same-sex desire, especially the same-sex desire that the freshly forged all-American teenager (almost always a boy) was designed specifically to exclude. These include the juvenile delinquent films of Sal Mineo and John Ashley, Ricky Nelson, and Billy Gray in nuclear family sitcoms, the crooning teen idols, the monsters threatening to eat the world, and the beach movies. The very attempt at exclusion often seems to subvert the heteronormativity it was meant to preserve. The gay rights movement made same-sex identities increasingly salient in mainstream culture. The biker-hippies and clean-cut Benjamin Braddocks of the Generation of Love gave way to the 1970s' androgynous, gay-teasing teen idols and a nostalgic backlash to a pre-gay 1950s' world. The 1980s witnessed the rigidly homophobic Brat Pack, and the 1990s a proliferation of teencoms and teensoaps jubilantly celebrating the triumph of boy- and girl-craziness.

This book analyzes the paradoxical correlation between intense heterosexual desire and critiques of heteronormativity in teenagers, mostly boys, as they appear in mass-media texts produced for teenage consumption during the last half of the twentieth century. Texts were presumed to be for teenage consumption if they were discussed in a convenience sample of teen magazines published between 1955 and 1995, or if they included teenage characters as protagonists. Though movies and television programs proved the most accessible and most popular, several other texts were analyzed, including comic books, young-adult novels, popular songs, radio programs, and a limited amount of physical ephemera (e.g., games, toys, costumes). To ensure a correlation between physicality and theory, the research was organized wherever possible around the careers of male performers whose teenage roles made them famous (e.g., Ricky Nelson, Billy Gray, Dwayne Hickman, Frankie Avalon, Tommy Kirk, Arch Hall Jr., Don Sullivan, Pat Boone, Fabian, and James Darren).

Textual analysis does not require a facile division of characters, scenes, situations, or desires into gay/lesbian and heterosexual. Many years ago Derrida told us that the text always means more than it is; it must necessarily include that which it is most precisely designed to eliminate. The reason, as poststructuralists note, is that every image is polysemous, capable of practically limitless meanings. Mass culture producers—the writers, directors, actors, choreographers, set designers, and so on—work together to imbed the image with enough context to delimit it meanings, to "fix the floating chain of signifieds in such a way as to counter the terror of uncertain signs."[7] However, signs are necessarily unfixed, especially in film and television. The consumer of mass culture images must depend upon intertextuality, the "recognition" of elemental bonds, desires, identities, relationships, and social roles derived from other texts in the genre.[8] Thus, Wolfgang Iser defines the text as a network, a "juncture where texts, norms, and values meet and work upon each other."[9] The network itself creates the system of meanings, the weltanschauung.[10]

Thus, Alexander Doty finds discourses of lesbian desire between the female duos on *I Love Lucy* and *Laverne and Shirley,* present not in the script nor even necessarily in the actors' intentions but in the dynamics of the interactions themselves, in "a place beyond the audience's conscious 'real life' definition of their sexual identities and cultural positions."[11] An incongruity in language, style, and the dynamics of homosocial interaction itself may allow for a "queer reading" of a text. Doty argues that it is not about resistance, tweaking, misreading, subcultural appropriation, or textual poaching: queerness is there, is *always there.* It is the very definition of heterosexism to assume that all characters in all texts are heterosexual unless they blatantly self-identify or conform to a narrow range of gender-transgressive character traits. All cultural texts are structurally and constitutionally "queer," expressing "all aspects of non- (anti-, contra-) straight cultural production and reception."[12]

The products of mass culture possess agency, volition, or motives. Sitcoms are suddenly exuding heterosexually desiring young boys deliberately to quell male homosocial panic or present an irreducible template for the production of tomorrow's capitalists. However, as Foucault notes in *The Archaeology of Knowledge,*[13] we can read statements as communicating the larger discursive practices that allowed them to come into being. However, some queer images are evoked only in order to civilize, control, and depower the "homophobic, heterosexual desire for homosexuality."[14] Judith Butler argues, for instance, that heterosexual-in-drag films such as *Victor/Victoria* and *Mrs. Doubtfire* provide "a ritualistic release for a heterosexual economy that must constantly police its own boundaries against the invasion of queerness."[15] Max Weber determined that in order for a system of meaning to legitimate action, it must be external to the system of action.[16] Mass culture must be complicit with other social institutions, education, religion, and the state, to constrain and delegitimate discourses of same-sex desire, restrict them, and especially make them linguistically deprived, lacking a language, and a vocabulary. Infusing teen culture with girl-crazy boys and boy-crazy girls is only one means of trying to eliminate the vocabulary of same-sex desire from conscious thought, and queering the text one means of restoring it.

Author's Note

Since many actors, from Frankie Avalon to Arch Hall to Andrew McCarthy, played the same sort of role over and over, it was often convenient to use the name of the actor rather than the name of the characters he played. I do not imply that any statements made on screen, either pro- or antigay represent the actor's actual sentiments, or that any relationships evidenced reflect his real life. Descriptions of the physical attributes of underage performers reflect only the way they are portrayed to a teenage audience, and are not meant to encourage or condone adult erotic interest in minors.

doi:10.1300/5484_b

ABOUT THE AUTHOR

Jeffery P. Dennis, PhD, is Visiting Assistant Professor of Sociology at Lakeland College in Sheboygan, Wisconsin. His first book, *The Boy Who Loved Robbie Douglas,* analyzed youth culture of the 1960s and 1970s.

Chapter 1

Devil on Wheels:
The Rise of Teen Culture

Maybe it began just after World War I, when William Sylvanus Baxter fell in love with a baby-talking girl next door in the Booth Tarkington bestseller *Seventeen,* and comic strip hipster *Harold Teen* first bought his best girl a Gedunk Sundae at the Sugar Bowl. Maybe it began in 1938, when Andy Hardy asked Dad to lend him $200 for a jalopy to ensure his big-man-on-campus status, and Henry Aldrich first ruined his social life with a voice-cracking "Coming, mother!" But we didn't really notice until after World War II, when the June 1945 issue of *Life* magazine devoted its cover story "the teen-age boy," and Paramount's musical comedy *Junior Prom* (1946) made extra sure we knew the word. The musical group was named "Freddie and the Teenagers," malteds were served at the "The Teenage Canteen," and the cast rolled its eyes every time a square used the outré "kids." Teenagers were a new and different breed, not children, not young adults, not even necessarily adolescents, and they needed their own name, their own vocabulary, their own hangouts, their own culture.

THE ADOLESCENT

Adolescents already existed. There were plenty in every society that requires a gap between physical and social maturity,[1] that is, between the onset of adultlike configurations of hair, muscle, and sex organs and the ability to buy a house, get a job, get married, and be called "sir" or "ma'am."[2] Most scholars follow Ariés[3] in asserting that traditional societies did not recognize such a gap, just a gradually increasing adeptness: boys were trained from birth in the pursuits of their fathers, and girls in the pursuits of their mothers, so they faced

doi:10.1300/5484_01

1

no abrupt driver's test, valedictory speech, or submission of resumes. Often, they never even established their own households. They continued to live in the kraal or the longhouse throughout their lives, so they faced no bank loans or year-leases, or Thanksgiving in the old neighborhood.

Though Hanawalt uncovered a gap between physical and social maturation as early as the European Middle Ages,[4] most scholars believe that it is limited to modernity, where complex knowledge must be acquired outside the home, through apprenticeship or school, and differentiation of labor makes children pursue careers different from those of their parents, and establish new households, sometimes miles away. Thus boys in the eighteenth-century German *hausmärchen* were continually marching off to seek their fortunes, never content to burn charcoal or cut wood like Mom and Dad, and girls waited in towers for princes to sweep them away to new kingdoms east of the sun and west of the moon. Stovkis finds adolescent boys in nineteenth-century Holland, and Haines in fin-de-siècle France, both caught up in a liminal moment between innocence and responsibility, adult in height, breadth, and manner yet not ready to buy houses or take jobs in the steel gray factories.[5,6,7] In the twentieth century, the future wage earners of late capitalism required a great deal of specialized training in Latin, algebra, grammar, and history, so those who did not want to burn charcoal, cut wood, or work in a factory all their lives had to postpone adulthood through the four years of high school. As Weber's iron cage tightened into hierarchies and bureaucracies, they had to go to college, and sometimes graduate or professional school. By the mid-twentieth century, fifteen-year-old boys who appeared adult in size, strength, voice, chest hair, and libido would not be ready to commence social adulthood until the ink was dry on their doctoral dissertation, a decade hence. The result was adolescence, a period that could not be explained as either a late childhood or an early adulthood, with its own distinct rules, hierarchies, commodities, transgressions, and myths.[8]

THE TEENAGER

However, not all adolescents had a culture of their own with distinctive stories and songs, myths and legends, norms and values that made them look and feel separate from both the children on their younger border and the adults on their older. American youth culture arose as early as the 1920s among young adults, in college or newly working, living on their own, with most of the social markers of adulthood passed and thus no obligation to ask Mom and Dad's permission before listening to jazz.[9] The lion's share of adolescents were *teenagers,* defined here as boys and girls 'twixt twelve and twenty still in junior high or high school, living under the care of parents, guardians, or in loco parentis colleges, with most of the social markers of adulthood unpassed.

Teenagers were generally excluded from youth culture, either because Mom and Dad said no or because the sheiks and shebas looked askance at children invading their turf. So they made do with childhood toys, or else appropriated the toys of the adults: Andy Hardy's jalopy was just some adult's roadster on its last wheels, and his dance of choice, "The Big Apple," actually belonged to the collegiate crowd. Even Freddie and the Teenagers in *Junior Prom,* lacked a teen-specific musical repertoire, so, beneath a sign exhorting the audience to "Get Hip!", they sang the spiritual "Crossing Jordan."

A culture designed specifically for teenagers rather than young adults did not arise until after World War II, when the number of real-life teenagers soared, and postwar prosperity meant that more of them could stay in school instead of dropping out at age sixteen to help with household finances. They had tons of free time for doing homework instead of working double shifts, and they had wallets and purses bulging with allowance money. Meanwhile, new venues of mass communication, especially television, the long-playing record, the transistor radio, and the drive-in movie theater, made nationwide and even worldwide transmission of cultural norms faster and more efficient than ever before. So, culture industries began to speak to the teenagers, giving them a name, a group identity, and a lot of things to buy: fashions that would look silly on children or adults, comic books about teenagers instead of adult superheroes and pip-squeak sidekicks, novels with teen protagonists, crooners who were (or who claimed to be) teenagers, and movies and television programs about high schoolers harassed by militant old fogies.

Though more than half of the teenagers were girls, the culture industries tended to portray "typical" teenagers as boys, perhaps because they had more money and power, or perhaps because the gap of adolescence required more of them. Postwar girls were encouraged to take home ec class, write in diaries, wait demurely for telephone calls, and be home in bed by 10:00, while boys were encouraged to select colleges and careers, play on teams, make the telephone calls, and roam wild and free through the countryside. Even the entry into adolescence was well-defined for girls with a vocabulary word, *menarche,* and a Disney documentary, *The Story of Menstruation* (1946), shown in classrooms, and television commercials about mothers and daughters sitting on porch swings discussing "freshness." However, for boys, adultlike physicality came unmarked and hushed, like a thief in the night, with no films, products sold only at porno shops, and no talks on porch swings about their restless, guilt-ridden nights. G. Stanley Hall's seminal *Adolescence* described his life as endless discontent and dread because its most salient characteristic, sexual potency, was an evil thing, a portent of madness, to be denied and restrained.[10] Others described adolescence as a form of dementia praecox. Even in the more enlightened 1960s, Erik Eriksen's *Identity: Youth and Crisis* explained that the counterculture's penchant for sit-ins and burning of draft cards was caused chiefly by the erotic turmoil of the developing self.[11,12]

However, adolescence was also troubling to the adults, primarily men, who wrote the scripts and marketed the songs of the new teenage culture. It was often achingly obvious that the fifteen- or seventeen-year old boys in their target audience had broader shoulders and stronger arms; they were agile and fearless; they prowled. Meanwhile, the adults were sitting at their drawing boards or behind their movie cameras, sagging, with potbellies and aching joints. The teenagers were bursting with life, while the adults were increasingly aware of their own mortality. The teenagers had all the world to decide, while the adults were increasingly trapped in houses and jobs. Men reach their sexual potency at age nineteen, said the myth, a myth that took on the power of common knowledge, so every year after nineteen, every year as an adult, even a young adult, represented decline and decay. The teenage boys in the target audience were no fragmented, ineffectual replicas: they were the real men, and the adults' simulacra. Though publicly adults might deride teenagers for their weird habits, their odd vocabulary, their unsophisticated tastes, and their utter lack of common sense, privately, in dreams, and in the stories and songs they wrote, they heartily desired teenagers, or their lives. Only in the gap, not a child but not yet a man, could a man be really free.

THE HETEROSEXUAL TEENAGER

Before World War II, that "gap" meant chiefly freedom from heterosexual desire. Though the sex phobia of the Victorian era was fading gradually in the wake of progressive sex manuals, Freudian psychoanalysis, and burlesque, the marriage bed was still considered a curse, a constraint of civilization, along with real estate, automobiles, liver pills, and lending libraries.[13] Husbands in comic strips and radio sitcoms hated their wives, longed for the escape of poker or bowling with male friends, and reminisced fondly the wild Tom Sawyer-freedom of their youth. Whatever adolescent boys were doing in real life (and in the Flapper era they were probably doing quite a lot), in the mass media targeted at adults or children, they lived in a homoromantic Eden, ignoring girls to form intimate, sensual bonds with one another.

Between 1935 and 1945, Frankie Darro played "woman-hating" adolescents some fifty times. Leo Gorcey and Huntz Hall led a gang of juvenile delinquents whose hearts of gold had no room for heterosexual romance, and Jack Armstrong (the All-American Boy), Tim Tyler (of *Tim Tyler's Luck*), and Terry (*Terry and the Pirates*) never gazed with longing at girls, either on the radio or in their movie serials. Sometimes a stammering Oogie Pringle or Henry Aldrich might ask a small-town sweater girl to the prom, but only to his peril, his heterosexual interest derided by parents, teachers, and peers alike as a signifier of childishness or effeminacy. Thus, in *Andy Hardy Meets Debutante* (1940), high schooler Andy (Mickey Rooney) must hide his scrapbook of photos of "it"-girl Daphne Fowler beneath a cover with the singularly uninteresting title *Botany,* lest his friends taunt him for being a sissy. But they discover his secret anyway:

POLLY: Of all the ridiculous little boy exhibitions! Collecting pictures of a perfectly awful girl that he's never seen!

BEEZY: [In a childish singsong] Andy's got a crush on Daphne Fowler!

The real, red-blooded, all-American boys had no time for such "ridiculous little boy exhibitions." They were busily fighting Nazis, gangsters, or spies, and if they happened to rescue a girl next door along the way, they would deposit her on her doorstep with a cheery "See ya" and fade out into the sunset with a buddy. In *Chasing Trouble* (1940), Frankie Darro befriends a girl his own age on his flower-delivery route. She needs a job and a boyfriend, so he promises to talk to his boss about hiring her as a receptionist. "And I might even get you a boyfriend!" he adds with a wink. Surely, a modern viewer concludes, Frankie plans to become that boyfriend. But no, in the next scene he is dutifully making a list of prospective *men* for her to date.

During and immediately after World War II, as movies, radio programs, pulp stories, and comic books about teenagers were increasingly sold not to children or adults, but to the teenagers themselves, we see a major change, boys who are not at all interested in girls gradually vanishing in favor of boys who are decidedly girl-crazy. In the spring of 1947, when Darryl Hickman starred in the early juvenile delinquent flick *Devil on Wheels,* audiences must have been shocked: the kid whose soulful eyes, cherubic smile, and nonstop wisecracks bedeviled Mickey Rooney, Jimmy Lydon, Jackie Cooper, almost every teenage actor working in the 1940s, was now a teenager himself. But he was hardly an insecure, voice-cracking bumbler. He strutted about like a runway model in a white T-shirt and tight chinos. He took ample time from the plot (a melodrama about driving Dad's car too fast and accidentally hitting his mother and best friend), to make it clear that he liked girls. *A lot.* And not for humorous effect, like Oogie or Henry Aldrich: he was a super confident heartthrob, experienced at making sweater girls swoon, at going steady and being pinned, at all manner of heterosexual practice. When his young-adult brother (James Cardwell) mentions his crush on a debutante named Suzie, Daryl happily trots out his many years of experience.

MICKY (DARRYL): Suzie's not a bad dish, but I like more meat on mine.

TOM (JAMES): Where do you pick up that kind of talk?

MICKY (DARRYL): Hey, am I a child? I know just what you're going through. I've been through it myself.[14]

Darryl (playing Micky) is not a child, he is a teenager, and he is not bragging: he has indeed "been through it." The viewer has seen him with girls, swaggering, posturing, flirting, not at all fumbling or shy. He necks with his girlfriend on the beach with an exuberance that is discomforting to watch, presaging the Freudian tidal smooch in *From Here to Eternity* (1953). Darryl (Micky) is certainly not a child, or a young adult; he is a teenage boy, being defined before our eyes as heterosexually aware, active, and adept.

But there is another difference. Darryl (Micky), his best buddy Robert Arthur (an innocent-looking twin of the next generation's Ron Howard), and his brother James Cardwell (Tom) spend about half of the movie in swimsuits, flexing and posturing at the country club pool, gleaming in firelight at a party on the beach. Shots of gleaming muscles are not necessary to the plot (in a movie about a "devil on wheels," scenes at a drive-in or in a parked car would make more thematic sense. Nor can we assume that they represent the interests of the cast (both James Cardwell and Robert Arthur came out years later, but in 1947 they were probably unaware that they were gay, and in any event hardly in the position to suggest beefcake shots), or even an attempt to sell more tickets. Since it was presumed that boys made most of the movie selections (girls stayed home until they received a phone call), and that they were all exclusively heterosexual, why emphasize the physicality of the boys in the movie over the girls? Instead, the muscles have a precise ideological function, to separate teenage heterosexual interest from its earlier association with childishness or effeminacy, to present boys who liked girls yet were strong, powerful, and masculine.

The year 1947 was full of retiring youth: Mickey Rooney's last portrayal of Andy Hardy, Johnny Sheffield's last portrayal of the jungle teen "Boy," Frankie Darro's last tough kid, Bobby Jordan leaving the Bowery Boys. They shifted from adolescent melodrama to adult buffoonery. The retiring youth were replaced by basketball star/romeo Johnny Sands wooing Shirley Temple in *The Bachelor and the Bobby-Soxer,* Jimmy Lydon (previously the stammering Henry Aldrich) wooing Elizabeth Taylor in *Life with Father* and kissing her in *Cynthia,* adults beaming their approval at the sight of gang leader Stanley Clements kissing his girlfriend in *Big Town Scandal* (1948). It was very important that the new breed of teenage boys be both heterosexually active and strong, powerful, and masculine, since in real

life teenagers faced a new peril. In *Junior Prom,* the patrons of the
Teen Canteen jokingly order adult alcoholic drinks, and the soda jerk,
Tiny, substitutes the soft-drink equivalent:

BOY: One ricky, please!
TINY: Lime ricky, oughter.
GIRL: Manhattan, free!
BOY: One glass of water.[15]

Frankie Darro, playing the roughneck, wrong-side-of-the-tracks
Roy Donne, orders "a beer" in a deep, gruff voice, and Tiny responds
"With root to boot," that is, root beer, and Warren Mills as wacky
sidekick Lee Watson flashes a limp-wrist gesture and lisps "Champaign frappé!" There is no such drink (a frappé is an ice cream soda);
Lee is inventing something that sounds feminine, to contrast with the
beer and position himself in opposition to strong, powerful, masculine Frankie. Tiny rolls his eyes and serves him a "Tutti-fruit!" to code
that he considers the opposite of strong, powerful, and masculine not
merely feminine, but a *fruit,* that is, gay.

Men with a feminine affect were quite common through the 1940s:
Jack Benny made an extremely successful career out of a limp wrist
and a prissy voice, Edward Everett Horton played dozens of "pan-
sies," and even Judge Hardy, Andy Hardy's father, minced rather than
sauntered. During the first half of the twentieth century, they were not
presumed gay—if they were white and middle class. Only ethnic minorities and immigrants, feared for their presumed clannishness, secrecy, and chaotic "social disorganization," were regularly suspected
of "deviancy," leaving the middle class, and especially middle-class
teenagers, free to luxuriate in same-sex behavior with few penalties.

Pre-WWII Hollywood was home to a thriving gay community. As
long as a very minimal heterosexual facade was maintained, gay people were free to seek each other out at exclusive parties held by the
movie elite, or else cruise Sunset Boulevard bars and nightclubs, and
even form permanent partnerships.[16] One is astonished by the many
casual references to the gay/lesbian subculture in the memoirs of actors who were adolescents before the war. Some are not particularly
enthusiastic: Jackie Cooper recalls being branded a "fag" because of
his friendship with actor Wallace Beery. Frank Coghlan describes
lesbian and transvestite sex shows, and notes that a costar propositioned

him on the set of *Blazing Barriers* in 1937. He paints the encounter as an attempted child molestation, but he was twenty years old at the time.[17] Somewhat more tolerant, Mickey Rooney mentions gay people frequently in his memoirs, and reprints the complete text of a love letter that "Andy Hardy" received from a gay fan in 1940. Even memoirs predating Stonewall mention gay people frequently. Bowery Boy Leo Gorcey includes several positive or neutral references to Hollywood's gay community, including: "most of the sex kings and queens fell in love everyday—the kings fell in love with the kings and the queens fell in love with the queens."[18]

The change began near the beginning of World War II, when yellow journalists and the medical establishment began to associate middle-class gay men with effeminacy, and therefore a threat to the hetero-masculine social order.[19] They were "sex criminals" as unreliable and potentially violent as cocaine fiends, and when they were recruited or enlisted into the war, their cowardice, unreliability, and attempts to seduce straight soldiers would compromise the Allied efforts. In 1942 Philip Wylie published *Generation of Vipers,* a bestseller for the next twenty years that pinned the fate of the free world on America's ability to produce "manly men," as opposed to the weak, girlish (i.e., gay) milksops currently being churned out by clinging mothers and workaholic fathers.[20,21] Perhaps the war intensified the "crisis of masculinity" that defined the Western, capitalist, political-economic systems in terms of sexual identity. That is, masculine/heterosexual in opposition to the feminine/homosexual of the Nazis and then the Communists.[22] Heterosexual desire was validated as normal and natural, "the American way of life," indeed inscribed within the very concept of desire itself, while same-sex desire was marginalized as abnormal, unnatural, infantile, a threat to the American way of life. Queer theorists note that same-sex desire blurs hegemonic polarities of public and private, stranger and kin, individual and the state. So, during political and economic crises it often takes on profound significance as the primary threat to the social order, civilization, and even human existence.[23]

The result of this "threat" was the construction of an American hetero-masculinity defined not through desire for women but through a flight from anything that might suggest a desire for men. Michael Kimmel observes that hegemonic heterosexuality is often reified to demonstrate not heterosexual desire but the lack of homosexual desire; the depiction of an inevitable hormone-drenched "discovery of girls" may erupt in part from a refusal to depict a "discovery of boys," a disavowal of the possibility that the homosocial might evolve into the homoerotic. Hyper-heterosexuality thus may be a negation of unstated homosexuality; absence informs presence, "ignorance and opacity collude or compete with knowledge in mobilizing the flows of energy, desire, goods, meanings, persons."[24]

One postwar consequence was the utter demise of Hollywood's gay community. The facade of heterosexuality became a mandate; all gay actors subsequently pretended to be heterosexual, even to their closest friends, even when everybody "knows."[25] Except for the superstars deemed worthy of exhaustive biographical research, most will stay closeted forever. Unless someone steps forward to say it, there is simply no way to determine if a director, writer, or actor active between 1947 and 1987 was gay. Many married multiple times, or stayed married to one person for thirty years, or carefully adopted a womanizing or man-hungry persona.

When comparing the memoirs of teen stars from the postwar period with those from before, the memoirs mention no gay people, no gay communities, nothing at all.[26] Dwayne Hickman starred in *The Many Loves of Dobie Gillis* (1959-1963) with Sheila James Kuehl, later the first openly lesbian member of the California State Assembly. In his memoirs, he asks himself rhetorically if he "knew" at the time and answers "To be honest, I never thought about it . . . someone's sexual preference was not the topic of conversation that it is today. It's not that we didn't know about gay men or women, it was simply that people kept a lower profile in those days."[27] Boze Hadleigh has published two books of heart-wrenching interviews of celebrities whose careers ended decades ago and need no longer fear homophobic blacklisting. Nevertheless, in the 1980s and 1990s, they send their life partners out of the room, peer over the top of the *Advocate* they're reading, and maintain a stubborn silence.[28]

But the teenage boy, trapped in a liminal space between caught in that moment of freedom between innocence and experience, between a presumably sexless boyhood and a presumably heterosexual adulthood, could not be silent, since no one believed that his desire for girls was innate or constitutional. It must be carefully nurtured from childhood through marriage, lest he fall prey to the innumerable pitfalls that could subtly shift his trajectory away from heterosexual destiny. The all-consuming fear of parents, teachers, almost all adults, as Benshoff notes, was that they might inadvertently instill "homosexuality" in their charges.[29] The fear was so great that child psychologists and pop sociologists dared not use the word (lest seeing it in print enact a subtle perversion), yet parents' magazines and self-help books overbrimmed with advice on how to avoid raising boys who were *that way*.[30] Fathers must be neither especially distant nor especially close, mothers neither cool nor clinging; friendships with girls should not be encouraged, nor should friendships with boys, nor should solitary activities. All things were suspect, all things were required, all things were forbidden. First dates, proms, pinning, and engagements became moments of profound relief, evidence that, at least for now, the boy was "normal," not perverted, not doomed.

The new teen culture addressed the fear of "homosexuality" by producing a new teenage boy: resourceful, industrious, wisecracking yet serious when it counted, cautious yet brave when it counted, smart but not an egghead, handsome but not matinee-idol pretty, sensitive but not a sissy, good to his mother but not doting, obedient to his father but not subservient. He was staunchly patriotic and vaguely Protestant, white, middle class, small town. He was friendly with his male peers, but rejected the intense same-sex bonds that earlier teenagers enjoyed. Most important, he could no longer ignore girls or treat them as sisters; he could no longer postpone heterosexual desire until adulthood. To avoid speculation that his life trajectory might be heading toward "perversion," he must demonstrate longing for girls right now. Jonathan Katz demonstrates how heterosexual practice began to be portrayed as "not only normal, but productive and fun," or as Gore Vidal says in his preface to *The Invention of Heterosexuality,* "the grail, the ultimate in human maturity and happiness."[31] So Darryl Hickman, Robert Arthur, James Cardwell, and the thousands of teenage boys who followed must kiss girls, or date them, or flirt with them, or at least double take as a bombshell (hired to prove them straight) sashayed past, as proof that they were not gay.

Adolescent characters were flashing limp wrists and prissifying their voices throughout the 1940s: a boarding-house boy toy made suggestive double-entendres in *Life Begins for Andy Hardy* (1941), and a femme farmboy bedeviled Nancy Walker with his Eleanor Franklin impression in *Broadway Rhythm* (1944). But the champaign frappé in *Junior Prom* ended the feminine posturing. The postwar teenage boy was loathe to display the slightest hint of femininity, joking or not, and even his masculine traits must be tempered, since exaggerated masculinity was itself a symptom of "homosexuality." Thus, he had to be muscular but not a bodybuilder (bodybuilders were emblematic of same-sex desire until Arnold Schwarzenegger heterosexualized them during the 1980s). As Dutton notes, he must express "the lithe muscularity of the athlete," reifying "the ghost of Donatello rather than Michelangelo."[32] So Darryl Hickman, Robert Arthur, James Cardwell, and the thousands of teenage boys who followed must find an excuse, any excuse, to take their shirts off so they could offer up well-toned biceps, triceps, pecs, and abs as proof that they were strong, powerful, and masculine, therefore, not gay.

However, same-sex desire is always present, even in the most clichéd of boy-meets-girl stories, in the form of buddies who rescue each other from the bad guy, same-sex friendships framed according to the generic rules of romance, whispered words, looks that "don't lie." When teenagers appropriated the cultural texts of children or adults, they found dozens of vaguely gay teenage boys, born out of the very anxiety that one false move by parent, peer, or teacher might turn a straight boy gay. In the cultural texts of their own, they often found the homoromantic Eden intact, a resistance to heteronormativity penned by the very adults who purported to love it, with only a tacked-on kiss in the last scene to "prove" that all teenage boys like girls. For the next fifty years, even when there were no gay teenagers at all in the texts, even when writers, directors, producers, and actors all strove mightly to ensure its silence, same-sex love always had a voice.

Chapter 2

Father Knows Best:
Learning Girl-Craziness on TV

Between 1949 and 1959, movie attendance dropped so precipitously that many commentators predicted the immanent death of Hollywood, but the percentage of American households with television increased from 8 to 83 percent. The reason is obvious: postwar mommies and daddies with two or three baby boomers in diapers had no time for the trek downtown to the Bijou, or money for tickets, so they were staying home to watch TV. At first they saw mostly amateur hours, game shows, and sitcoms about wacky wives (*Burns and Allen, I Married Joan, I Love Lucy*), but then, in the early 1950s, Senator Joseph McCarthy began shifting the Communist Menace from far-off countries with unpronounceable names to subversives operating undercover in our very neighborhoods, teaching our children, writing our books and our television scripts (he even witch-hunted America's favorite redhead, Lucille Ball). Liberals were so terrorized by threats of being labeled communist or homosexual (more or less the same thing) that crotchety war-hero Eisenhower bulldozed the 1952 presidential election, with 442 electoral college votes to progressive Adlai Stevenson's mere 89.

As worries of a communist-homosexual conspiracy infiltrating Everytown peaked in 1952 and 1953, television began to promote a remedy: the nuclear family—Dad, Mom, and Kids living in a split-level ranch-style house in a faceless small town or suburb. Dad, Mom, and Kids, a little empire, sufficient unto themselves, with grandparents, uncles, aunts, and cousins absent or resented intrusions, and friendships forged only casually, with neighbors or co-workers. Dad with an organization-man type job, emblematic of the postwar reorganization of masculinity from production to consumption, a "personality market"[1] that required business meetings and bringing

doi:10.1300/5484_02

clients home for dinner. Mom spearheading neighborhood charity drives and having coffee every morning with Madge next door. Kids playing on teams (if they were boys) or with dolls (if they were girls), learning life lessons in preparation for the day when they would become Dads or Moms in split-level ranch-style houses of their own.

A few variations existed. A small town instead of a suburb, a widowed Dad or Mom, a job as a nightclub performer rather than an organization man, but nothing was allowed to contract the essential benevolence of the Nuclear Family. An intertwining of capitalism, consumption, and heterosexual practice, it provided the only reliable protection against the seething communist-homosexual monster.[2] Furthermore, it was praised as the epitome of human society, infinitely more modern, more evolved, than the extended families of the urban ethnic minorities, the loose, messy friendships of the Beat Generation, and the sinister farming collectives behind the Iron Curtain. Happiness, contentment, and indeed normalcy (in a world obsessed with deviations) depended upon growing up in a nuclear family and establishing a new one in adulthood.[3]

Teenage boys appeared in thirteen of the nuclear family series premiering between 1952 and 1959, and often stole the show, becoming standout stars and icons of teen culture.[4] But they did not fit well into the ideological structure of the nuclear family. They were already adultlike in configuration, so they could not be presumed asexual, like Kids; yet they could not be presumed heterosexual, either. As we have seen, heterosexual desire was not yet modeled as integral to the teenage boy, his "discovery of girls" an inevitable result of puberty; it was fragile and contingent, requiring constant prodding, cajoling, coercion, and encouragement. Yet he must experience that desire in order to become a happy adult, that is, to have a wife and children. Not only his emotional health, his protection against "homosexuality," was at stake. Even unhappy, miserable, homosexual adults needed jobs, but jobs were open only to "family men," that is, men with wives and children, so his economic future, his protection against communism and homosexuality, was also at stake.

In the nuclear family model, Mom and Dad had the responsibility of drawing Junior from childhood latency to heterosexual destiny, but they could make thousands of seemingly minor mistakes. A mother might easily be too clinging, a father too distant, a chore too girlish, a punishment too severe, a word said or left unsaid, and the boy's trajectory would shift, subtly but surely, away from his happy, well-adjusted, prosperous future toward perversion. Thus, nuclear-family television, especially the series that became part of teen culture, constantly evoked the fear that the teenage boy might be turning out "wrong," might be becoming gay.

RICKY NELSON

Bandleader Ozzie Nelson and his wife, singer Harriet Hilliard, began playing themselves on a radio sitcom, *The Adventures of Ozzie and Harriet,* in 1944. At first, their children, David and Ricky, were portrayed by actors, but the real boys took over as soon as they were able to read a script. After the exploratory movie *Here Come the Nelsons* became a minor hit in the spring of 1952, the clan moved to television, where they lasted for fourteen seasons, the longest-lasting fictional family in mass-media history.[5] Though often uncritically presented as staid and predictable, the emblem of Cold War conformity, *Ozzie and Harriet* was actually quite hip, incorporating dream sequences, parodies, and self-referential "in" jokes.[6] Virtually every episode was written and directed by Ozzie, a self-described conservative Republican in an era when even liberal Democrats worried about the "threat of homosexuality." Though nothing was ever said openly—just saying the word could lead to perversion—his scripts and direction frequently evoke the contemporary anxiety that teenagers, however nicely parented, might turn out gay. Fifteen-year-old David began dating girls before the family leapt onto television, so most of the anxiety fell upon Ricky.

Oddly, in the early seasons, Ricky is presented as intensely girl-crazy. As early as *Here Come the Nelsons,* the eleven-year-old "wowed" at the sight of a hot female houseguest descending the stairs, and elaborated "Now that's like the pictures in *Esquire* magazine!"[7] In "The Party" (September 1953, dir. Ozzie Nelson), the thirteen-year-old Ricky receives a letter "from one of my girlfriends" and offers to read it aloud, but advises "it might be a little mushy—don't blame me if you get sick." He is not joking. He really does have girlfriends, and the letter is indeed somewhat mushy. Ozzie, somewhat old-fashioned, thinks that girl-craziness is a symptom of effeminacy, and tries to steer Ricky toward football as a masculinizing remedy. However, next-door neighbor Thorny is ecstatic: "You should be tickled to death that Ricky is so easy in mixed company! [He's] quite the lady killer!"

By the third season, when he was fourteen years old, Ricky had grown from a smart-aleck, girl-crazy preteen into a shy, conflicted teenager with no apparent interest in girls. He could easily appear today on a teensoap as the stereotypic shy, conflicted gay guy. He continued to resist his father's push into football in favor of gender-transgressive music and drama until, in "Ricky, the Drummer" (April 1957), he performed the Fats Domino standard "I'm Walkin'" and demonstrated that he could pull in a teenage audience. Thereafter he sang in most episodes, with or without plot justification, becoming more famous as a teen idol than as a TV actor. However, his performances in character differ considerably from his performances as a teen idol; his teen idol performances are oddly detached, not connecting with anyone in particular, while an audience of both boys and girls gaze at him, love struck.

The teenage Ricky was soft and malleable, his dark eyes and pouting lips delicate, almost pretty, in remarkable contrast to brother David's athletic hardness, and his sexual energy was undirected, variegated, and somewhat disturbing, suggesting a passion that could not fit into the cookie-cutter simplicity of the nuclear family. The actor himself was probably heterosexual. He lost his virginity to a prostitute at the age of fourteen, and he was married to Kristen Harmon for nearly twenty years.[8] But the television character obviously prefers the company of boys. In the sixth season, he keeps a large photograph of a boxing match over his bed, emphasizing beefcake where other male adolescents might hang pictures of girls.

Ricky tags along with David in "little brother" style well into his teens, and often his jokes depend upon an implication of same-sex desire, suggesting an unease in the fraternal relationship and an awareness of homoromantic bonds. For instance, when David shows up unexpectedly at a party, Ricky quips "Did you come to ask me to dance?" When he sees David preening before a mirror, he asks "Did you win a beauty contest?" In "Sea Captain" (October 1959, dir. Ozzie Nelson), David considers taking a job on a merchant ship, and dream sequences chart his family's reaction to his potential absence. Nineteen-year-old Ricky dreams that David is a bejeweled Middle Eastern potentate, fanned by scantily clad harem girls. A giant urn arrives labeled "Happy Birthday," and Ricky pops out! The parallel to a girl jumping out of a birthday cake is obvious, and not counter-manded by the girls suddenly turning their fawning attention to Ricky. He is dreaming of a way to maintain their relationship by be-coming an object of David's erotic interest.[9]

Ricky also has a series of nonfraternal best friends, at first hunky boys next door like Micky Darby and Will Thornberry, but then the portly, comic-relief Wally. As plotlines increasingly pair him with boys, his expression of interest in girls decreases. In the fourth sea-son, the fifteen-year-old Ricky rarely mentions girls at all, even as friends. No episode in the fourth or fifth season and only two in the sixth involve him dating or expressing an interest in girls, and the dat-ing episodes are both setups. In "Who Is Betty" (February 1958), he is importuned by a girl to attend his school's Sadie Hawkins dance, and in "Ricky Is Micky" (May 1958), Harriet arranges the date, like a good 1950's mother concerned about her son's lack of heterosexual interest.

Parental anxiety over Ricky's potential gayness is foregrounded earlier in the sixth season, in "Ozzie's Triple Banana Surprise" (No-vember 1957, dir. Ozzie Nelson). After eating two triple-banana sur-prises (e.g., ice cream sundaes) before bed, Ozzie's indigestion pro-duces a dream of a tropical island, where he is surrounded by flirting, grass-skirted native girls. His heterosexual revel is interrupted when the phone rings: David's car broke down, and he is stranded with his date, Helen, at a distant diner. But just as Ozzie throws on his bath-robe and starts his rescue mission, David walks in. His date is over; he had no car trouble, and he never telephoned.

Ozzie concludes that it must be seventeen-year-old Ricky, not Da-vid, who is stranded with Helen at the distant diner. But why was he unable to recognize his own son's voice? Did he just assume that it was David, because Ricky never dates girls? Confused, he follows the phone call's directions to a nightmarish diner where a sultry blonde waitress claims that she saw no one, knows nothing, and an effemi-nate man in a cape claims that he is Helen's father but knows no Ricky. Ozzie has no choice but to go home. He receives another phone call, Ricky and Helen are stranded in the midst of their date at a distant auto garage. Again he finds a dead end, a surly auto mechanic who saw no one, knows nothing. Ozzie has been drawn into a film noir in which everyone is hiding something and nothing is what it seems, the sexual ambiguity of the man in the cape hinting at a gay demimonde. In a real film noir he might spend months trudging through sinister gin joints and pool halls, searching for his missing son and uncovering clues about his secret life.

But, this is a sitcom, so Ozzie goes home to bed. In the morning, he investigates and discovers that the diner burned down two years ago, and the garage closed at 6:00 p.m., so he could not have visited either. It was all a *Twilight Zone* episode, or a dream. What about Ricky's stalled date with Helen?

OZZIE: Didn't you go out on a date last night?

RICKY: [Hesitates] Well, sorta. . . .

OZZIE: With a girl named Helen?

RICKY: [Hesitates, then decides to confess] I was over at the Darbys' watching television.

Ricky's attempt at evasion seems odd. He knows that Ozzie uses the term *date* to mean "date with a girl," as everyone on the series does, but nevertheless he tries to expand the definition to include non-girl evenings. Obviously he is somewhat ashamed of his "failure" to express heterosexual interest by dating a girl on a Saturday night, like his brother David, but there is a more subtle deception: Ricky admits that he was *at* the Darbys', but does not say whom he was with. Most likely he was not socializing with the middle-aged couple, but with their teenage son Mickey, who appeared several times during the season as his best friend. Why would he hesitate to admit to an evening with a buddy, unless it emphasizes that he prefers Mickey to Helen, "dating" boys to dating girls?

Of course, Ozzie knew that Ricky was at the Darbys' last night. No dutiful 1950's parent would fail to inquire about where his underage son was going. His dream begins with a celebration of his own heterosexual identity only to underscore his anxiety over his failure to adequately ensure Ricky's heterosexual development. Thus, he gives Ricky a female date instead of the buddy-bonding evening with Mickey, and goes through a lot of inconvenient and dangerous travail to "save" him. He still fails, struggling through a world of sexual ambiguity, unable to find Ricky or ensure his heterosexual redemption.

When the eighteen-year-old Ricky goes to college in October 1958, he finally begins to express significant heterosexual interest: ten of the thirty-six episodes in the seventh season, nearly 30 percent, have Ricky trying to impress a girl, stealing a buddy's girl, having his girl stolen by a buddy, in hot water because his girl thinks he's cheating, in hot water because his girl thinks he's serious, and so on, while his parents sit back, grinning in palpable relief. Yet they still are not entirely certain. In "Rick Gets Even" (December 1959, dir. Ozzie Nelson), Harriet announces that she has sent his good gray suit to the cleaners, and in a scene reflective of "Ricky Is Mickey" (a year and a half before), Ricky realizes that she is pressuring him to date a girl.

HARRIET: [Coyly] It will be back in time for the dance. . . .

RICKY: Thanks. [Annoyed] How'd you know I'd have a date?

HARRIET: Oh, I just had confidence in you.

Even in the tenth season, Ozzie and Harriet occasionally express uneasiness about whether Ricky is sufficiently heterosexual. In "Lonesome Parents" (March 1962), Harriet is writing a letter to her mother. When Ricky mentions that he is going bowling with "Terry," she excitedly records that Ricky has a date with a girl. She specifies *with a girl,* though elsewhere in the series "date" almost always means a boy-girl outing, as if to express her relief at this validation of his heterosexual interest. Then Ricky refers to Terry as "he," and a disappointed Harriet corrects herself in the letter: he is *going out with a boy.* Finally, Terry calls and cancels the evening, and Harriet tears up the letter in frustration.

The sequence is mystifying. Teenage boys on TV in the 1950s traveled in packs with other boys, and spent evenings alone only with girls. Sometimes they might spend an evening alone with a male friend, but only a very, very close friend, and only after they had established that they were heterosexual by complaining that they would vastly prefer to be with a girl. Terry is obviously not a close friend, or Harriet would know him, and Ricky has made no complaint. Though the writer (Ozzie) obviously did not intend the evening to be read as a romantic date, the scenario described, with Ricky "asking out" a new acquaintance, who then cancels, certainly has the proper dynamics, and Harriet plays along, treating Terry-the-girl and Terry-the-boy as equivalent "dates" and tearing up the letter when Ricky is rejected. His heterosexual desire is still tentative, an accomplishment to be proud of, a parental dream that might *not* be realized, up until the

October 1963 episode titled "Ricky's Wedding Ring," in which the law student suddenly arrives for the new season a "married man," his entry into a new nuclear family a fait accompli.

BILLY GRAY

Robert Young, veteran of eighty-odd movies and later *Dr. Marcus Welby,* co-produced and starred in a sitcom called *Father Knows Best* in the last days of network radio (1949-1952). It was a show about a father who didn't necessarily know best, his canny wife, and their wisecracking kids. After the 1954 jump to television, *Father* bombed in the ratings, perhaps because CBS stuck it in late-night Sunday dead time, or perhaps because it critiqued rather than promoted the myth of the nuclear family. Jim Anderson had a requisite organization-man job as an insurance agent, but he was rather stupid, his wife Margaret (Jane Wyatt), with an accent out of the New York Social Register, seemed too sophisticated to relish being a small-town hausfrau, and their teenagers, overachieving straight-A student Betty (Elinor Donohue) and shy, conflicted sissy Bud (Billy Gray), were not only wisecracking but actively resistant to their futures as Moms and Dads in staid Springfield.

As a child actor, Billy Gray starred in over thirty movies, working with such big names as Doris Day, Bob Hope, Abbott and Costello, and Gene Autry. It is perhaps no accident that, as he entered his teens in the early 1950s, his characters were frequently upset by or threatened by the insistence that his future depended on girl-craziness. *By the Light of the Silvery Moon* (Warner Brothers, 1953, dir. David Butler) is based on a Booth Tarkington story about a girl-crazy preteen, but director David Butler gave fifteen-year-old Billy's character no girls to ogle, just a shrill protest against his nuclear family future: "I'm never gonna be a father! I hate fathers!" In *The Girl Next Door* (1953), Billy sings "I'd rather have a pal than a gal—anytime!"[10] He does ogle showgirls in *The Seven Little Foys* (1955), but only after he had already played Bud the sissy.

Denis and Denis protest that Bud Anderson "is not a closet gay."[11] However, in the first season, Bud is shy, quiet, frequently called a "sissy," and full of secrets; he spent a lot of time hiding in the basement (or, rather interestingly, in closets). He has no interest in sports (Betty is the avid football fan) and his mother overprotects him, two key 1950's signifiers of gayness. He has a series of best buddies, but no interest in girls: he'd rather have a pal than a gal—anytime. The family responds, not by trying to jump-start his girl-craziness, like Ozzie and Harriet, but by urging Bud to play the game, to acquiesce to his heterosexual destiny in spite of what he may or may not feel.

In the premiere episode, "Bud Takes Up the Dance" (October 1954, dir. James Neilson), Bud locks himself in his room and makes odd noises, and when he realizes that the family is getting suspicious, arranges a secret meeting with a friend named Joe. Before the viewer can wonder what Bud and Joe might be planning that requires a locked door and odd noises, sister Betty sleuths out the truth: Bud is learning how to dance (so Bud and Joe were waltzing around the room). The family is elated, presuming that the sixteen-year-old has "discovered" girls and wants to date them. But the secrecy, the male partner, and even the episode's title play with an explanation that is quite different. Bud may not be studying "dancing," in preparation for heterosexual practice at sock hops, but "the dance," an art form that instantly codes its male performers as gay. When Bud finds out that the family knows his secret—or at least part of it—he is so upset that he hides in the basement (evidently his common practice). Little sister Kathy yells down a taunt of "sissy," but Jim stops her before the insults become more specific. "This is a situation that has to be handled with the utmost diplomacy," he intones, suggesting that Bud may have a "problem" more severe than embarrassment. The episode ends conventionally, with Betty teaching Bud to dance so he can ask a girl for a date. But the question of potential gayness will linger in the air through the first season, along with its solution: play the game.

In "Bud the Snob" (January 1955, dir. William D. Russell), the family learns that Bud never talks to girls at school. Again, the problem could have two possible explanations: Bud may not like girls, or he may like them so much that he gets tongue-tied. His admission during a man-to-man talk with Dad that he "wants to talk to girls real bad" is inconclusive. Does he want to talk to girls because he likes them, or because it is a requirement of 1950's teenage normalcy? The family's solution is to compel the talking to girls, regardless of its motivation. Betty reasons that he may be able to talk to girls on the telephone, but he stammers and squeaks and heads for the closet. "You can't keep running away!" she yells. When a girl comes to the door, Bud emerges from the closet wearing a Sherlock Holmes mask—and now he is relaxed and charming. This is a few years before the metaphor of the closet became commonplace, but it is obvious that Bud can display heterosexual interest only if he hides his true self behind a mask. The family obligingly throws him a costume party.

Bud continues to be a sissy, with no or ambiguous interest in girls, through the first season. In "The Matchmaker" (February 1955, dir. William D. Russell), Margaret tries to get her cousin's boyfriend to propose because, even though he ecstatically describes his new car and fishing trips with the boys, she believes him to be "lonely and miserable." Bud declares that he never intends to marry, arguing that being single does not necessarily mean being lonely or miserable. Jim does not insist that his future depends upon wife, kids, house, and job, all end results of a successful expression of heterosexual desire, but tells him "You haven't got a chance!" Bud is destined to marry, regardless of his interests or intentions. "You see, women have a peculiar attitude toward unattached males. If a man wanders around unmarried, every woman in the world takes it as a personal insult." In the next episode, Bud acts as a gender-bending bridesmaid for his cousin, he can't hold out forever. Sooner or later he must learn to play the game.

At the end of the season, *Father Knows Best* was canceled, but NBC picked it up and moved it to Wednesday nights at 8:30, prime nuclear family viewing time, and made some not-so-subtle changes. It became deadly earnest, without a tongue-in-cheek moment or a hint of resistance: Father really did know best, Mother was happily subservient, and the Kids were aching to grow up and become Moms and Dads of their own. Bud was no longer a sissy, as attested by a new obsession with sports and painstaking attention to his muscles. He wore extremely tight T-shirts, bounded down the stairs shirtless, stripped down to change clothes, got a seminude massage in the locker room, as if obsessed with demonstrating his strength, power, and masculinity. In contrast, Ricky Nelson of *Ozzie and Harriet* and Tony Dow of *Leave It to Beaver* never appeared shirtless on the small screen, except when they were children.

A few glimpses of the potentially gay Bud remain. In "Bud the Wallflower" (February 1956), the eighteen-year-old declares that he does not like girls, and plans a camping trip with his friends to avoid a Sadie Hawkins dance. But his friends drop out one by one, admitting that they prefer dancing with girls to buddy bonding at the lake. When best friend Kippy (Paul Wallace) accepts a date right in front of him, Bud is heartbroken. Again, the viewer is unsure whether he is upset because of Kippy's rejection, or because no girl has invited him to the dance. In "No Apron Strings" (September 1956), a girl rejects Bud because he is too close to his mother, thus reflecting the common ideological position that "mama's boys" were inappropriate candidates for future Dads. Soon Bud was drawn as indefatigably girl-crazy. In the fourth season, in addition to the usual dates and ogling at pretty young things, he falls in love with an older woman, he takes up the bongo drums in order to impress a girl, and he has the standard sitcom dilemma of dates with two girls on the same night. In "Bud the Romeo" in the fifth season (February 1959), Bud is so effective in wooing girls that he must turn down potential dates, and they get even by going on an "anti-Bud" strike. He becomes both masculine and heterosexually adept. He has arrived.

The revamped *Father Knows Best* prospered for three years on NBC (and returned to CBS for two). It was nominated for eighteen Emmies, (winning six), and it always trounced the competition in the ratings, becoming practically an archetype of the nuclear family. Years later, Billy Gray revealed that he knew it was all a hoax, that they were misleading people into imprisoning themselves and lying to their children, but he could hardly state his concern at the time: he was only a teenager, and an outsider.[12] His relationship with the rest of the cast was cordial, businesslike, and somewhat strained, for reasons that he still doesn't understand or won't talk about. About a year after the show ended, in 1962, he spent three months in jail for possession of marijuana, and no one from the show came to visit him except for the prop man. Today, after a long career in music and motorcycling, Billy Gray barely mentions *Father Knows Best* on his Web site. Instead, he represents his acting career with a photo from *The Day the Earth Stood Still.*[13]

JERRY MATHERS

Fresh from producing *The Private War of Major Benson* (1955), a movie about Charleton Heston as a military school commander in charge of preteen cadets, Joe Connelly and Bob Mosher tried to compete with *Ozzie and Harriet* and *Father Knows Best.* They came up with *Leave It to Beaver* (1957-1963), a nuclear-family series that emphasized the children (junior-high Wally, grade-school Beaver) rather than the parents (Ward and June Cleaver). Junior-high Wally would be played by twelve-year-old Tony Dow, new to acting, but an expert swimmer and diver, a jock for the young Beaver to look up to. Nine-year-old Jerry Mathers was hired for the most important role, that of the Beaver. During his audition, he sounded natural, like a real kid, even though he had been working for years for such luminaries as Nicholas Ray and Alfred Hitchcock.

In spite of the laugh track and the jaunty theme song, "The Toy Parade,"[14] *Leave It to Beaver* was serious business. Small-town Mayfield was considerably darker and more threatening than the Springfield of *Father Knows Best* or the Hollywood of *Ozzie and Harriet*. Greed and malice hid behind every smiling face. Everyone was after something, everyone had an angle. Friends, classmates, and co-workers would backstab you in an instant, take credit for your accomplishment, blame you for their mess, goad you into disaster, make time with your girl, dump you for another boy, all the while maintaining a cool civility. The myth of the nuclear family requires such a menacing world, of course, with outside friendships casual, tepid, and suspicious, and the only strong emotional ties between Dad, Mom, and Kids. But the Cleavers had little emotional connection. The Andersons and the Nelsons attended parties and ball games together, but the Cleavers rarely socialized as a group. Bud on *Father Knows Best* was always hanging around with Jim Anderson, chatting with him while he was dressing or puttering around the house, but Wally and Beaver never chatted with their father; they sought out his advice and feared his punishments. Ward always approached them with an undertow of hostility, perhaps anger over dreams deferred by his entrapment in suburbia.

Beaver's popularity among teenagers derived from the character Wally, a fourteen-year-old played by a twelve-year-old when the series began, yet presented from the start as strong, powerful, masculine, and girl-crazy. Tony Dow soon became the darling of the teen magazines, though he responded to the media attention with bewilderment. He never recorded any teen-idol songs, and never appeared shirtless or in a T-shirt once he began to bulk up. Though he is the object of constant swooning teenage-girl infatuations, Wally is absurdly attractive to everyone, boys and girls, men and women. Perhaps

conniving best-buddy Eddie Haskell (Ken Osmond) is the most blatant, just barely hiding his affection behind barbs and put-downs. In
"Bachelor at Large" (November 1962, dir. Hugh Beaumont), he invites Wally to his new apartment with a coyly suggestive, "You could
drop by for dinner, and spend the night." What does he expect them to
do all night? We get a clue as he exits, singing the Rosemary Clooney
number that hit the charts in 1951 in spite of (or perhaps because of)
its suggestive lyrics: "Come on-a my house, my house, I'm-a gonna
give-a you candy." Lest his intentions become too obvious, he omits
the concluding line, which promises "I'm gonna give-a you *everything.*"[15]

Though Wally was girl-crazy from the start, Beaver, as a kid, was
required to *dislike* girls. If male adolescence is a time of intense, single-minded, and unique heterosexual interest precipitated by a pubescent "discovery" of girls, then preteen boys could never "wow" over
hot houseguests like Ricky Nelson did in 1952. They must ignore
girls completely as an undiscovered country. Indeed, they might even
express anti-girl hatred, to make their later transformation into girl-
crazy teenagers more dramatic: "Go see a girl? I'd rather smell a
skunk!" Beaver snarls. "If I had a choice between a three pound bass
and a girl, I'd take a three pound bass!"[16] More often Beaver is perfectly willing to have girls as friends; he merely disdains heterosexual
practice. In "Her Idol" (November 1958, dir. Norman Tokar), for instance, the ten-year-old happily befriends Linda Dennison (Patty
Turner), until his classmates ridicule him with the anti-heterosexual
taunt "She's your girl!" To avoid the stigma of being a preteen heterosexual, he calls her a "smelly ape." The teacher suggests that, though
they need not become mushy, boys and girls should learn to get along,
so they can "grow into the kind of men and women we want you to
be." That is, they need not be heterosexual now, but they should
practice for their heterosexual future.

To further emphasize the difference between asexual child and
girl-crazy teenager, Beaver develops strong same-sex bonds. Like
Ricky and David Nelson, Beaver's relationship with Wally fits more
of the generic cues of romance than brotherly affection, perhaps more
obviously so because they are not really brothers (in real life). The
two enjoy an easy, almost jubilant physicality, a closeness not ex-
plainable by the conventions of the stage. In July 1959 *TV Star Parade* ran a feature titled "Who Needs Girls? The Beaver and TV

Brother Enjoy Carefree Bachelor Life," coding them in precisely the same terms used to hide other "confirmed bachelors" of the period. Jerry Mathers recalls Tony Dow in 1959 as "an incredibly good-looking 14-year old boy," casting his affection in terms that fall just short of the homoerotic.[17]

The anxiety for Ward, June, and Wally is that Beaver might not adequately "discover" girls, abandoning childhood same-sex bonds for girl-crazy adolescence. Gender-transgressive activities are the most troubling, coding Beaver as feminine and therefore unqualified to make the adolescent "discovery" of the feminine. In "Party Invitation" (January 1958), Beaver happily accepts a party invitation, but his parents are shocked to discover that he will be the only boy there. In "School Play" (December 1958, dir. Norman Tokar), Ward (Hugh Beaumont) is upset to discover that Beaver will be playing the part of a bird, a role somewhat too femme for his tastes. At least he could have been cast as a macho bird like a bald eagle, but no, he's a prancing yellow canary! June (Barbara Billingsley) cautions him to be kind—Beaver is excited about the role—but Ward worries about what his co-workers will think, raising a son who is a canary (after all, it rhymes with *fairy*). They all go to the performance anyway, and June gushes "He was so sweet, it almost makes up for not having a girl!" before they discover that Beaver traded places with another boy just before the curtain went up. He was really playing an undeniably masculine mushroom.

In "Beaver's Doll Buggy" (June 1961, dir. Anton Leader), Beaver needs some wheels for his soapbox car, and a girl donates her old doll buggy. As he wheels the buggy down the street, everyone assumes that the eleven-year-old is playing with dolls. His peers laugh, tease, yell, and pick fights, and an adult recoils in homophobic panic: "The new generation has gone sissy on us!" Eddie Haskell is too stunned to wisecrack, and Wally solemnly advises that he discard the buggy in order to make it home alive. "Guys always pick on someone who's different," he says, quietly considering the possibility that his little brother might be gay.

Though Jerry Mathers is fourteen years old when the series ends and physically adolescent, grown taller, his body noticeably harder and tighter, his voice noticeably deeper than in the season before, Beaver never "discovers" girls. A few episodes in the spring and fall of 1962 have him walking girls home or going out on dates with them, but attached to plotlines that only serve to reestablish the emotional bond between Beaver and Wally. In "Brother versus Brother" (May 1962), for instance, Beaver is attracted to Mary (Mimi Gibson) who in turn has a crush on the "high school man" Wally. Beaver is furious, accusing his brother of "stealing his girl"; but the two quickly reconcile. When Mary sends Beaver a note in class offering to return to him, he gleefully responds "Drop dead!" The episode ends with girls rejected, and the brothers lying casually against each other on Wally's bed.

In spite of the dating and walking-home episodes, Ward and June spend the last season increasingly worried about Beaver's lack of interest in girls, and Beaver became increasingly adept at feigning interest. In "Beaver's Autobiography" (December 1962, dir. David Butler), June wonders why he is so late at the library, and Ward avers that he must be there to meet girls. He even stakes their relationship on it, jokingly but with his usual undertone of hostility: "If [Beaver] hasn't discovered the romantic advantages of studying in the library by this time, he's *not his father's son!*" But Beaver was not trying to meet girls—he finds girls "creepy." He does submit to the attention of love-stricken Betsy (Annette Gorman), but only so she will write his class assignment for him. So Beaver is obviously *not* his father's son. Who is he?

In "The Mustache" (January 1963, dir. Hugh Beaumont), June is perplexed because Beaver and his buddy Gilbert (Stephen Talbot) failed to go to the high school to watch Wally's basketball practice, their usual practice (she assumes without question that they would be interested in ogling Wally and other high school hunks in revealing uniforms). Beaver says that they were planning to go, but they changed their mind when they realized that a lot of girls would be watching, too.

Alarmed, June asks: "You mean you and Gilbert don't like girls?"

Realizing that to not like girls at his age would be a transgression, Beaver quickly backtracks: they like girls fine, he explains, but not combined with sports.

"Don Juan Beaver" (May 1963) is a masterpiece of feigned girl-craziness. With family and friends all agog over the upcoming Sadie Hawkins dance, Beaver claims enthusiastic interest, and accepts invitations from two girls. When they discover his two-timing, they dump him, and he's left alone in his room, dateless on the night of the big dance. We see him happily dancing the twist by himself, with music popping from his record player. Then he hears Ward coming to check on him, so he quickly switches off the record player and sits on the bed, looking dejected. Ward invites him downstairs to be with the family, but Beaver refuses, saying that he would rather be alone. Ward leaves, and Beaver jumps up and starts dancing again, grinning broadly. It is a remarkable scene. Why is Beaver so obviously happy, when the most one should expect from a girl-crazy teenager is a brave front, an attempt to have fun in spite of his dating failure? Why does he want Ward to believe that he is miserable? The deception makes no sense unless Beaver has cleverly achieved what he wanted all along: he has met the social mandate to display girl-craziness without having to actually date a girl.

During the last two seasons, the adolescent Beaver was usually paired with Gilbert in a precise parallel to Wally's pairing with a girl: that is, Wally takes a girl to the movies, and Beaver takes Gilbert; Wally is on the telephone with a girl, and Beaver is on the telephone with Gilbert. Some of the scenes between the two are charged with an erotic energy that the actors themselves seem to find uncomfortable; more than once, Gilbert casually rests a hand against Beaver or lies beside him on the bed, and after a moment Beaver moves away. In "Uncle Billy's Visit" (March 1963, dir. David Butler), Gilbert seems to have a specifically physical interest in men. Caught sneaking into the movies, he explains "I guess I wanted to see Tony Curtis real bad." Tony Curtis was one of the premiere pretty-boy heroes whose ambiguous sexuality made early 1960's audiences swoon. The poster outside the theater promotes the explicitly homoerotic *Spartacus*. But more intriguingly, Wally's friendships with other boys are often circumscribed by manipulation and deceit. Gilbert and Beaver seem to genuinely care for each other, establishing the series' only strong emotional bond outside the nuclear family.

In an oddly serious episode, "Beaver on TV" (February 1963), Beaver announces that he has been selected to participate in a panel discussion program, *Teen Forum*, so practically everyone in town tunes in. But no one realizes that the program is taped a week in advance, so he will not be on *today's* episode. When they fail to see him on TV, Beaver's friends angrily reprimand him for lying. Beaver *knows* that he was on the show, and they *know*, just as certainly, that he was not. Doubting his sanity, Beaver runs away. Wally looks for him in his little-kid hangouts, but to no avail. Only Gilbert knows where to look. Then, quietly, even lovingly, he tries to help Beaver make sense of this seemingly impossible situation.[18]

"Beaver Sees America" (June 1963), the last episode except "The Clothing Drive," which is out of sequence, and the retrospective "Family Scrapbook," does give Beaver an oddly gender-transgressive heterosexual interest. He falls under the spell of man-hungry vamp named Mary Margaret (Lori Martin), who femininizes him with her manipulations. For instance, she complements him on his glamorous "perfume" instead of cologne. When she begins working on Gilbert as well, Beaver fears that he will lose her if he goes away for the summer, so he cancels the cross-country bus trip he has been planning. Ward solves the problem by arranging for Gilbert to go on the trip as well. When they discover that Mary Margaret has played them both, they swear off girls, resisting their heterosexual destiny, at least until after they have spent a final idyllic summer together.

DWAYNE HICKMAN

The younger brother of Darryl, Dwayne Hickman started his television career as Chuck, a high school boy who lives with his widowed mother and sleazy photographer uncle in *The Bob Cummings Show* (1955-1959). At first Chuck is interested in hot rods and rock and roll but not girls, somewhat transgressive for a boy with a wolf for an uncle, but he adapts with old-fashioned Yankee capitalism. In "The Wolf Sitter" (December 1955), he starts a service that pairs high school boys with beautiful models, so the boys can get reputations as heterosexually adept, and the models can go out on the town without being constantly hit on.

Nevertheless, Uncle Bob is concerned, and tries to instill in his charge an appreciation of "the important things in life," e.g., girls. Since his job involves drooling over, gaping at, and sometimes photographing swimsuit models, he's something of an expert at girl-craziness, and he has spent many episodes promoting heterosexual activity among gay and gender-transgressive colleagues: his mannish secretary (Alice B. Davis, later the maid on *The Brady Bunch*); a mannish female buddy (gay actress Nancy Kulp, later Miss Hathaway on *The Beverly Hillbillies*); and a "girl-shy" male buddy (King Donovan).

His overenthusiastic attempts to induce girl-mania in Chuck, especially when their bond is avuncular rather than parental, looks uncomfortably like an attempt to displace his own homoerotic attraction. Even the teen magazines seemed to notice, treating the two as a couple. The December 1957 issue of *'Teen* shows Uncle Bob and Chuck slurping on ice cream sundaes, gazing into each other's eyes like an archetypal Mickey Rooney and Judy Garland, while wearing matching, extremely effeminate fur coats (actually raccoon coats: the tagline tells us that "the Roaring 20's Raccoon Rage Returns"). Eventually, Chuck went off to college and returned as an occasional guest star, his girl-craziness still inchoate and tentative, and Uncle Bob settled in for more seasons of ogling.

Meanwhile, humorist Max Shulman hired Dwayne Hickman for the film version of a suburban sex comedy, *Rally Round the Flag Boys*. It bombed at the box office, but when *Bob Cummings* ended, Shulman grabbed up Dwayne and director Rod Amateau for a sitcom adaption of his *The Many Loves of Dobie Gillis*. Dwayne was twenty-five years old, and his Chuck character nearly ready to graduate from college, but he would be playing a sixteen-year-old high school junior. Tuesday Weld, his *Rally* costar, would play his gold-digging love interest Thalia Menninger, future playboy Warren Beatty his spoiled-rich-kid nemesis Milton Armitage, and future Gilligan Bob Denver a rare 1950's sitcom sidekick, the beatnik Maynard G. Krebs.[19]

In the original stories, Dobie's heterosexual interest is acceptable in college, but in high school it causes him to be shunned as a sissy, so the series begins with a confessional. In the first season's introduction, the blond, not unattractive Dobie sits beneath a statue of Rodan's *The Thinker* and defiantly proclaims:

> My name is Dobie Gillis and I like girls. What am I saying? I love girls! Love 'em! Beautiful, gorgeous, soft, round, creamy girls. Now, I'm not a wolf, mind you. No, you see, a wolf wants lots of girls, but me? Well, I just want one. One beautiful, gorgeous, soft, round, creamy girl for my very own.

In a society where many teenage boys like girls, such a proclamation would be unnecessary, but Dobie's world is peculiarly low on straightness. Maynard G. Krebs shrinks away from the word "girl" as timidly as from the word "work," both symbols of the nuclear family, of heterosexual destiny. Bob Denver notes in his memoirs that he had played beatniks before, whereas the writers had no idea what beat-niks were, so he mostly created his own character. Many of the beat-niks of the late 1950s, like their spiritual progenitors, the Beat Gener-ation, were ambisexual or gay, shunning heterosexual practice as a tool of oppression and promoting instead the manly love of com-rades. Bob Denver's watered-down version was simply uninterested in girls, expressing heterosexual interest only a few times, and usu-ally in the first season, when his character was not yet fully formed. In "The Gigolo" (February 1961), Maynard becomes sought after as a date because his lack of heterosexual interest makes him safe. In "Girls Will Be Boys" (February 1962), he falls in love with a masculine-acting girl, and loses interest when a makeover turns her feminine. Scripts sometimes "explain" this lack of interest as shyness, but Den-ver insists that Maynard "isn't afraid of girls; he just wants to pursue his own way of life."[20]

The girls in Dobie's world are no comic-book Betty and Veronica, wild eyed with hetero horniness. Tomboyish Zelda Gilroy (Sheila James Kuehl) expresses an unrequited crush on Dobie with theatrical flourish, but withdraws in horror whenever he pretends to acquiesce; it is not difficult to imagine that she is using the crush to avoid any more realistic heterosexual practice. Other girls accept dates not be-cause they are attracted to boys, but because boys are necessary for an affluent future. In "A Taste of Lobster" (December 1959), Dobie fi-nally meets a girl who is not interested in the size of his wallet—until her sister starts going on fancier dates with a rich boy. In "Taken to the Cleaners" (March 1960, dir. Ralph Francis Murphy), Thalia Menn-inger famously quips: "Even if my father had kidneys of steel, my mother was younger than springtime, my sister was married to a trillionaire and my brother was president of Harvard, I'd still want money!"

Foppish Milton Armitage similarly seems uninterested in girls for their own sake, merely using them as tools to one-up Dobie. They even compete without girls as an impetus in "The Smoke-Filled Room" (December 1959). After the first season, Warren Beatty went on to other projects, and Milton Armitage was replaced by his even more foppish (i.e., gay) cousin Chatsworth (Steve Franken), a mother-obsessed milquetoast who doesn't bother with the pretense of girl chasing. Instead, he openly competes with Maynard for Dobie's af-fection. In "Jangle Bells" (December 1960), he tries to lure Dobie away from Maynard by inviting him to a spectacular Christmas party. In the spring of 1961, high school graduates Dobie and Maynard join the army for an extended story arc, leaving Chatsworth behind,[21] but four episodes later, he enlists, ostensibly so the character can stay in the series, but really because he rather likes Dobie.

Even the intensity of Dobie's attraction to girls is open to dispute. The "I Love Girls!" manifesto was dropped after the first season, and most episodes were about groups of friends rather than heterosexual machinations. Sometimes Dobie is even suspected of being gay. In "The Flying Millicans" (October 1959), Dobie dates a girl (Yvonne Craig) who belongs to a family of trapeze artists. They wander around the house in flimsy togas, discussing the benefits of "the Greek way," a riff on the Edith Hamilton best seller, but also an oblique reference to the legendary homoerotic appetites of the ancient Greeks. To demonstrate their enthusiasm for Dobie, Dad (gay actor Francis X. Bushman) and the hunky brothers mob him and rip his clothes off. But they do not intend a free-form Greek orgy; they are merely fitting Dobie for a toga of his own. Mr. Gillis arrives, mistakes the togas for dresses, and concludes that Dobie has "gone fruity" in a household of drag queens.

Since Mom and Dad are off in the background and Dobie an only child, it can be argued that Dobie Gillis is not a nuclear family series at all, but an early example of a new breed, the "teencom." So, why would they be so extremely lax in promoting girl-craziness? The answer lies in the teenage reaction to the nuclear family ideology. *Ozzie and Harriet, Father Knows Best,* and *Leave It to Beaver* were targeted at parents and children, with teenage interest addressed only by accident, or through a single character. Cultural texts produced specifically for 1950's teenage audiences, such as *Dobie Gillis,* often expressed less anxiety over a possible gay life trajectory than a desire for the homoerotic Eden, with teenage boys forming intense, intimate bonds with one another and ignoring the girl next door.

Chapter 3

Sal Mineo and Friends:
The Juvenile Delinquent Films

Before 1945, the East Side Kids, the Little Tough Guys, Frankie
Darro's tough kids, and Mickey Rooney's boys born to be hung nego-
tiated adolescence on mean streets and tenement flats. Dad was in the
slammer and Mom looked about ninety from bending over laundry
baskets all day. Or, both were dead and Big Sister was working double shifts at the plant to make ends meet. They were loud, exuberant,
young toughs with hearts of gold, getting into mischief rather than
trouble, suspicious of cops and sissies but always eager to help a pal
or sleuth out a mystery. The biggest fear of the adults and the audience was that they would fall prey to the gangsters who offered cars,
zoot suits, and dough in exchange for a few minor "jobs," but all they
needed was a caring newspaper reporter, cop, or priest to tough love
them onto the straight and narrow.

When the nuclear family myth began to dominate the mass media,
poor, urban, Irish-Catholic tough guys vanished. The East Side Kids
transmutated into the post-adolescent Bowery Boys, Frankie Darro
started playing suburban high school hooligans, Mickey Rooney grew
up, and no one could believe that pretty-boy Tony Curtis was really bad
in *City Across the River* (1949), nor the gang in *Bad Boy* (1949), when
it consisted of "Henry Aldrich" Jimmy Lydon, "Little Beaver" Tommy
Cook, and Valentino-eyed waif Dickie Moore. A new type of bad boy
called a juvenile delinquent appeared to take their place, adopting the
costumes, gestures, and slang of the mean streets, as Corber notes.[1]
Nevertheless, they were decidedly white, middle class, Protestant, and
suburban, a twin to Ricky Nelson or Wally Cleaver. The modern juvenile delinquent had his own room, his own bed, a wad of allowance in
his pocket, a car for his sixteenth birthday, Dad reading the paper downstairs, Mom in the kitchen cooking dinner, no one dead, overworked, or

in prison, no deprivation, no poverty, nothing to get upset about, nothing to rebel against. But, nevertheless he *did* rebel. He ignored the debate team and his college applications, his future wife, kids, and job, his entire heteronormative future, to drive hot rods, listen to cacophonous music, smoke, drink, vandalize, brawl, have illicit sex, and die young. He was not Ricky Nelson. He was not Wally Cleaver. Something had gone horribly wrong.

The new bad boy first appeared during World War II in women's magazines and movies like *Youth Runs Wild* (1944). These were latch-key kids with fathers overseas and mothers working double shifts at Lockheed, who might succumb to the temptation to wear zoot suits or listen to boogie-woogie music. The new bad boy appeared intermittently in the first days of the nuclear family myth, in classroom instructional films, pulp fiction, *Devil on Wheels,* and J.D. Salinger's *The Catcher in the Rye* (1951). On December 30, 1953, *The Wild One* Marlon Brando swaggered into a sleepy desert nowheresville in tight jeans, black motorcycle jacket, and savagely erotic gaze; he had an iconic figure and a face. An explosion of juvenile-delinquent movies began in 1955, as Eisenhower was being elected to a second term and nuclear families were gaining ground on the small screen: *Six Bridges to Cross, Blackboard Jungle, Running Wild, Teen-age Crime Wave, Teenage Devil Dolls,* and of course *Rebel Without a Cause.* Between 1956 and 1959, teenager bad boys and girls starred in fifty-eight feature-length movies, mostly in drive-ins for audiences of teenagers looking for ways to define themselves while Mom and Dad stayed home with *Father Knows Best.* Interest began to falter in 1960, and only a dozen or so juvenile delinquents raced hot rods and back talked to Mom and Dad through the years of John F. Kennedy's Camelot.

Many scholars have commented on the primacy of middle-class bad boys in the mass media of the late 1950s. Charles Acland finds five primary, often overlapping causes "ordinary" teenage turmoil, bad-seed genetics, demonic possession, childhood deprivation, or social apathy. These causes suggest anxieties concerning the inefficiency of several social institutions, including medicine, religion, psychology, and the nuclear family, in producing the mature, responsible, well-adjusted, happy adults they had promised.[2] For girls, the primary aberrant life course was premarital heterosexual activity, which would lead to pregnancy or an inability to secure a respectable, middle-class husband. For boys, it was "homosexuality."

The male juvenile delinquent often displayed no interest in girls, and even when he dated or slept with them, his primary emotional bonds were with a sidekick or with an amorphous, all-male gang, both offering presumably dead-end alternatives to the heterosexual nuclear family. In a 1959 study of real-life youth gangs, psychologists Block and Niederhoffer noted with some dread their "homosexual ambivalence."[3] In *The Vanishing Adolescent* (1959), sociologist Edgar Z. Freidenberg[4] concludes that their frequent lapses into "homosexuality" were caused by fear of adult responsibility and the need to defy authority. Juvenile delinquent movies usually gave a "nice girl," that is, a girl who was not heterosexually active, the responsibility of drawing the juvenile delinquent away from his defiance, fear, and rebellion and make him acknowledge the necessity of heterosexual adulthood. Usually she succeeded, and the boy abandoned his buddy or gang joyfully to hold her in his arms, with marriage, family, organization-man job, and split level house in the suburbs to follow. In *Young and Dangerous* (1957), for instance, nice girl Lili Gentle (playing Rosemary) convinces sullen Mark Damon (playing Tommy) to abandon his teen gang, marry her, and go to college; thus he has rejected his same-sex bonds for a life trajectory leading to a nuclear family. Sometimes the girl was inept or conflicted, or parents or other authority figures unwittingly ruined her plans, and the bad boy failed to become good, that is, heterosexual. In *The Delinquents* (1957), parents force Tom Laughlin (as Scotty White) and his girlfriend to break up, leaving him no choice but to drift into a gang. The juvenile delinquent films constantly reworked the theme of girl who draws the bad boy away from his homoerotic Eden. Though the result was always marriage/family or death, the teenagers in the audience could watch strong, intimate, same-sex relationships, drawn in loving detail, sometimes with a barely concealed erotic urgency, and wonder if Father really knew best after all.

JUVENILE DELINQUENTS

Marlon Brando

The first bad-boy icon of the 1950s was hardly a teenager and far from unknown: the twenty-nine-year-old Brando had already

received three Oscar nominations for four starring roles. Perhaps
more significantly, he was not only bisexual but astonishingly open
about it, welcoming the subtle media suspicions of his relationships
with Tennessee Williams, James Baldwin, Leonard Bernstein, and
roommate Wally Cox.[5] He moved openly through the gay subcultures
of New York and Provincetown as a guest, a visitor, an experimenter.[6]
In his early movie roles, Brando deliberately positioned himself as a
sexual outsider to the 1950's heteroconformity, infusing a dangerous
sexual ambiguity or an even more dangerous gay presence to his nomi-
nally heterosexual characters. In discussing *A Streetcar Named Desire*
(1951), Derek Jarman writes that, "The modern queer was created by
Tennessee Williams. Brando in blue jeans, sneakers, white T-shirt, and
leather jacket. When you saw that, you knew that they were available."[7]
In blue jeans, sneakers, white T-shirt, and leather jacket, copying
Montgomery Clift's "cruising sexual swagger," Brando was the image
of the macho gay man that arose after World War II in the hot spots of
London, Amsterdam, Berlin, and New York, immortalized by the increasingly erotic magazine illustrations of Tom of Finland.[8]

In *The Wild One,* as McCann notes,[9] Brando's stage presence (as
Johnny) gives "unmistakable signs that he needs the adoration of both
sexes," but there are perhaps more signs that Brando is playing not
ambiguously bisexual, as usual, but gay. In spite of the tagline "Hot
cycles, hot blood, and cool, cool dames," there are few cool dames in
the movie. Though there are women in the rival motorcycle gang,
Brando's gang is exclusively male. The boys flirt intermittently with
local girls, but they seem quite content with their own company, and
they actively embrace gender transgression. During a night of revelry
and vandalism, one unidentified gang member is seen wearing a
dress, and another, played by Darren Dublin, emerges from a beauty
salon in a wig:

DINKY (Dublin): [Preening, in a falsetto] Mildred gives the craziest
    permanents!
DEXTRO: [Pretending to be interested] Honey, let's dance!
DINKY: Oh, I've been tapped![10]

They dance a parody of a 1940's swing, one pretending to be the
girl, while the other gang members laugh. But in a later scene, Dublin
has abandoned the wig, and they are dancing for real, swinging

energetically. Same-sex couples also danced together during a Christmas party in *Stalag 17* (1953), but only because no women were available, and they danced with grimaces or blank stares, as if they detested one another's touch. These boys are having fun, and the other gang members are watching nonchalantly, as if same-sex dancing is an ordinary part of their juvenile delinquent weekends.

Brando himself has two encounters with girls, but neither suggest that he is heterosexual. Yvonne Doughty, the moll of a rival gang named Britches, reminisces about the last time they met, evidently several years ago, when she was new to the motorcycling lifestyle. She acts like an old girlfriend, or at least a one-night stand. But what precisely happened during their encounter?

BRITCHES: We really got ourselves hung on the Christmas tree, didn't we? Boy, was I green. Was I really green! I thought I was really livin' it up. I had me a guy and we were really gonna go. But we had a lot of yaks, anyway, didn't we, Johnny?

JOHNNY: [Dismissively] What do you want me to do, send you some flowers?

Doughty's comment that "I had me a guy" and the crack about sending flowers imply that they had a romantic liaison, but other statements point to an ordinary motorcycle ride. "Hung on the Christmas tree" means crashing through bushes or shrubbery,[11] and "was I green" surely implies that she was inept at motorcycle riding, not at sex. It seems likely that she was "hung up" on Johnny, who was oblivious to her. The scene fails as an attempt to establish Brando's heterosexuality with a back-story girlfriend.

Brando displays heterosexual desire more successfully in his encounter with the "sad girl," Kathie (Mary Murphy), who works in the local diner. She is the one who will ideally draw him from the homoerotic and gender-trangressive freedom of the youth gang into a stable, responsible, heterosexual adulthood. Brando describes his interest in Murphy as a new experience, parallel to the pubescent "discovery" of girls in nuclear family narratives, as if the twenty-nine-year-old has never been interested in girls before. "I can't explain it," he says in the opening voice over. "But somethin' changed in me. She got to me."

Brando's heterosexual destiny is as contingent and inchoate as Ricky Nelson's. He takes Murphy to a secluded park and tries to hug and kiss her. When she responds favorably, he breaks away, shocked, and decides to take her home. Murphy—and the viewer—wonders why he would initiate a romantic liaison if he didn't want her to acquiesce.

KATHIE: It's crazy, isn't it? You're afraid of me. I don't know why, but I'm not afraid of you now. You're afraid of me.
JOHNNY: I'm afraid of you? Are you cracked? Come on, get on.
KATHIE: I wanted to touch you. I wanted to try anyway.
JOHNNY: Try what?

Now she tries to touch him, and he moves away. He will not let a girl touch him. In the last scene, when the gang is ordered to leave town, he stays behind long enough to give her a trophy he stole from a motorcycle competition earlier. But he does not stay behind long enough to marry her and look for an organization-man job. He has flirted with the possibility of abandoning the homoerotic Eden of his gang for the smile of a "sad girl." But then he rides off again.

Sal Mineo

It may seem that James Dean should come next as the American icon, emblematic of teenage rebellion, and again as openly bisexual as one could be in the 1950s. But when Dean died two weeks before the premiere of *Rebel Without a Cause,* he became a myth; costar Sal Mineo lived, and had to negotiate the tricky terrain of being a gay teen idol. James Dean was white bread, middle class, zooming down the rural roads of Kansas or Nebraska; but Sal Mineo, slim, dark, with moist, puppy-dog eyes, was the dark dreaming other. He was sometimes cast as Italian, sometimes as Native American, sometimes as Jewish, sometimes as Arab. In real life, he joined a gang at the age of eight, and started taking acting and dancing lessons at the age of ten. He was already torn between gang and girl in his earliest roles when he starred with Tony Curtis in *Six Bridges to Cross* and with Tim Considine in *The Private War of Major Benson.* Then came *Rebel.*

Director Nicholas Ray specialized in incorporating transgressive, often homoerotic images into workmanlike plots.[12] Critics have often noted the barely cloaked attraction of attorney (played by) Humphrey Bogart for street punk (played by) John Derek in *Knock on Any Door*

(1949), or between Mercedes McCambridge and the gender-bending Joan Crawford in *Johnny Guitar* (1954), or between has-been rodeo star Robert Mitchum for ranch hand Arthur Kennedy in *The Lusty Men* (1952). The homoeroticism of *Rebel* is so integral to plot and characters that to call it subtext is a misnomer.[13] Kashner and MacNair indicate that the overtness of the same-sex desire is what makes *Rebel* "truly revolutionary and perennially fresh."[14] Ray seems to have deliberately cast actors who would assist in adding a homoerotic center to a conventional heterosexual romance: Bisexual rebel-actor James Dean as bisexual rebel-teenager Jim Stark, and Sal Mineo, gay but not out, in love with Dean, as Plato, gay but not out, in love with Jim. Although McCann suggests that their profoundly erotic attachment was based on a real-life affair during filming, Mineo told his biographer, "If I'd understood back then that a guy could be in love with another one, it would have happened. But I didn't come to that realization for a few more years, and then it was too late for Jimmy and me."[15] More likely it was based on deliberate acting decisions: both Nicholas Ray and James Dean instructed Mineo to emphasize Plato's romantic attachment to Jim Stark.[16] Because of *Rebel*'s profound impact on Hollywood and on America, that attraction became emblematic of the juvenile delinquent genre.

James Dean died two weeks before the premiere of *Rebel,* but Sal Mineo busily reprised his Plato role in *Crime in the Streets* (1956) as Baby Gioia, the doting right-hand man of teen gang leader Frankie Dane (John Cassavetes). After a minor role as the aggressively girl-crazy Angelo Barrato in *Rock, Pretty Baby* he returned to overtly homoerotic, love at first sight with ex-con James Whitmore in *The Young Don't Cry* (1957). Even in the Disney western *Tonka* (1958), he bonded with a horse rather than a girl. In 1957, he initiated a musical career, but his record singles charted poorly. "Lasting Love" hit number fourteen in October 1957, and "Little Pigeon" never rose above number forty in the spring of 1958, in spite of teen magazine acclaim (the cover story of the June 1958 issue of *Hep Cats* named him "America's Top Teen Singer"). He was a competent performer, and in a field where looks counted far more than vocal ability, he might have become a major teen idol, but the unspecified rumors beginning to emerge in the yellow press coupled with the standard sexual ambiguity of the teen idol's stage presence (see Chapter 4), and lyrics that never specify that the "Lasting Love" is with a girl, brought the "possibility of possibility" too close to the surface, and Sal began to display an aggressive heterosexual façade.

To establish himself as heterosexual, Sal made the rounds of Hollywood hot spots in the company of teen starlets, notably Darlene Gillespie of the *Mickey Mouse Club,* and he began putting his barbell-toned physique on display in nearly every performance. Even the biopic *The Gene Krupa Story* includes extensive shirtless and underwear scenes, an early example of an equation of nature, nudity, and heterosexuality, contrasted with an equation of artifice, costume, and gay identity, that will appear frequently in teen productions. His screen characters became voraciously heterosexual, but their practice was oddly organized around triangulations: he bedded the girlfriends of James Darren in *The Gene Krupa Story* (1959) and Gary Crosby in *A Private's Affair* (1959). He was nominated for an Academy Award for his role as a young Jewish terrorist in *Exodus* (1960), mostly for a scene in which he tearfully admits that the Nazis treated him "as a woman." In *Who Killed Teddy Bear* (1965), he suffered from heterosexual "sexual problems," but his obsession over Juliet Prowse can easily be seen as displaced homoerotic passion.

John Saxon

Long before his kung fu match Bruce Lee in *Enter the Dragon* (1973) and his career as an action-adventure and horror staple, John Saxon was a struggling actor working as a beefcake model. In 1955 he was grabbed off the cover of *True Romance* to bring a sexually provocative, tight-chino swagger to *Running Wild,* Universal's stab at the juvenile delinquent genre. He played doting sidekick to gang leader Jan Merlin (who had just finished a run on TV's *Tom Corbett, Space Cadet*) and ignored the ladies prowling about, including famously busty Mamie Van Doren. Released a few weeks after *Rebel* in November 1955, *Running* proved so successful that Universal cast Saxon in its next juvie, *Rock, Pretty Baby* (dir. Richard Bartlett, 1956).

Saxon is the only dark, brooding, fisticuffs-prone rebel-without-a-cause in a high school jazz combo otherwise composed of "nice" (e.g., girl-crazy) teenagers. In *Listen to the Warm* (1976) poet Rod McKuen has two girlfriends,[17] Sal Mineo dozens, and they spend every moment not performing or practicing on the beach, necking in swimsuits to demonstrate that they are strong, powerful, masculine, and heterosexual. But Saxon repeatedly asserts that he has no interest in girls, explaining that he wants to concentrate on his music. He accepts the friendship of girl-next-door Joan (Luanna Patten), an aspiring musician who has been accepted to a prestigious music conservatory in San Francisco, only because she offers to help the combo with musical arrangements. He pointedly ignores her romantic hints, refusing a good-night kiss after a practice session even though Sal Mineo is smooching enthusiastically with a girl in the backseat to model the appropriate behavior.

The other members of the combo do not accept Saxon's "concentrating on music" rationale for failing to smooch, and variously tease, belittle, and attack him. Even mild-mannered Ox (Rod McKuen) yells: "You knucklehead, you gotta stop acting like dames were never invented!" At the beach, they grab him, pin his arms behind his back, and invite the girls to gather around and kick start his heterosexual desire. Finally Dad, a kindly physician played by Edward Platt (the juvenile officer in *Rebel,* and later the Chief on TV's *Get Smart*), has a heart-to-heart with the boy, like Jim Anderson addressing Bud's girl-shyness on *Father Knows Best,* and convinces him that he cannot resist his heterosexual destiny.

Suddenly the scales fall from Saxon's eyes. He rushes to Patten's house and exclaims "There's so much I want to tell you!" They run hand in hand down to the deserted beach at night without swimsuits, but oddly, now that Saxon wants to kiss, Patten refuses. She doesn't trust herself to keep the kiss from escalating.

JOAN: How do we know it's love? All I can think about is necking and petting!
JIMMY: That's because we held back so long.
JOAN: But what about our plans?

Finally they do kiss, but carefully. It is the girl's responsibility not only to elicit heterosexual desire, but also to stave off its practice (other than kissing and hugging) until she has a wedding ring, a mortgage, and a career as a wife and mother. If she errs in either direction, their plans will be ruined. In the morning, she decides that the men aren't really worth it, and leaves to take that scholarship and embark on a non–wife-and-mother career of her own.

His entry into heterosexual adulthood stymied, Saxon again becomes sullen and despondent, and prone to pick fights. To make matters worse, he is missing band practice, and the combo is scheduled to perform at a big competition in a few days. Another heart-to-heart talk with Dad about accepting one's responsibilities proves fruitless. Saxon insists that career success and loyalty to one's friends are both meaningless without a girl. Then, at the last moment, Patten gives up her career goals to become a wife and mother after all, Saxon happily rejoins the combo, and everyone (except the girl) gets to have their cake and eat it too. One suspects that everyone would have been much happier if Saxon had remained true to himself and not let Dad talk him into liking girls.[18]

John Ashley

A tall, beefy Oklahoman with a gravely drawl and an oddly ostentatious garnet ring, John Ashley has accumulated a remarkable body of myth work for a nonsuperstar, including two discovery stories rivaling Lana Turner sipping a soda at Schwab's.[19] In the discovery story, the twenty-year-old Oklahoma State University undergrad, vacationing in Hollywood, wanders onto the RKO lot, where John Wayne is filming *The Conquerer.* Seduced by his beefcake physique, cowboy accent, and sultry homoerotic gaze, the Duke hires him on the spot for the television series he is bankrolling, *Men of Annapolis* (1956-1957).[20] In another story, Ashley wanders onto the lot of the newly formed, teen-oriented American International Pictures (AIP) (actually just a building), where his girlfriend is auditioning for *Dragstrip Girl.* Staff writer Lou Rusoff is seduced by his beefcake physique, cowboy accent, and sultry homoerotic gaze, and hires him on the spot.

However he was discovered, John Ashley spent 1956 being heavily promoted as a teen idol. He sang as "himself" in AIP movies, as if he were already a big star; he cut six records, and posed endlessly for teen magazines.[21] Yet he never rose beyond the bottom rungs of the ladder that led past Rod Lauren, Sal Mineo, Johnny Crawford, and Johnny Tillotson to the ethereal heights of Fabian, Bobby Rydell, and Frankie Avalon. His greatest fame came in movies. He spent forty years as an actor, director, and producer, first in the United States and then in the Philippines. Though his adult roles featured lots of groaning, sweating, bare-breast-and-bottom sex scenes with girls, mostly in the jungles of the Philippines, his teen roles constantly favored homo-erotic bonds over heterosexual practice. Actually, they rarely in-volved any heterosexual practice at all: in his eighteen teenage roles between 1956 and 1965, Ashley necks with girls only three times, al-most as if someone at AIP was deliberately trying to reveal the pres-ence of boys who are not interested in girls.

Dragstrip Girl (dir. Edward L. Kahn, AIP, 1957) turned out to be less about the girl than about the two boys she dates. John Ashley plays wealthy pretty boy Fred, whose sizzling attraction to his wrong-side-of-the-tracks buddy, the blond, buffed Jim (fellow teen-idol wannabe Steven Terrell), has become increasingly overt and increas-ingly dangerous as they move through their teen years, realized mostly through reckless hot rodding through public streets. When kicks-happy Louise (Fay Spain) moves to town, she happily dates them both. Oddly, at the end of the date with Ashley, she refuses to kiss him:

FRED: [Pouting] I bet it'd be all right if it was Jim.

LOUISE: Can't you find anything else to talk about? I think you've got an obsession with Jim! What kind of threat is he to you?

Jim (Terrell) indeed kisses Spain, and he finds heterosexual prac-tice sufficiently satisfying to abandon Ashley, along with their hot rodding, and joins a hot-rod club that races on a safe track. Rejected, Ashley finds a new best friend in another blond, buffed, hot rodder, played by future real-life hot rodder Tommy Ivo. They challenge Terrell to a "chickie run" (made famous in *Rebel*) and conspire to beat him in the upcoming race, with a college scholarship on the line that wealthy Ashley doesn't even need.

Meanwhile, at the local teen hangout, twenty-three-year-old Frank Gorshin in his pre-*Batman* (Riddler) days dons a mop wig and tablecloth dress to sing a drag version of the theme song "Dragstrip Girl," coyly evoking the gender disruption of hot rodding even as he enjoys a love-hate relationship with a girlfriend. Ashley also seems aware, on some level, of the homoerotic implications of the race. He taunts Terrell that his team colors are "yellow" (because he's chicken) and "uh . . . what was that other one?" Terrell decks him before he can say the other color he has in mind. Surely the sudden fury of the easygoing Terrell suggests that he expects Ashley to say something like "lavender."

As Terrell moves closer to the girl, the hot-rod club, and adult heterosexual responsibility, Ashley's behavior becomes increasingly obsessive. Ivo breaks his leg during the chickie run, but it is Terrell, not his "best friend" Ashley, who rushes to the rescue. Later, Ashley kills a pedestrian in a hit-and-run accident, and tries to lay the blame on Terrell. When Spain discovers the truth, he tries to kill her. The movie ends with Ashley being led off by the police, wondering how his life fell apart. The teen audience knows how: he failed to reject the homoromantic (indeed, homoerotic) bonds of childhood for a future with girls.

John Ashley and Steve Terrell reprised the plot, with different character names and motorcycles instead of dragsters, in *Motorcycle Gang* (1957). Terrell retired from teen idoling to become a real race car driver, and John Ashley continued playing pretty-boy teenagers with barely suppressed homoerotic longings and, evidently, an ironclad clause in his contract stipulating that he never had to kiss a girl. In *Hot Rod Gang* (1958), he plays a sissified boy who leads a "double life." In the daytime, he wears suits and plays the violin to appease his maiden aunts, Abigail and Anastasia; but at night he wears tight jeans to play rock and roll and race hot rods. Although he flirts with girls, his main interest is in buddy Mark (Steve Drexel), another teen-idol wannabe and the leader of the gang. When Ashley goes under cover as a rock singer to help Drexel raise money for a new hot rod, his aunts discover his "secret life." To his surprise, they are tolerant and supportive.

Next, Ashley starred in the Korean War movie *Suicide Battalion* (1958), in which he keeps hanging out by himself while his foxhole buddies are smooching with the local girls, explaining rather unconvincingly that he's staying faithful to his fiancée (when he is finally reunited with the girl, they conveniently never manage to find time alone for kissing). He also starred in the horror films *How to Make a Monster* and *Frankenstein's Daughter* (see Chapter 5). He returned to the juvenile-delinquent genre one last time for *High School Caesar* (dir. O'Dale Ireland, Marathon, 1960), which is a sanitized *Rebel* with no puppy shooting, no guns, nobody killed except in an accident, and a popular teen star instead of an outcast. It also trivializes the heterosexual practice of the earlier film, making it only a necessary triangulation for same-sex love. Ashley plays Matt, a wealthy yet troubled high school boy who spends the first ten minutes or so of the movie extorting money, selling black-market tests, rigging the student body elections, and hugging a petite, androgynous buddy with the odd name Cricket (Steve Stevens, then far more famous than Ashley for his work opposite Annette Funicello on *The Mickey Mouse Club*). Their interaction becomes amazingly erotic.

CRICKET: Do you really think I'll get to be student body treasurer?

MATT: I think so. You'll be even more important to me then. [Caresses his face]

Stevens and Ashley are rather obviously playing a romantic couple, constantly linking arms, touching shoulders, grabbing at each other; at the school dance and the local teen hangout, they stand on the sidelines, watching while the heterosexual couples swing. They do express some minimal girl-craziness: Ashley occasionally puts his arm around (but never kisses) the creepy, semi-comatose Daria Massey, who looks like Vampirella without the cleavage. Stevens wants to be seen on the arm of the new girl, blonde bombshell Judy Nugent. Ashley promises to acquire her for his buddy, but she refuses to accept the dates.

The Ashley-Stevens bond parallels the bond between current student body president Kelly (Lowell Brown) and his buddy Bob (Gary Vinson). They are similarly inseparable, always touching and hanging out together; but while Ashley uses Stevens' adoration to maintain dominance, Brown encourages Vinson to think and act for himself. When Vinson notes an interest in Wanda (Judy Nugent), Brown prompts him with "All you have to do is ask her!" This approach works. Upset that Brown is more successful in mentoring buddies, Ashley tries to run him off the road; the car spins out of control and into a ditch, and Brown is killed.

Stevens is upset that Ashley has been unable to acquire the girl for him, "I thought you were a big man!" So Ashley kidnaps her, orders Stevens to drive him to a secluded park, and initiates a date rape (without kissing her). Stevens objects—this is hardly an approved method of acquiring a girlfriend—but Ashley orders him out of the car. He is clearly planning the rape to maintain his dominance over Stevens. But his plan backfires: betrayed, Stevens sobs, "You said that we were . . ." and runs to the teen hangout to apprise the other teens of his malfeasance. Meanwhile, the girl escapes, and runs to tell on him also. The teens reject him one by one; Stevens is the last. The film ends with Ashley on his knees, sobbing, in the light of a streetlamp near the deserted teen hangout.

JUVENILE DELINQUENCY HEATS UP

As teenagers began to lose interest in the juvenile delinquent movies, producers tried to heat it up with more shirtless shots and rock-and-roll music. The homoerotic bond between the boy and his buddy became increasingly overt, the ministrations of the girl increasingly ineffective, and the penalty for failing to embrace heterosexual destiny increasingly brutal. Actor Warren Berlinger played sad, doomed sidekicks with crushes on best buddies in *Blue Denim* (1959) and *Because They're Young* (1960). In *Platinum High School* (1960) the buddy is murdered, and Warren is adopted by his distraught father, played by Mickey Rooney. In *The Girl in Lovers Lane* (dir. Charles R. Rondeau, Filmgroup, 1959), a beefy drifter played by Brett Halsey sleeps cuddled up with his partner, the wealthy young runaway played by Lowell Brown. He jealously sabotages Brown's attempts to meet girls twice, even dragging him bodily out of a small-town brothel, and is so immersed in an underwear-clad heart-to-heart that he stands up a date of his own. At the end of the movie, after being unjustly accused of rape and beaten to a pulp by the townsfolk, Halsey no longer even pretends to be heterosexual. He meekly accepts when Brown takes him by the arm and says "Come on, Bix [Halsey], we're going home."

Arch Hall Jr.

Western actor Arch Hall Sr. doted on his sixteen-year-old son, Arch Hall Jr., so much that he was unable to objectively evaluate the boy's charisma, looks, or talent, and bankrolled starring roles for him in six movies (1961-1965), one each of juvenile delinquent, teen horror, rock-and-roll, thriller, secret-agent spoof, and Western. They were surprisingly successful at the box office, earning over a million dollars each on miniscule budgets, perhaps because of their earnestness and chutzpah, or perhaps because of the sheer spectacle of

Arch Jr., who can't act and never wanted to, being forced to emote on cue. He was no Steve Reeves (and for that matter, no Dwayne Hickman, either), yet in every scene he was shoved into tight jeans and T-shirts or a swimsuit so the camera could linger over every inch of his body, blatantly inviting an erotic gaze made somewhat creepy by the realization that his father was standing behind that camera. Though adequately established as strong, powerful, and masculine, he always ignored his bombshell girlfriends, finding his most honest and intense bonds with men.

In his juvenile-delinquent entry, *The Choppers* (dir. Leigh Jackson, Rushmore, 1961), Arch Jr. played Jack Cruiser, a member of a juvenile-delinquent gang lead by muscular Ricky Nelson look-alike Robert Paget. The gang demonstrates heterosexual interest through flirting with a waitress ("It's not that I like girls so much, but there's something about the way they look!"), but meanwhile they denigrate a couple kissing in their car:

TORCH: Get a load of big smooch! Talk about tall in the saddle!

TOM: Couple of fanatics! They go wall to wall!

Hall's girlfriend Liz is played by Marianne Gaba, a former "Miss Illinois" and *Playboy* playmate who in real life dated a number of sexually ambiguous teen hunks, including Sal Mineo. When she tries to initiate a romantic liaison, he ignores her, preferring to lounge around the pool, displaying his unremarkable chest and reading car magazines:

LIZ: That's what I don't understand about men. We have a pool and a hi-fi, and you're talking about an axel!

JACK: And that's what I don't understand about women. You're always nagging!

He only puts down the magazine when Gaba challenges him to a race across the pool, a competitive sort of dating activity not likely to lead to romance.

But Hall is heavily punished for his flirtation with the gang. Instead of becoming a bona-fide gang member, he is forced to keep a lookout while the Choppers drive around in a poultry truck, stripping abandoned cars for parts. The police, anxious to apprehend this gang of hardened criminals, finally corner them in the junkyard where they sell the parts. Paget and the sleazy same-sex couple that runs the junk-yard are killed, and the other three, including Hall, are dragged off to life in prison, while Dad looks on somberly and Gaba sobs, their dreams of a "normal" heterosexual life for the boy ruined.

Chapter 4

Teenage Zombies from Outer Space:
Monster Movies

Before 1957, horror and sci-fi movie heroes, villains, scientists, scientists' daughters, and townsfolk were always adults, with occasionally a child or a very young, barely pubescent teenager, like thirteen-year-old Billy Gray in *The Day the Earth Stood Still* (1951). Actors were thrown in to innocently befriend the alien or chase a stray softball into the monster's lair. Then Samuel Z. Arkoff of American International Pictures cast a sullen, morose, high schooler into Universal's 1941 classic *Wolf Man.*[1] Michael Landon's confessional *I Was a Teenage Werewolf* was filmed in a week on a budget of $82,000, and grossed $2 million, becoming number five at the box office in 1957, followed closely by its drive-in double-bill, *Invasion of the Saucer Men,* about the teenagers from *Dragstrip Girl* defeating bug-eyed monsters by shining car headlights at them (so parking at lovers' lanes had some benefit after all). In November 1957, AIP hit gold again with more teenagers inserted into classic monster movies, *I Was a Teenage Frankenstein* and *Blood of Dracula* (originally *I Was a Teenage Dracula*), and soon dozens of young adults were being snapped up from modeling agencies, actor's studios, and the casts of juvenile-delinquent movies to play teenage monsters, monster hunters, classmates, buddies, and girlfriends. Evidently the teenagers buying drive-in movie tickets liked being scared, or laughing at silly special effects, or watching themselves literally transformed into the sexually ambiguous monsters that Ozzie and Harriet feared they would become.

doi:10.1300/5484_04

TEENAGE WEREWOLF

In *I Was a Teenage Werewolf* (dir. Gene Fowler Jr., AIP, 1957), Tony (Michael Landon) has been raised by a single dad in a nuclear-family society where two parents of complementary sexes are essential to guard the tykes against perversion, so it is little wonder that he has grown into a sullen, sensitive, "confused" (i.e., gay) high schooler. "I say things, I do things, I don't know why," he explains without explaining anything. "I get certain feelings." He overcompensates for his "certain feelings" by picking fights with any boy who touches him, even by accident. "I don't like to be touched [by boys]!" he yells. He doesn't mind when girls touch him, since they represent no danger, but a same-sex touch signifies something intolerable, the possibility that "certain feelings" will rise to the surface.

Scholars often find homoerotic undertows in horror films as stylistic devices meant to accentuate dread. Twitchell argues that the genre encodes patterns of "normal" sexuality and makes the monster inappropriately or perversely sexual.[2] Benshoff points out that the AIP horror quartet (*Werewolf, Frankenstein, Dracula,* and *How to Make a Monster*) involves mad scientists transforming boys (and one girl) into perversely sexual monsters, "a metaphorical reworking of the increasingly common idea that older homosexuals were out to recruit young people into their ranks."[3] Asked about the formula, producer Herman Cohen argues that the mad scientist was not the root cause of the monstering at all. The teens transformed into werewolves, Frankensteins, and Draculas were outsiders from the beginning:

> Somebody wants love, somebody is ugly, somebody doesn't fit in, somebody is an introvert, somebody has a father and mother divorced. I speak in front of colleges and universities at times . . . and the comment is made quite often, "Gee, Mr. Cohen, we noticed that the kid is always being turned bad by doubt."[4]

In *Teenage Werewolf,* long before the mad scientist appears, Landon's character is overwhelmed by doubt about his trajectory into heterosexual adulthood, trying unsuccessfully to exhibit "normal" girl-craziness and punishing the licit same-sex contact of a buddy. Dad tries to help by advising him to play the game, just as Jim Anderson advised Bud in *Father Knows Best:* "Sometimes you just have to do things the way people want them done!" But Landon continues to ignore his girlfriend, and picks fights with his male friends. He seeks help from psychiatrist Dr. Brandon (Whit Bissell), who mad scientists him down the evolutionary ladder to a prehistoric werewolf ancestor. However, wolfing out only makes the attacks deadly, and now Landon specifically targets classmates who may be gay.

The teenagers in *Werewolf* attend two different rock-and-roll parties, and everyone pairs off into heterosexual couples except Frank (Michael Rougas), whose only nod at heterosexual practice is to agree to dance with (Ken Miller) Vic's girlfriend while he is busy playing bongos. After the second party, Landon and his girlfriend Arlene (Yvonne Lime) offer him a ride home, but he refuses. He's going to walk through the woods instead. One wonders why he would turn down a ride home, unless he has some special reason for wanting to walk through the woods in the middle of the night. Is the woods some sort of special place, a 1950's cruising ground? Landon must wonder, too. He hurriedly drops off Lime, not even bothering to kiss her good night, and rushes off to the woods. Obviously, he intends to meet Rougas there, but why? He just saw him a few minutes ago. If he is expecting the boy to *touch* him, his plans are stymied when he turns into a werewolf and guts Rougas instead of kissing him.

Landon's next victim is played by Dawn Richmond (who coincidentally was the *Playboy* Playmate of the Month in May 1957, a month before *Teenage Werewolf* premiered). One day after school, she is in the gymnasium, practicing on the parallel bars and responding with grins and giggles to the overt flirtation of the mannish, suit-clad (i.e., lesbian) principal. Landon sees the exchange, and when the principal leaves the room for a moment, he morphs into a werewolf and kills the girl. Biskind calls the attack a sexual assault precipitated by Landon's uncontrollable heterosexual desires: he is "turned on by a nubile bobbysoxer."[5] But he has not been watching the bobbysoxer: he has been watching an arguably romantic interchange between the girl and the principal. The monster attacks a girl who has not adequately displayed heterosexual desire, and indeed may be subject to "perversion" by the older woman. He is attacking someone gay. In effect, he is attacking himself.

The monster's third and final victim is a janitor at the police station, who is from the old country and knows all about werewolves. Perhaps this attack is a form of self-defense, or perhaps the janitor's lack of heterosexual interest and eye-shimmering admiration for

Seargent Donovan (Barney Philips) codes him as gay also. Afterward Michael himself is killed, his chaotic inner nature unable to survive in the clean, orderly world of the 1950's teenager.

TEENAGE FRANKENSTEIN

In the second in the quartet of teenage monster movies, *I Was a Teenage Frankenstein* (dir. Herbert L. Stronk, AIP, 1957), Whit Bissell plays an overtly gay, mad Dr. Frankenstein, a descendent of the original (whom no one has ever heard of). So dedicated is he to his mad-scientist experiments that he ignores his clinging fiancée, played by Phyllis Coates, and finally disposes of her in the alligator tank under the house. When he reads of a track team dying in a plane crash, he exclaims "All those fine athletic bodies gone to waste!" and hustles out to the cemetery to collect the choicest parts. His creature is not to be the original groaning, green-faced slug of the Universal classic, but a teenage jock with "the hands of a wrestler" and "the legs of a football player." Though the tagline reads "Body of a boy! Mind of a monster! Soul of an unearthly thing!" the monster actually created has the body of an athlete, the mind of a genius, and a quiet, sensitive soul.

Producer Herman Cohen denies that there was anything special about Gary Conway, hired to play the monster: they just went down to Muscle Beach in Santa Monica and grabbed the nearest hunk. Surely it is no coincidence that the twenty-year-old Conway was studying art at UCLA (a gay-coded major), and that he was earning extra money by posing in gay-oriented physique magazines, including a cover of the June 1956 issue of *Body Beautiful*. The Athletic Model Guild's *Physique Pictorial* included "codes" on each photo specifying the model's sexual orientation and bedroom interests, and Gary Conway's photo's in October 1964 issue are marked with the astrological sign for male pointing straight up, signifying heterosexual. However, being an art student, a model in publications aimed at gay men, and member of a bodybuilding subculture where same-sex activity was conducted more or less openly from the 1940s through the 1960s, the young Conway was often assumed gay, and this may have been Cohen's motivation in selecting him, even though he had no previous professional acting experience. The monster would be gay not by artifice or perversion, but by being portrayed by a "gay" actor.

Conway as the boy monster has a hideously disfigured face but a beautifully sculpted body, which is displayed as he lifts weights, shirtless, in his cell (Dr. Frankenstein insists that "our main concern is your physique!"). He demonstrates that he is strong and powerful, but falls short of 1950's macho masculinity when, understandably upset over being made up of the miscellaneous body parts of dead athletes, he begins to cry. The doctor is delighted that his tear ducts work, but muses "It seems we have a very *sensitive* teenager on our hands." *Sensitive,* code for gay, was evidently not part of the master plan, but comes as an unwelcome surprise.

The boy monster can still achieve a heterosexual life trajectory if he "discovers" girls, so he ambles out to the nearest apartment complex. He spies a young lady primping at a mirror and breaks in to see more. She screams, he protests, and in the confusion, he accidentally strangles her. But he never intended a sexual assault. He does not seem either violent or hetero horny; he might easily have peered in the window next door instead, and invaded the apartment of a young man preening.[6]

To remedy the problem of his deformed face, the boy monster and Dr. Frankenstein go shopping for a new one. They park at a lover's lane. The pair is an oddly incongruous same-sex couple among the heterosexual teens necking to big band music. One wonders why they don't just grab a star athlete from a locker room. Evidently, they need someone who has engaged in heterosexual practice to give the boy monster a heterosexual "face," a facade to present to the world like the Sherlock Holmes mask Bud Anderson wore. So they unglue a blond pretty boy from his girlfriend's lips and take him back to the lab to become a face donor. However, after the operation, the boy monster is still not a man: he can't stop staring at his image in the mirror and stroking his cheeks. "Quite handsome!" Dr. Frankenstein agrees. "Quite, quite handsome!" Of course, the boy monster is not looking at his own face at all; he is admiring the beauty of the blond they harvested last night. That is, he is expressing a homoerotic interest. He is still a monster, not because he is violent or disfigured, but because he has failed to express the heterosexual desire "necessary" to become a real boy. The film ends quickly and ludicrously when Dr. Frankenstein decides to take him to England, but instead of buying a ticket, he plans to disassemble him, ship the parts to England, and reassemble him there. The boy naturally disapproves and feeds Dr. Frankenstein to the alligator. Then he is accidentally electrocuted, dying because he cannot live. Like Michael Landon's Werewolf, there is no place for him in the teenage world.

THE MONSTER MASH

Teenagers starred in a quarter of all horror and sci-fi releases in the United States in 1958, and fully a third in 1959. Studios even began to use *teenager* as an all-purpose draw, transforming *Meteor Man* to *Teenage Monster* (1957) and *The Gargan Terror* to *Teenagers from Outer Space* (1959), and announcing *I Was a Teenage Gorilla* (1961) before saner heads suggested *Konga* (1961). Interest began to wane in the early 1960s, along with the juvenile-delinquency genre, until the percentage of horror and sci-fi movies starring teenagers dropped to about 10 percent and stayed there until Jamie Lee Curtis fought off Michael in *Halloween* (1978).[7] At the same time, Vampira, Zacherley, Ghoulardi, and dozens of costumed ghouls began to host late-night "creature features" on local TV. Thousands of horror comics, though toned down a bit when the Comics Code took charge in 1954, attracted both children and teenagers. Bobby Pickett's "Monster Mash," number one on the charts in October 1962, became the most famous of horror-spoof singles.[8]

The sudden surge of media monsters cannot be attributed to the real monsters thought to walk the earth in the late 1950s, since their activities, poisoning the water supply and filtering propaganda into history textbooks, were far removed from most teenage interests. Instead, we can find a clue in the monster movies' settings, which are never Mars or the Moon, or even the exotic jungles where Johnny Sheffield's teenage Bomba (of the popular *Bomba the Jungle Boy* series) fought off poachers, but nuclear-family, small towns and suburbs like those where Jim Anderson sold life insurance, and Ward and June fretted about the Beaver. The teenage monsters or monster fighters were juvenile delinquents, swaggering about in T-shirts and leather jackets, listening to rock-and-roll music, and raging inarticulately against the constraints of the adult world. Like the AIP horror teenagers, they were unable or unwilling to express the "proper" level of girl-craziness, even though scenes near the beginning of the movies usually showed girlfriends trying to jump start heterosexual desire. They were not punished for their transgression. Instead, once the saucers land, the organization-man capitalist bureaucracy proves too stupid, disbelieving, ineffectual, or bound by red tape to adequately defend the world, so the teenager calls on his buddies or the gang, and the same-sex bonds that the adults revile as disruptive and chaotic demonstrate their superiority over office-man job, house, wife, and kids.

In *The Blob* (dir. Irwin S. Yeawood, Fairview, 1958), Steve's (Steve McQueen) buddies mock his interest in his girlfriend and then set out on a late-night mischief raid to disrupt the heterosexual practice across teendom: they steal a boy's car while he visits his girlfriend (so he will be unable to neck with her later?) and invade a lover's lane, dragging a boy from his girlfriend with the quip "Excuse me, we're looking for a monster." One of the buddies does display a bit of heterosexual interest, going to a midnight movie in search of girls (and finding one), but the other two, Mooch (James Bonnet) and Al (Anthony Franke) always interact as a couple: they sit together at the movie, grab at each other outside, and pair up to warn the townspeople about the blob.

In *Teenage Zombies* (dir. Jerry Warren, EMB Productions, 1959), a movie about a water-skiing expedition to the evil Mullet Island that goes horribly wrong, a young teen named Morrie (Jay Hawk), with very fey mannerisms (and an ostentatious ring), approaches the tall, gangly Reg (Donald Sullivan), his buddy Skip (Paul Pepper), and their two tepid, ornamental girlfriends (evidently there because boys may not go water-skiing by themselves), and bemoans the fact that he has plans with his girlfriend or sister (one can't really tell which) which will keep him from the relationship he is really interested in:

MORRIE: [Hopefully] How about you and the other guys going horse-back riding with me and Dot?

REG: I can't do it. We're going to go water-skiing.

GIRLFRIEND: Do you want to come along?

MORRIE: [Excited, then remembers] No, I promised Dottie.

REG: I tell you what. I'll pick you up at 4:00 at the stables, and we can go to the drive-in [later].

MORRIE: You'll pick us up for sure?

REG: You know I wouldn't hang you up. [Morrie leaves]

SKIP: How weird can you get?

Though Skip disapproves of the attachment, Morrie would obviously prefer to be with Reg. One wonders why he is dating Dottie at all, or if it is a date at all. Later, the four older teens go on their waterskiing expedition and are abducted by the mad scientist. But instead of drawing them away from buddy bonding, she draws them away from their heterosexual loves, housing the boys and girls separately. When Reg, Skip, and the girlfriends are captured by a lady mad scientists who wants to transform them into zombies, it is Morrie's concern about Reg, not any ruminations after girls, that motivates him to go to the police, and then (after the adults give him the runaround) to save the day.

In *Teenage Cave Man* (dir. Roger Corman, AIP, 1959), earnest cave-teen Son of the Symbol Maker (twenty-five-year-old Robert Vaughn) is pressured by his girlfriend, the Blonde Maiden, to move in to their own cave. "It would be a good thing," she notes seductively. He is obsessed with the Land Beyond the River, with its quicksand, giant iguanas, and gesticulating "tree thing" "that gives death with its touch," so he conducts a secret expedition with his "gang" of young men, one of whom, the Curly-Haired Boy (Jonathan Haze), keeps his hand permanently attached to his arm or shoulder. The expedition results in death and ostracization, but he continues trying to convince the adults that "the laws are old. But age is not always truth," his heterosexual interests long forgotten.

Teenage monster fighters usually have a single adult ally in their attempt to save the world, an older teenager, sheriff, doctor, or scientist sent down from the state university. He is rarely married, nor does he display any heterosexual interest of his own; he is too busy playing surrogate father or big brother to the monster fighter, offering so many adult gifts, freedom, responsibility, noble and important work, and of course homoerotic buddy bonding that the boy's incipient girl-craziness falls to the wayside.

In *The Blob,* police lieutenant Dave (thirty-eight-year-old Earl Rowe) is a boyish, innocent, wifeless, childless, middle-aged man in a small town consisting only of teenagers and their nuclear-family parents (who look and act about eighty years old). Dave is the only one inclined to believe Steve's story—that a glob of red ooze from a meteorite is eating people. Their bond is intense and intimate, and seems to transgress the buddy roles available for teenagers and adults during the period. When the Blob traps Steve and the others in the basement of the small-town Cosmopolitan Diner, Dave is unable to maintain his professional demeanor: he needs comforting by another cop. But he is not necessarily distraught over the *others*. When they all escape, Dave runs past the others to embrace Steve. The last scene of the movie shows Steve standing next to Dave, not next to his girl-friend, his entry into heterosexual adulthood postponed or waylaid by a demonstration of the power of same-sex bonds.

In *The Giant Gila Monster* (dir. Ray Kellogg, Hollywood Pictures, 1959), Donald E. Sullivan plays Chase Winstead, a teenage auto me-chanic living with his widowed mother and his crippled sister (to whom he sings the horrible "Mushroom Song," about God ordering children to laugh). He is dating a French foreign-exchange student, but he is always surrounded by older men, sometimes with an inti-macy that leaves little to the imagination. While driving his tow truck, for instance, he meets the brash, bragging Horatio Alger "Steam-roller" Smith (Dallas radio personality Ken Knox). Since he is too drunk to drive any further, Chase invites Smith to spend the night in the spare bed in the auto garage. The next morning, Smith wakes up to find Chase getting dressed. Obviously, he also spent the night there, but why didn't he just go home? He is much too trusting to stay up all night guarding the garage. Could they have slept together?

SMITH: How'd you ever get me in that bed?

CHASE: I carried you in there, and I sat on you until you fell asleep.

SMITH: [Chuckling] That must have been quite a chore. Next time you're in town, there's my card, look me up, will ya?

Most of Chase's buddy bonding occurs with another adult, Sheriff Jeff (Fred Graham), who keeps dropping by the auto garage to in-volve Chase in long heart-to-heart talks and inviting him to tag along on investigations. Perhaps not coincidentally, he tends to call Chase during dates, requiring him to choose between the buddy and the girl, and instead of saying "Sorry, I'm busy at the moment," Chase drops the girl instantly, without hesitation, to rush to the buddy's side. Oth-ers in the community are aware that the sheriff has an intimate, argu-ably romantic interest in the teenager: Businessman Mr. Fisher thinks that Chase knows something about the disappearance of his daughter (eaten by the giant Gila monster), and accuses the sheriff of lying to protect him. Nor is Chase completely oblivious. In a scene pivotal for revealing plot exposition, he sits atop a desk, inches away from the sheriff, his legs extended, his hand absently stroking his thigh as if he is teasing or inviting, an odd position for the discussion of giant Gila monsters. Then suddenly the sheriff dismisses him, saying abruptly "Go out and have fun!" as if Chase has become uncomfortably close.

When the giant Gila monster finally shows itself, it breaks through the wall of a barn full of teenagers (it is attracted to the noise of the wild applause as Chase reprises "The Mushroom Song"). Chase takes charge, crashing a jalopy full of nitroglycerine into the monster (to explode it), while the sheriff covers crowd control. The monster transforms into a flaming carcass, and everyone in town is jubilant even though several of their teenagers have been eaten. Mr. Fisher offers Chase a job if he comes around "first thing in the morning," and the sheriff exclaims "I'll bring him around myself!" Why is he in the position to bring Chase around "first thing in the morning"? Will they be spending the night together (in that spare room in the garage)? Then he goes to Chase, watching the flaming lizard with arms around his girlfriend and his little sister. He touches Chase on the shoulder; getting no response, he moves away, then touches him again and moves away again, despondent. Their relationship is over. Chase has embraced heterosexual destiny, producing a nuclear family, and the sheriff has no place in his new post-Gila monster world.

Arch Hall Jr.

After *The Choppers* (See Chapter 3), Arch Hall Jr. found a new career as monster fighter in *Eegah* (dir. Arch Hall Sr., Fairway, 1962). Hall plays as eighteen-year-old high school student/grease monkey Tom. He had developed an acceptable physique (again treated by director-daddy as magnificent, deserving of constant swimsuit closeups), and again, his relationship with girlfriend Roxy (Marilyn Manning) seems tepid at best: the two never kiss except for a peck on the cheek, nor does he express any attraction to her other than polite "you look nice" comments at the beginning of their dates. However, he does express considerable interest in her father, Dr. Miller (played by his own father, Arch Hall Sr.). He brags to a fellow gas station attendant: "That's my girl. Her father is Robert L. Miller, [who] writes all those adventure books. You oughta see her swim!" This is an odd non-sequiter: Tom discusses the father first, and when he gets to the girl the only compliment he can think of is her athletic ability. Clearly his interest in Roxy is predicated on his interest in Dr. Miller.

Tom invites Dr. Miller along on both of his dates with Roxy, and when he arrives to pick them up, he makes a point of chitchatting with Dad first, before he even acknowledges Roxy's presence. However, Dr. Miller is clearly uncomfortable with his interest: he frequently insists that the two "kids" go off by themselves, and refuses invitations to see Tom alone, without Roxy. He tries to discourage the boy with a series of jabs at his musical taste, driving ability, and teenage slang, but Tom is not dissuaded:

TOM: [Hopefully] I've got my dad's wheels tonight, Mr. Miller.

MILLER: Your dad's *wheels?* What did you do with the rest of his car?

TOM: [Stares for a moment, then laughs] You're real funny, Mr. Miller!

Indeed, the movie is less about the caveman Eegah (seven-feet two-inch Richard Kiel in bearskin and fright wig) than about Dr. Miller attempting to deflect Tom's attention away from himself and onto Roxy. During a date with Tom and Dr. Miller, Roxy describes her first encounter with Eegah on a deserted highway, and Dr. Miller decides to go out looking for the creature. Tom is eager to go along, perhaps because he likes adventure, or perhaps because he wants to spend a few days alone with Dr. Miller.

MILLER: I'm going up on Shadow Mountain with a camera.

TOM: I'll take you up there. My dune buggy is all ready to go!

MILLER: [Hesitates] No, thanks.

TOM: [Angrily] It is! I just gave it the works!

MILLER: No offense, son, but I'd like to take this trip in something a little safer. [Tom turns away, pouting]

When Dr. Miller hires a helicopter to fly him to Shadow Mountain, Tom whines "A helicopter is safer?" Perhaps it is . . . depending on what Dr. Miller wishes to be safe *from.*

When the airport calls to say that the helicopter cannot make the journey to pick him up, Tom is delighted. He exclaims, "We'll get the dune buggy and we'll whiz right out there!" Of course, Dr. Miller does not arrive at the agreed-upon rendezvous point: he has been captured by Eegah. Tom and Roxy wait up for him all night, giving Tom an opportunity to sing, and Eegah an opportunity to capture Roxy.

Instead of going back to town for help, Tom spends the next twenty-four hours running around the desert, encountering iguanas and rattlesnakes and looking stalwart, while the camera zooms in on his pale legs and tight white shorts, inviting us to swoon over this underfed Adonis. Eventually, he rescues them (Dr. Miller first, of course), and they return to the dune buggy. With Eegah in hot pursuit, the question of who will ride shotgun seems irrelevant, but Dr. Miller takes the time to make sure that Roxy sits in the middle, between him and Tom.

They arrive back home just in time to dress for a party. While Tom is singing yet again, Roxy tells her father that she has fallen in love with the caveman! Oddly, Dr. Miller does not attempt to dissuade her from this unlikely choice of romantic partner. He only points subtly in the direction of Tom: "[Worrying about you is] my job for about two more years. Then it will be up to someone else. [Sees Tom approaching] Maybe him, huh?"

Dr. Miller obviously wants to resolve an Oedipal crisis by releasing the emotional responsibility for his daughter to another man, but Tom cannot be that man, since Tom is more interested in Dr. Miller. This dilemma is emphasized later, at poolside, when Tom and Roxy are dancing, and another boy cuts in. Tom merely dances on her other side—he is more than willing to "share" her with the other boy, even if the triangulation implicates them in a homoerotic relationship (in the background, two boys are dancing together with no girl nearby). After awhile, he retrieves Roxy, and they begin dancing together again. The interloper is upset, shouting "I'm gonna deck you!" and instigates a fight. Clearly, Tom was not at all distressed.

A moment later Eegah arrives, having tracked them down, and grabs Roxy—another man unwilling to "share" her. Yet the police, who have been chasing him all over the city, shoot him, and he falls into the pool. Roxy screams in horror at the death of her "lover," and Tom puts his arm around her. "Remember, I love you," he says in an odd, childlike voice, offering support rather than commitment, as if they are best friends. Dad solemnly intones "There were giants in those days." Now, we have only Tom, so rapt over an adult friend that he is unwilling or unable to express the single-minded devotion to heterosexual practice required of teenagers.

In his later films, Hall's characters were no longer teenagers, but they were still obsessed with older men (or they were the obsession of older men). In *Wild Guitar* (1962), for instance, sleazy agent Mike McCauley (Hall Sr.) displays a sleazy, erotic interest in rising country-western singer Bud Eagle (Hall Jr.), moving him into his "own" apartment and sabotaging his relationship with his girlfriend, for no apparent reason except jealousy. In one scene, Bud even meets one of McCauley's previously kept boy stars. In *The Sadist* (1963), Hall plays a psycho killer (based on real-life mass murderer Charlie Starkweather) who intimidates a trio of stranded high school teachers. The fact that he concentrates his abuse on the handsome, muscular Ed (Richard Alden), all but ignoring Doris (Helen Hovey) or the elderly Carl (Don Russell) suggests a sadism rooted in irresolvable homoerotic desire.[9]

Rod Lauren

Sometimes the teenagers were threatened by adults without being turned into monsters. A hunky, teen-idol wannabe (whose "If I Had a Girl," charted at number thirty-one in January 1960), twenty-two-year-old Rod Lauren made his film debut in *Terrified* (1962). After a mysterious hooded figure drags a boy into a graveyard and buries him in wet cement, his sister Marge (Tracy Olsen) decides to investigate. She drives out to an old ghost town with two college-student friends in tow: Ken (Rod Lauren) and David (Steve Drexel). Neither seem to be her boyfriend; in fact, they seem quite taken with each other. After presenting himself as an object of desire by displaying his manly chest, Rod gets captured by the psycho, who makes scary noises, locks him in a room full of spiders, and threatens to drown him. The culprit turns out to be the owner of the local teen hangout, who has the remarkably gay-coded name Wesley Blake (Stephen Roberts). An ex-vaudevillian and ventriloquist, Blake is not interested in murdering the boys so much as terrifying them, thus feminizing them and drawing them away from their heterosexual interests. Unfortunately, he feminizes Ken to death before David and Marge can mount a daring rescue, so they settle for each other.

Next, Lauren starred in *The Crawling Hand* (dir. Herbert L. Stronk, Hanson Enterprises, 1963), a movie about the disembodied hand of a dead astronaut taking on a life of its own. In the first scene, college student Paul (Rod) chases Marta (Sirry Steffin), his Swedish girl-friend, across some sand dunes on a beach at night. After a change-of-clothes scene which amply displays both bodies, they kiss for a long time, thus demonstrating that they have adequately acquired teenage heterosexual interest. Paul notes that most men pretend to be gay so the women can "cure" them: "I know now the secret of how to be successful with a woman. You have to be weak, pathetic, so they feel sorry for you."

The heteronormative idyll is interrupted when Paul finds a disembodied astronaut hand in the surf, and instead of calling the police, takes it home to study. That night the hand comes to life and strangles Paul's aunt, then works on possessing him. He receives the assistance of a pre-*Gilligan* Alan Hale Jr. as the doting male sheriff, as well as the two astronauts assigned to retrieve the hand, but not before he attacks a local ornery soda jerk. He heads out to the junkyard, removes the hand, and lets cats eat it. And peace is restored.

In *Black Zoo* (1963), Lauren plays the mute teenager Carl, who displays no heterosexual interests, relying only upon his intimate adult "master," a zookeeper named Michael Conrad (Michael Gough). Conrad runs an animal-worshipping cult and wants to unleash an army of mutant animals onto the world. After *Black Zoo,* Lauren tried his hand at various genres, including several Westerns, a war movie, a beach movie, and a rock-and-roll musical before relocating, like John Ashley, to the Philippines.

THE END OF THE MONSTER MASH

The monster movie genre lasted only about as long as teen idols— four or five years. The new generation of teenagers wanted something new, and saucer-men and zombies belonged to the last generation. Some spoofs and short subjects appeared, such as *The Incredibly Strange Creatures Who Stopped Living and Became Mixed-Up Zombies!!?* (1963) and prime time's nuclear families with fangs, *The Addams Family* (1964-1966) and *The Munsters* (1964-1966),[10] but overall, teen monsters and monster hunters were forgotten. Vincent Price became the star of AIP's horror movies, his nemeses all adults.

In the opening scene of *Jesse James Meets Frankenstein's Daughter* (1966), Miss Frankenstein leers at an uncredited teenager in tight jeans, shirtless and comatose on her slab, but decides that he's unsuitable and opts to make a monster out of the adult Cal Bolder (playing Hank) instead. *The Navy vs. the Night Monsters* (1966) features the middle-aged Lt. Brown (Anthony Eisley) and Bobby Van, (Rutherford Chandler) as well as Billy Gray (Fred Twining) of *Father Knows Best,* now a seasoned twenty-eight-year-old. Teenagers could no longer look to the skies, or to a caring local sheriff for escape from their heterosexual destiny. But they still had the teen idols and the beach.

Chapter 5

Heartbreak Hotel:
The Teen Idols

Before 1955, most teenagers appropriated their music from Mom
and Dad, who listened mostly to silky-voiced crooners like Nat King
Cole, Doris Day, and even Frank Sinatra. Then, rock and roll ex-
ploded onto the musical scene almost overnight. Elvis and Pat Boone
sanitized it sufficiently for middle-class living rooms, and suddenly
dozens of young rock and rollers were aimed directly at the pages of
teen magazines: Paul Anka and Ricky Nelson by 1957, Frankie Avalon and Bobby Darin by 1958, Fabian by 1959. These new "teen
idols," as they were eventually called,[1] differed significantly from the
performers of the past. Rudy Vallee first crooned through a mega-
phone for a national audience at age twenty-seven, and Frank Sinatra
cut his first record at twenty-four, but the teen idols were eternally
sixteen,[2] able to reference drive-ins, sock hops, and algebra homework without the slightest nostalgia or condescension.

Likewise, Rudy Vallee and Frank Sinatra performed for adults, and
were surprised and incredulous when teenyboppers asked for their
autographs. The teen idols were explicitly niche marketed to teenagers, especially white, middle-class teenagers, through jukeboxes at
high school hangouts, teen-oriented record stores, Top 40 radio sta-
tions, and TV appearances. Bobby Vinton appeared on *The Patty
Duke Show,* James Darren on *Where the Action Is,* Fabian on *The Vir-
ginian,* Frankie Avalon almost everywhere; Ricky Nelson, Paul Pe-
terson, and Johnny Crawford actually started their careers as TV
heartthrobs. Dozens of new teen-oriented magazines appeared on
newsstands, with articles on grooming and fashion subsidiary to gossip columns and beefcake pinups.[3] Soon an encyclopedic knowledge
of the teen idols' biographies, discographies, filmographies, romantic
entanglements, and physical attributes became requisite for place-

doi:10.1300/5484_05

ment in the most popular cliques in the high school cafeteria, as important as slang, fashion, and foodstuffs as signifiers of teen identity. The rare adult who expressed an interest in a teen idol was unwelcome, an interloper, an oldster embroiled in a midlife crisis, or worse.

Nineteen major and innumerable minor teen idols appeared between 1956 and 1963, almost all male and almost all white, though they often covered songs made famous by black R&B performers.[4] However, they were not as doggedly middle class as their target audience. Instead, they usually came from working-class, big-city neighborhoods, and from the ethnic roots carefully excised from the nuclear families and juvenile-delinquent pictures (James Darren, Frankie Avalon, Fabian, and Bobby Rydell grew up within a few blocks of one another in Little Italy of south Philadelphia). Thus they could add a sensuous exoticism to their stage presence, absent since Frankie Darro and Billy Halop stopped playing "Tough Kids," yet still be sufficiently crew cut and clean scrubbed to avoid the middle-class outrage that kept scruffier rock and rollers under wraps. They usually performed as soloists so fans could pretend that they were alone, the sole recipient of the singer's passion, his heart speaking only to *you.*

What the teen idol's heart spoke was a pitch, repeated in 243 top-of-the-chart songs over the eight-year period, as loud, abrasive, and unrepentant as Howdy Doody encouraging peanut-gallery tykes to whine for Wonder Bread.[5] There was little wordplay, little metaphor, not a hint of irony or ambiguity to detract from the pristine clarity of the pitch: if you are a boy, get a girl; if you are a girl, get a boy. Heterosexual romance is your reason for living. No other interest, no sport, hobby, academic subject, or friendship, is worth bothering with unless it will help you meet, impress, or maintain a member of "the opposite sex."

There is no room in the pitch for anxiety about potential problems teenage boys may experience en route to their heterosexual destiny; no clinging mother, absent father, or subversive homosexual-communist infiltration of the public school curriculum could possibly deflect their life trajectory. Any teenage boy who seems impervious to girls is just being cool, any who protests lack of interest is simply lying. Though adult performers of the era, such as Sinatra, were often portrayed as prowling playboys, only a few of the teen idols express a promiscuous desire to kiss every girl on earth. In "Travelin' Man" (1961), Ricky Nelson has girls in every port, from Alaska to Berlin, and in "The Wanderer" (1962), Dion insists that he'll have sex with any girl who offers, no matter if they don't even know his name. Otherwise, heterosexual practice is tepid and unsatisfying, merely a time filler until the teen idol finds *the one* girl whom he was meant to be with, the one girl who will give his life meaning, "the mate that fate created me for," as Bobby Rydell sings ("That Old Black Magic," 1961).

After the teen idol meets *the one,* all other girls instantly become repulsive, or else he is simply unable to notice them. This is not the result of individual volition, a deliberate choice to remain loyal to one's girlfriend, but an unconscious change, rooted in the mysterious underpinnings of the universe. Over 30 percent of the songs proclaim that *you* are the one, my sole purpose, my reason for living. Some of the teen idols are more insistent about the exclusivity, permanence, and mystical underpinnings of their love than others. Frankie Avalon proclaims it in 58 percent of his songs, Ricky Nelson in 48 percent, but Fabian in only 14 percent, and James Darren not at all.

In spite of the "teen angel" clichés, none of the teen idols mourns dead girlfriends, but they do lose *the one* frequently, to moving away, parental disapproval, or simple rejection. Such losses are much more painful in the pitch than they might be in real life, since even after *the one* is gone, the teen idol still finds other girls repulsive, or is unable to notice them. Thus he can never find another love; he is destined to be lonely and miserable for the rest of his life. Bobby Rydell insists "I'll Never Dance Again" (1962), but he means more than that: he will spend every Saturday night henceforth reading Agatha Christie whodunits instead of sock hopping. Since *the one* is his sole reason for living, he will never find the slightest joy in anything else, a career, political activism, hobbies, sports, or friends. The entire world will be dreary and meaningless forever. Thus Paul Anka keeps praying "Every Night" (1962) for *the one,* "because I know that my life would be worthless without you." In spite of the extreme consequences, *the one* is lost in 20 percent of the teen idol songs (not counting instances in which the teen idol initiates the breakup). Johnny Tillotson loses most often, in 75 percent of his songs; Bobby Vinton loses in 44 percent, Bobby Vee in 33 percent, but Ricky Nelson in only 7 percent, and Fabian, Johnny Crawford, and Tommy Sands never.

TEENAGE BOYS IN LOVE

The pitch was repeated incessantly, in hundreds of songs played dozens of times a day for endless weeks, a background blur in bedrooms and soda shops, school gyms and drive-ins, throughout all of those crucial years 1956 to 1963. At the same time, Ricky, Bud, and the Beaver were learning that they must like girls or pretend to, and down at the drive-in, juvenile delinquents were torn between gang and girl for the same reason. Teenagers were moving closer and closer to the edge of the nuclear family womb, closer to the roaring, ravenous world outside. Every day they were wandering farther afield, spending time with their friends instead of the family, at the soda shop instead of in their rooms, until Mom and Dad offered no protection at all against subversion or perversion. So the protection must follow the teenagers, becoming a background as they roamed the world, and reinforcing the nuclear family ideology by reducing Mom, Dad, kids, house, car, lawn, and career to one essential dynamic—a boy and a girl. The boy would then select a career, buy a house, and father children to please the girl, and the girl would find her sole existence in the children and in his arms. Most teen idols were boys singing to girls. Real-life girls had the hard and noble job of drawing real-life boys away from chums and hot rods.

Teen magazines and teen idol biographies usually insisted that there were no male fans at all, that girls bought every record, posted every pinup, fed every dime into a jukebox, and solicited every autograph. Even today, concert photographs from the era are commonly captioned, newsreels narrated, and memorabilia on eBay advertised as if the teen idol was dogged by armies of "hysterical girls" but not a single boy. Instead, boys were portrayed as actively hostile to the teen idol, constitutionally unable to appreciate his music. If he happened to buy a Frankie or Fabian record by mistake, hidden away amid a pile of Connie Stevens, or if he was dragged to a concert by an insensitive girlfriend, he would judge the teen idol hideous, not "dreamy," and cringe at the cacophonic wailing that passed for song. Dozens of movies and television programs from the early 1960s, including *Beach Party, Palm Springs Weekend, The Beverly Hillbillies, The Lucy Show,* and even *Gilligan's Island,* show girls screaming and swooning over parodic teen dreams, while the boys dry heave and cover their ears.

Yet the narrations, captions, teen magazines, and eBay advertisements are all lying, very obviously and very deliberately: teen idols had many, many boy fans. Looking beyond the caption about "Hysterical Girl Fans" at the actual photographs shows as many boys as girls. They are having fun, not sullen and resentful at a threat to their masculinity. Even photos of the backstage fans show boys interspersed among the girls, equally jubilant at the proximity of their idols, equally eager to solicit an autograph or rip off a shirt. Today, many men and women who grew up in that era recall teen idols' sensual, androgynous performances on TV or in live concerts forty years ago. The straight men and lesbians not quite able to squeeze their erotic adulation into the "hero worship" or "buddy" categories available to them.[6] The gay men and straight women were both certain that they were numbered among the *yous* that made the idol's life worthwhile.

The reason behind the pretense that boys never appeared in a teen idol's fan base is obvious. Though he promoted a graphically gender-polarized world of strong boys and swooning girls, the teen idol was pretty, androgynous, even feminine, with a soft, sensual public persona that would foreground same-sex desire if ever a boy as much as grinned at him. It is no wonder that many teen idols were rumored to be gay, or "funny," as the slang of the day might term them. The teen magazines seemed to actively encourage such rumors, omitting any reference to wives or girlfriends, and characterizing each teen idol, regardless of his real personality, as shy, quiet, sensitive, artistic—all code terms for gay. Elvis performed with swiveling hips and fluttering wrists, gestures so flamboyant that he had to be surrounded by a dozen girls at all times just to minimize suspicion.[7] Bobby Rydell and Fabian appeared in ridiculously effeminate hairdos suggestive more of Liberace than Jerry Lee Lewis. Though sold as "all-American boys," the teen idols rarely displayed the hard muscles that would suggest strength, power, and masculinity, at least not until they moved from music into acting. Instead, they swayed gently in full-body shots, or sometimes in misty close-ups, with no distracting subsidiary performers and no props, not even a guitar to mask their physicality, just a phallic microphone drawn close to the mouth. The teen idols did not grin or swagger; sometimes they managed shy smiles, but mostly they were in pain, vulnerable and wounded even in the midst of a song about how *you* have made their life complete, as if they didn't really believe the sales pitch they were trying so hard to foster, as if the audience didn't really believe them. As if something essential had been left out.

In their pitch, the teen idols eliminate the possibility of male same-sex desire, even in the form of homosocial friendship, by presenting a world in which no boys exist. Only twenty-seven of the teen idol songs allude to boys at all, in twenty-two, including Bobby Vee's "Staying In" (1961), Pat Boone's "Johnny Will" (1962), and James Darren's "Pin a Medal on Joey" (1963), boys are reviled competitors, lying in wait to steal the girl and walk off with her. Again, some artists were more worried about the male interlopers than others: Del Shannon fought off (or lost to) other boys in 60 percent of his teen-idol romances, Bobby Vee in 33 percent, Johnny Tillotson in 25 percent, but Frankie Avalon, Paul Anka, and Fabian, never did (since they were generally deemed the most attractive of the teen idols, perhaps no one could believe that they had competition).

Five songs mention boys who are not reviled competitors. In "Poor Boy" (Elvis, 1956), "Ten Lonely Guys" (Pat Boone, 1962), and "Drip Drop" (Dion, 1962), buddies commiserate with the teen idol over his loss of *the one,* and the other two, a pitiably small number, contain vague allusions to same-sex practice. In "Jailhouse Rock" (1957) which became a hit after Elvis performed it in the movie of the same name, Elvis evokes a dance at the county jail, an all-male preserve, and specifies that prisoners vie for the most attractive dance partners: "Number 47 said to Number 3, 'You're the cutest jailbird I ever did see!' " Less suggestive but more homo-romantic is Bobby Darin's "Nature Boy" (1961), a cover of a 1948 Nat King Cole song about a "very strange enchanted boy" from far away, "a little shy and sad of eye," like the sad, shy, pretty boys who linger at the margins of the heteronormative myth. Nature boy visits Bobby on "a magic day" and, during their time together, tells him: "the greatest thing you'll ever learn is just to love and be loved in return." Perhaps the song managed to pass into the pitch because the boy could be interpreted as a little boy, advising Bobby to find a girl. Yet according to Nat King Cole's biography, the boy is an adult, one of the long-haired, sandal-clad Nature Boys, forerunners of the hippies, who wandered Los Angeles in the 1940s. And he never says "get a girl." He wants the teen idol to love *him.*[8]

The possibility of same-sex love is evoked in less than 1 percent of the teen idol songs, but many more subtle critiques of heterosexual destiny are audible. The boy usually falls in love through a passive rush of emotion, unexpected and overwhelming. He waits by the phone for the girl to call; he sobs into his pillow when she breaks up with him. When Ricky Nelson whispers "I wanna be kissed until I tingle" ("I Wanna Be Loved," 1959), he wants to be kissed rather than initiate the kissing, to be embraced rather than embraced. This part of the pitch is so directly opposed to the aggressive striving expected of gender-polarized boys in 1950's society that one really can't imagine an "all-American boy" behaving this way with a girlfriend. However, he might well behave this way with another boy.

In the teen idol songs, the boy falls in love instantly and stays in love for the rest of his life, but the girl plays games, flirts, lies, cheats, pretends to be in love when she is not, sees other guys on the side, toys with him. Elvis moans "Don't Be Cruel" (1956) and merely "Don't" (1958); Ricky Nelson is a "Poor Little Fool" (1958); Bobby Vee warns that no matter how hard his girl works to cover up her philandering, "The Night Has a Thousand Eyes" (1963). Dion has probably the worst luck of any teen idol, getting his heart ripped out by "Runaround Sue" (1961), "Little Diane" (1962), "Sandy" (1963), and "Donna the Prima Dona" (1963). Cruel, deceiving, cheating, unfaithful girls appear in 14 percent of the teen idol songs, with James Darren, Johnny Crawford, Dion, and Elvis particularly susceptible. Again, this part of the pitch is the opposite of standard 1950's gender polarization in which women wait at home experiencing everlasting love, while men hound dog around, suggesting that the "all-American boy" would more likely have such a boyfriend than a girlfriend.

Another critique of heterosexual destiny can be made, especially evocative when one compares the teen idol songs with other genres of teen culture in the 1950s. The teen idol is surrounded by parents, teachers, and coaches who hate the heterosexual desire they have long since abandoned, and try to stifle it through harsh curfews, withdrawn car and telephone privileges, insistence on ugly costumes and hairstyles, and the incessant chant that the boy is "too young."[9] In 1957 Pat Boone insisted that "April Love (is for the very young)", and in 1959, he specified that it is designated for those "Twixt Twelve and Twenty." Frankie Avalon sang "Bobby Sox to Stockings" and Paul Anka sang perhaps the theme of the first half of the 1960s, "Puppy Love." Perhaps because he roiled against Ozzie approving his every performance, Ricky Nelson recorded three anti-adult anthems, "I'm Not Afraid," "Young Emotions," and "A Teenager's Romance."

Although only 7 percent of the teen idol romances specify adult opposition, that opposition seems extraordinarily severe. They accuse the teenager of being simply too young, unwisely deciding on *the one* before they have completed high school or selected a career; their loves are abnormal, unnatural, evil, and wrong. Gene Pitney sings "If we stop to gaze upon a star, people talk about how bad we are" ("Town Without Pity," 1961). In "A Teenager's Romance" (1957), Ricky Nelson sings:

> They tell us we're different
> We haven't the right
> To decide for ourselves, dear
> What's black and what's white.

He doesn't say "our love is different," but *we're* different. Perhaps significantly, Ricky does not mention a girl in the song.

The penalty for teenage romance is also surprisingly severe, more than mere grounding or refused permission to attend the prom. In "Stranger in Town," Del Shannon and his love (again of unspecified gender) are on the run from a killer hired by their parents. What parents would want their child killed for a hetero-romance, however premature? He is clearly talking about something more significant than a boy-girl crush. Though appearing to reinforce the nuclear family myth by promoting heterosexual romance, teen idol songs often offer a subtle resistance, coding the teen idols as gender-trangressive, potentially gay, looking beyond the girls in the audience to find boys as well.

TEEN IDOLS ON SCREEN

Hollywood generally offered teen idols contracts the moment their first mug shot appeared in a teen magazine, first in small roles designed to draw teens into mainstream productions, and then in their own twixt-twelve-and-twenty vehicles. But feature-length movies could hardly reproduce the circumscript world of the teen idol songs, with only one boy and about a gazillion girls (though both Elvis and Pat Boone tried). There had to be male buddies, roommates, classmates, and co-workers, if only to give the boy someone to discuss girls with. Yet allowing a performer to maintain a soft, vulnerable, androgynous stage presence during buddy-bonding scenes necessarily foregrounds a homoerotic potential, especially when that buddy is also a soft, vulnerable, androgynous teen idol, as in the pairing of Sal Mineo and James Darren in *The Gene Krupa Story* (1959), Fabian and Tommy Sands in *Love in a Goldfish Bowl* (1961), Paul Anka and Sal Mineo in *The Longest Day* (1962), or Fabian and Tab Hunter in *Ride the Wild Surf* (1964). Plotlines that simply added songs to juvenile delinquent themes only made matters "worse," contrasting tepid boy-girl romances with same-sex friendships blinding in their intensity and passion.

Pat Boone

In the early days of his career, Pat Boone was not marketed as white-bread Republican, but as a sullen, sultry Brando wannabe, a teenage rebel in tight jeans. Though the twenty-three-year-old spent 1957 invoking the pitch with "I'm Waiting for You," "Remember You're Mine," and "Love Letters in the Sand," in his film debut, *Bernardine* (1957), he does not fall for a girl; instead he queerly facilitates the romance of the titular dream girl and Dick Sargent (the gay actor who would become the second Darrin on *Bewitched*). In *April Love* (1957), Pat plays a juvenile delinquent exiled to a Kentucky horse farm curiously lacking in boys, thus allowing for no homoerotic distractions in his romance with Shirley Jones. He buddy bonds again as a Virginia Military Institute cadet vacationing at *Mardi Gras* (1958) with fellow teen idols Tommy Sands and Gary Crosby (plus Dick Sargent again), and the mistaken-identity romance with Christine Carère virtually an afterthought.

In *Journey to the Center of the Earth* (1959), the homoerotic potential of the teen idol persona is foregrounded. Playing a nineteenth-century University of Edinburgh fratboy, Pat has a girlfriend for only the opening and closing scenes. Otherwise, he conveniently leaves her at home to follow his uncle-professor (James Mason), their beefy Icelandic guide, Hans (Peter Ronson), a widow (Arlene Dahl), and a duck (Gertrude) through a rabbit hole and deep into an underworld of lost or suppressed desire. As they descend, Pat loses his shirt, and the camera moves from close-ups of his pretty-boy face to concentrate on his small, firm biceps and lean, tight chest. Yet there is no heterosexual interest to correspond to his depiction of strength, power, and masculinity. Pat flees from a giant lizard, almost suffocates in quicksand, and is shot by the bad guy, consequently requiring rescue and cradling in the strong arms of the professor. He and Hans (also shirtless, for reasons required by the plot) smile at each other, touch arms and shoulders, hug, and dance together on the shore of a warm subterranean sea. Back in the daylit world, Pat proposes to his girlfriend, the professor woos the widow, and Hans woos the duck. They embrace their heterosexual destiny (kind of) only after they have spent ninety minutes celebrating the manly love of comrades.

Perhaps learning his lesson, Pat omits buddies, especially teen-idol buddies, from his films for the next few years. Fellow teen Bobby Darin appears in *State Fair* (1962), but only as competition for Ann-Margret. Sexual ambiguity intrudes with a vengeance in *Goodbye, Charlie* (1964). The titular womanizing cad character, shot and drowned by a jealous husband, comes back to life (Debbie Reynolds), who, though "the same old Charlie," is now interested in men. So, a suitor comes forward, Pat, as Bruce Minton, with a name already doubly gay coded (*bruce* and *mincing,*) and a litany of gay-coded traits: he is an antiques buff, a hypochondriac, a mama's boy, an over-the-top parody of Tony Randall's gay heterosexual characters. Yet (Virginia/Charlie) Debbie prefers former best buddy George (Tony Curtis), then a cute young thing who spent the early 1960s in sex comedies being hit on by guys (by mistake in *Some Like It Hot,* but not in *The Great Race*) or mistakenly assumed gay (in *Boeing Boeing,* for instance, his fiancée repeatedly catches him in suspicious-looking clenches with Jerry Lewis; she finally cries "What I suspected is true!" and demands that he choose between them). Tony falls in love with him/her even after being apprised of the switch. Evidently true love doesn't care about gender, but Pat did: he soon retired from acting, except for a few religious films and the campy documentary *The Eyes of Tammy Faye* (2000).

Fabian

Though the sixteen-year-old Fabian really couldn't sing, his dark curly hair, heavy-lidded gaze, and buffed physique practically created the teen magazine market, with beefcake pinups boosting the subscriptions of *Teen Magazine, Teen Live, Seventeen Movie Teen Illustrated, Hollywood Teen Album,* and many others. He became a Hardy Boys-style sleuth in *Keyhole Mystery Magazine* (1960), and even got his own magazine, *Fabian: Boy of Mystery.* After his film debut in *Hound Dog Man* (1959), buddy bonding with Stuart Whitman, he played sissified, androgynous, and girl-crazy against any number of "men's men:" Robert Mitchum, Bing Crosby, Stewart Granger twice, John Wayne three times. The only break in the string of macho companions was with fellow teen idol Tommy Sands in *Love in a Goldfish Bowl* (1961).

Surrounding a fey teen idol with all that brawn created a problem: the boy simply did not seem straight, especially when he sang, regardless of how often he flexed his biceps or ogled girls. When Henry Koester at 20th Century Fox costarred him twice with Jimmy Stewart, he simply gave up. *Mr. Hobbs Takes a Vacation* (1962) has Fabian on stage for only about five minutes, long enough to dance with Jimmy Stewart's wallflower daughter and sing a duet with her, "Cream Puff" (about cutesy pet names, not about being gay, though it was composed by gay thesbian Johnny Mercer). He gets slightly more air time in *Dear Brigitte* (1965), but no songs, and though he buddies around with Jimmy Stewart's daughter, he is never identified as her boyfriend and exhibits no romantic interest in her. Instead, his part of the plot involves exploiting eight-year-old math prodigy Billy Mumy for capitalist gain.

In *Ride the Wild Surf* (1964), the twenty-one-year-old Fabian drops out of college to hit Hawaii's North Shore with heartthrob buddies Peter Brown and Tab Hunter. Surfing was still being positioned as an all-male pursuit, and director Don Taylor knew it. He crowded North Shore with male surfers and spectators, (only a few girls), and when we see the details of surfing for the first time in a mainstream movie, it becomes an intensely homoerotic spectacle. The surfers paddle out prone until the beach is a vague line in the distance. Then they stand, their power distilled into the sharp thrust of their surfboards, and explode toward the shore, all bronze chests and thick biceps glistening in the sun, war whooping a triumph over the elements that has nothing to do with the wiles of civilization.

Later in the movie, there are some concessions to heterosexual destiny: each of the three boys hooks up with a girl, and Fabian eventually chooses college, with its end result of wife, kids, and house in the suburbs, over the male preserve of beach bumming. Yet the movie does not end with a kiss and hand-in-hand walk into a heterosexual sunset; instead, Fabian wins a surfing contest and is enveloped by his jubilant buddies, all hugging and hollering, a solid mass of men as the camera pans out to a wide-angle shot of surf and sky.

James Darren

In 1957, screenwriter Frederick Kohner published *Gidget—the Little Girl with Big Ideas,* a surprisingly graphic novel about a Malibu high schooler for whom heterosexual desire—indeed, heterosexual practice—is so ordinary as to be unworthy of comment. She disapproves of wearing "falsies" (fake breast enlargements), for instance, because a boy "will find out sure as hell the first time he takes you to a show";[10] that is, a movie date implies breast fondling just as much as popcorn. On the prowl for the working-class toughs who hang out on the beach, Gidget flirts with an older surfing bum named The Big Kahuna, but he insists on treating her like a little sister. Instead she has her summer fling with a rich college boy named Moondoggie.

Transforming this text into a movie comedy seems risky, since in the 1950s only sexploitation flicks showed "nice girls" doing anything more intimate than a doorstep kiss. In April 1959, Columbia released a watered-down *Gidget* (dir. Paul Wendkos), with fifteen-year-old Sandra Dee playing the girl-midget as considerably less hetero-horny than her fictional counterpart. In fact, she is one of the few girls in the mass media of the 1950s whose "discovery of boys" is problematic. She thinks dating is "icky" and has to be dragged onto the beach for a "manhunt." Her butch yet boy-crazy friend B.L. (Sue George) quips, "You need a few hormone shots!" Gidget worries that she will never "discover" boys, but Mom, who has no doubt been paying attention to the teen idol songs, assures her that heterosexual desire will soon kick in; it's inevitable, a fact of life. "That's a relief!" Gidget sighs. "I saw myself pickled in a jar at Harvard!"

While the other girls are oozing over the boys, proto-feminist Gidget tries to be admitted into their all-male preserve by learning to surf. Kahuna, a professional beach bum played by thirty-four-year-old Cliff Robertson, takes a big-brotherly interest in her, and she falls, on schedule, for his protégé Moondoggie (James Darren, not yet a teen idol), oblivious to the fact that the two men are obliquely coded as gay. Kahuna notes that he is deeply involved "in the life," a contemporary term for the gay subculture. Completely excluded from the heteronormative life of career, marriage, and family, he has "no connections." He never dates, nor does he express any interest in girls. The younger Moondoggie, a rich kid who dropped out of college to spite his father, is trying to model his life on Kahuna's. He does date girls, but only because he is not fully committed to "the life"; he's not fully integrated into the subculture. At the end of the summer, Kahuna and Moondoggie plan to go away together.

When Gidget first falls for Moondoggie, he ignores her, so she tries to incite his interest with the curious strategy of asking him to pretend an interest in her to make Kahuna jealous. "You can't get him jealous," Moondoggie protests. "I know, because we're two of a kind." What kind of boy will not get jealous over a buddy's liaison with a girl? He doesn't specify. He agrees to the deception—for the money, he thinks, but he is mistaken. Kahuna may be too cool to get jealous, or simply not interested in girls, but Moondoggie eventually falls for Gidget.

The pivotal scene comes when, rejected by Moondoggie, Gidget decides to "become a woman," that is, have sex, so she invites herself to Kahuna's beach house for "one of his private parties." We have not been told about these private parties before, but Moondoggie knows all about them, and has no doubt been a guest. When Gidget arrives, Kahuna is not interested in romance, but he plays along in hopes of scaring her off. She persists in flirting in spite of the dimmed lights and soft music, so he simply tells her "It's time to go home." Moondoggie arrives a moment later, seething with jealousy. Ostensibly Moondoggie is angry because he believes that Kahuna took advantage of an innocent Gidget, so why does Kahuna not simply tell him that nothing happened? And what does all of this have to do with being "in the life"? Perhaps Moondoggie is angry because he believes that Kahuna has been with someone else. In homophobic fantasy, older men like Kahuna are responsible for initiating innocents like Moondoggie into "the life." They fight, and Kahuna sadly concludes that the boy is not yet ready to sever his ties to the "straight" world. The next morning, Moondoggie arrives at Gidget's door as Jeff, a clean-cut college student ready for career, wife, house, and kids. Kahuna, too, takes a real job, as an airline pilot. Gidget's heterosexual awakening has successfully ended the homoerotic Eden of the beach.

James Darren's sullen good looks and magnificent physique, well suited to an angst-ridden conflict between homoerotic partner and gender-transgressive girl, made him the hit of the movie and a fixture in the teen magazines for years to come. His teen idol career began in 1959 with the *Gidget* theme song, and lasted until about 1963. He specialized in amazingly hostile accusations at the girls who led him on, or the boys they cheated on him with: "Goodbye, Cruel World," "Pin a Medal on Joey," and "They Should Have Given You the Oscar." Meanwhile, he continued to take movie roles in which his characters fail to exhibit significant interest in girls, but fall in love quite openly with boys. When his characters are sexually ambiguous, as in the Gidget series and *Let No Man Write My Epitaph* (1960), he rarely disrobes, even at the beach, but when he plays aggressively heterosexual, as in *Diamond Head* (1963), he rarely appears with a shirt, another example of the common equation of nature, nudity, and heterosexuality, contrasted with an equation of artifice, costume, and gay identity, which will appear frequently in teen culture through the 1980s.

In *The Gene Krupa Story* (dir. Don Weis, Columbia, 1959), Darren plays Eddie Sirota, who accompanies best buddy, drummer Gene Krupa (Sal Mineo), to New York to make it big in the Roaring-Twenties jazz scene. Darren is astonishingly unoffended when Mineo starts making time with his girlfriend, "Eth" (Susan Kohner), nor does he ever appear in the company of another girl during the sixteen-odd years covered by the story (1929 to mid-1940s). Instead, he is perfectly content to fifth wheel with the couple, making do with an occasional sultry look. When Mineo is boy-toyed by a fast-track jazz club singer and her cronies, it is Darren, not Kohner, who feels betrayed. "Those girls meant nothing to me!" Mineo protests, again as if it is Darren, not Kohner, who requires an explanation. After many heart-to-hearts and admonitions, both "friends" tire of Mineo's self-destructive boozing and partying, and leave, and at the end of the movie, both reconcile with him. Though the requisite fade-out scene involves man and woman walking off toward hetero-domesticity, it is clear that Darren has eyes only for Mineo.

Though Sandra Dee had dropped out of the Gidget franchise, Darren continued to play Moondoggie through *Gidget Goes Hawaiian* (1961) and *Gidget Goes to Rome* (1963), always treating his Gidgets (Deborah Walley and Cindy Carol, respectively) with bald-faced hostility. Moondoggie acts as if he hates being in love with them, but couldn't help himself, and variously baits and snubs his buddies (Michael Callan and Peter Brooks, respectively) as if desperate to keep them at arm's length. Only in his final teen role, *For Those Who Think Young* (1964), did the twenty-eight-year-old manage to reconcile both worlds, buddy bonding with Bob Denver (between girl-phobic sitcom roles as Maynard G. Krebs and Gilligan) while they both try to score with coeds.

Elvis

Elvis worked the hardest of any teen idol to replicate the one-boy-multiple-girl world of the songs. Though he played literal teenagers in only four of thirty-one movies, he was always a symbolic teenager, lost in the gap between childhood and adulthood, living with parents or next door to a parental figure, with a job that seemed more like a high school extracurricular activity (water skiing instructor, photographer, scuba diver) and no political interests or any awareness of the world outside (except for occasional, fleeting digs at big business or government bureaucracy). But while juvenile delinquent movies locate resistance to heterosexual destiny in the homosocial bonds of gang or the buddy, Elvis resists, ironically, by luxuriating in heterosexual horniness. Maguffins[11] about winning the big race or buying the boat are always smothered beneath countless scenes of Elvis wandering the beach amid scads of bikini babes, singing about how much he wants to kiss them. Then, the teen-idol pitch kicks in and he is thunderstruck by a vision of *the one,* played by the starlet du jour (Tuesday Weld, Stella Stevens, Ursula Andress, Ann-Margret). After flirting, bickering, tantrums, and breakups and reconciliations, he abandons his fun job, nonstop smooching, and freewheeling adult adolescence to marry *the one.* He finds an organization-man job, buys a house, and raises some kids in some suburb nowhere near Acapulco (but not to worry, in four months there'll be another movie, and Elvis will be wandering the beach again amid more *Girls! Girls! Girls!*).

The sheer proliferation of scenes of Elvis chasing, being chased by, kissing, dancing with, winning, or merely ogling girls means that there are few scenes left for developing the male characters necessary for the plot. Elvis always has best buddies or business partners (Gig Young, Gary Lockwood, Gary Crosby, Bill Bixby), but they enter his life with only a line or two of back-story exposition, or none at all, meeting him and instantly becoming his constant companion. When two people become intimate instantly, without a scene explaining that they have been friends for years or establishing their growing friendship, the most obvious explanation is erotic passion: the two have fallen in love at first sight. So in striving so mightily to immerse Elvis in a two-hour long *Sports Illustrated* swimsuit issue, the director, screenwriter, or editor (or Elvis himself), unwittingly foregrounds the possibility of homo-romance.

In *Viva Las Vegas* (dir. George Sidney, MGM, 1964), Elvis (as Lucky) accidentally encounters fellow race-car driver played by Cesare Danova, at an auto garage. They know each other by reputation, but they have never met before. Danova offers him a job driving in the big race, and Elvis refuses. However, the association doesn't end there: they spend the next ten minutes of the movie, several days in movie time, hitting Las Vegas night spots, ostensibly looking for dream girl Rusty (Ann-Margret), but obviously having a fabulous time without her. Their revel ends in Danova's hotel room, in the morning, as they are getting dressed. Are we to assume that they have been sleeping together? Elvis says that it's time to say good-bye, but he doesn't leave. The two supposed antagonists cling to each other like long-lost brothers for the rest of the movie, competing affectionately over the race and the girl, and in the final fade-out wedding, Elvis, Danova, and Ann-Margret are so tightly enclenched that one wonders who is marrying whom.

Clambake (dir. Arthur H. Nadel, United Artists, 1967), one of the last teen idol movies, came near the end of Elvis' film career, when the cast is obviously tiring of the formula, and the crew is becoming bored and sloppy; thus they are less careful than usual about obfuscating the homo-romance. As a Texas oil tycoon's son, ("Scott") Elvis heads out to nowhere to cut Dad's apron strings, and at a roadside diner he meets the poverty-stricken gay played by Will Hutchins (as "Tom," a lanky, amiable, nice-guy fixture of the era). Will wishes he had Elvis's money to score with babes and Elvis wishes he were poor so girls would like him for his good looks rather than the size of his wallet. So they pull a Prince-and-Pauper switch: Elvis hands over his super-sized wallet, Jaguar keys, and Texas tycoon outfit, and in exchange gets Will's clunker-motorcycle and poor-person's job as a waterskiing instructor at a resort hotel in Miami Beach. However, after the switch Will doesn't disappear forever, like most amiable young men who receive windfalls at roadside diners; he goes to the same resort hotel, name drops his way into a V.I.P. suite, and attaches himself firmly to Elvis.

For the rest of the movie the two are inseparable, hanging out in the V.I.P. suite together, playing together, singing together, or simply staring at each other and grinning as if delighted by some secret joke. They call each other "old buddy" and "old pal" and evidently mean it, though they have been acquainted for only a few days. The two actors had worked together before on *Spinout,* but in the context of the film their sudden, amazingly close friendship makes no sense, and indeed, it makes the entire premise senseless. Elvis cannot experience the joys of poverty when he spends every moment with a "rich" buddy. We might assume that Elvis just wants to keep a close eye on his money, but Will is the one who monitors the arrangement. He is constantly reminding Elvis that it is temporary, and he is the one who insists that they switch back. One suspects that Elvis would be perfectly content staying poor forever, especially when he can stay in a "rich" buddy's V.I.P. suite.

Other guests at the hotel are astonished at how well the rich boy and poor boy have hit it off, and some even seem to conclude that they are a romantic couple, or for some other reason off limits to potential suitors. When golddigging Dianne (Shelley Fabares) ignores "tycoon" Will, he asks "How come she never made a play for me?" Elvis replies, "Too much competition!" Competition from whom? Certainly not from other girls—Will has not dated up to this point. Perhaps she believes him too attached to Elvis to be interested in girls. After the titular clambake, Will manages to pry himself away from Elvis long enough to invite a girl to "look for buried treasure" down on the beach. As they walk away arm in arm, Elvis looks dejected, and Shelly Fabares mistakenly concludes that he is upset because Will is abandoning him. "You should get a *girl,*" she advises, emphasizing the *girl* as opposed to a boy.

The heterosexual horniness that carried Elvis through nearly thirty movies is certainly retained in *Clambake,* with both Elvis and Will talking about, longing for, and eventually kissing girls, but still, bits of stage business constantly evoke—or forget to hide—the possibility that they are romantically involved. After Elvis, Will, and four bikini babes help refurbish a race car, Elvis sings, begging them to line up behind a counter so he can kiss them, one by one. Will lines up along with the girls, as if he wants his turn, and indeed, why would he line up with the rest unless he expected a kiss? It's a short sequence, and he could easily have just stood aside. Elvis kisses the first, second, and third girl, while Will watches with an amazing intensity, aching for his kiss—he is next—and then the scene falls apart. Three different takes are jumbled together, with characters in different positions— Will in fourth or fifth place, Elvis walking toward him or walking way, the last girl sitting or standing. Why the chaotic editing? I do not suggest that one of the takes had Elvis actually kissing Will—but surely something went wrong, some of the takes made the homoerotic implication of Will *waiting for his turn* uncomfortably obvious, and trying to hide it without reshooting the whole sequence resulted in a cinematic breakdown. When order is restored, Elvis has shoved the fourth girl into Will's arms, offering her as a substitute for his own kiss.

However, it is an inadequate substitution. The penultimate scene of the movie has the two boys discussing how important they are to each other. Though they have switched back to their original lives, they will not be parting; they toast their relationship with champaign. Then Elvis takes a drive with Shelley Fabares and tells her that he can accommodate her gold digging because he's rich. She doesn't believe him—having a rich buddy doesn't count, regardless of how close they are. So Elvis displays his oil-tycoon driver's license. She faints. The camera pans out with Elvis trying to revive her and apologizing for being rich, while the cars stuck behind him begin to honk. This is one of the few Elvis movies that ends on a joke rather than a wedding; but perhaps the wedding came before, with the two men sipping champaign and promising to stay together as the era of the teen idols faded away.

Chapter 6

How to Stuff a Wild Bikini:
The Beach Movies

In January 1961, young, handsome, man-about-town John F. Kennedy and his glamourous First Lady, Jackie, moved into the White House and sent the elderly Ike and Mamie back to Kansas, a triumph of beauty over age, optimism over crankiness, tolerance over bigotry (since JFK was Roman Catholic in an era of know-nothing populism), and perhaps most importantly, the nuclear family over all. David Eisenhower was long grown up and moved away before his dad took the Oath of Office, but JFK and Jackie had toddlers, four-year-old Caroline and babe-in-arms John-John. The First Family was presented in the press as simply the Nuclear Family writ large, Dad going to work every day while Mom stayed home to redecorate, the pinnacle of human happiness achieved and visible. There were a few problems left in the world, especially the Cold War, but surely all the Soviets needed was a demonstration of American youth, vigor, and fecundity. So, the President's Council on Physical Fitness ensured that all American schoolkids could do push-ups, the Peace Corps sent smiling young missionaries out to preach the American Way in countries straddling the fence, and NASA launched square-jawed cowboys Alan Shepard and John Glenn into space after ensuring that they were more photogenic than the Soviets' Yuri Gagarin.

It didn't work. The Cold War raged on. Just a few months after he took office, JFK mounted a war-whooping "intervention" of Cuba that failed miserably, and in October 1962 his showdown with the Soviets over Cuban missiles brought the world closer to Armageddon than ever. In September 1962, JFK published a letter in *Life* magazine urging families to dig fallout shelters in the backyards of their split-level suburban houses, prompting a "shelter-mania" that raged through the summer of 1963. That summer was especially tense: on June 20, a

doi:10.1300/5484_06

83

hotline opened between the White House and the Kremlin, to ensure that the world did not end by accident, and on June 26, Kennedy gave his famous "Ich bin ein Berliner" speech, defiantly proclaiming West Berlin a symbol of freedom in the midst of Soviet tyranny. Worried or oblivious, the teenagers of Camelot hit the beach.

The Beach Boys' "Surfin" barely charted in 1962, but in 1963, their "Surfin' U.S.A." stayed on the charts for sixteen weeks, peaking at number two and inspiring competing songs by Jan and Dean ("Surf City"), The Surfaries ("Wipe Out") and The Chantays ("Pipeline). Teen movies sometimes set scenes on the beach before, but only so juvenile delinquents could walk around feeling morose or monsters could rise up out of the surf to grab at swimsuit-bare bodies; even in *Devil on Wheels,* Darryl Hickman's weenie roast and surf smooch portends tragedy. The beach was rarely a site of fun and escape until *Beach Party* premiered in June 1963.[1]

AIP President Sam Arkoff stated that it was a deliberate marketing strategy. The horror genre had run its course, and he needed something else to draw teenagers to the drive-in. Teen idols sold tickets by singing and doffing their clothes, so he hired fading teen idol Frankie Avalon, whose last hit peaked at number twenty-one in 1960, Disney good-girl Annette Funicello, and some miscellaneous pals and gals. They dressed in swimsuits, and sang on the beach at Malibu. Writer/producer Lou Rusoff borrowed some plot motifs from juvenile delinquency and monster movies (a boy torn between the gang and the girl, a mad scientist-anthropology professor leering at the teenagers through binoculars), director William Asher (soon to hit it big with the TV series *Bewitched*) added moments of slapstick comedy, and the singing swimsuit teens became the summer's runaway hit, netting $4 million on a budget of $350,000 (meanwhile *The Great Escape* cost $4 million to make, and barely grossed $5.5 million).

The beach-movie craze began with a popularity unprecedented by the juvenile delinquents and monsters.[2] For the next four years, AIP kept Frankie, Annette, and company busy with a dozen beach movie sequels; if Frankie was unavailable, Dwayne Hickman or Tommy Kirk was consigned to fill his Speedos, and Deborah Walley or Yvonne Craig stood in for Annette. Other studios immediately began churning out their own teen-idols-in-swimsuits movies, even though they quickly ran out of teen idols. 20th Century Fox got Bobby Vinton for *Surf Party* (January 1964), but had to settle for one-hit wonder Rod Lauren, currently eking out a living in monster movies, for *The Young Swingers* (July 1964). *For Those Who Think Young* (July 1964) starred James Darren, and *Ride the Wild Surf* (August 1964) both Fabian and Tab Hunter, but *Beach House Party* (August 1965) was stuck with a Dean Martin hanger on named Frankie Randall. *Beach Ball* (September 1965) had Edd "Kookie" Byrnes from the TV series *77 Sunset Strip,* and *Winter A Go-Go* (October 1965) had James Stacy, best known at the time for being married to teen dream Connie Stevens.

The plot of the AIP beach movie, a flimsy device on which to hang swimsuits and jokes, is about the same in each installment. A gang of teenagers arrives at Malibu for a joyful summer or spring break vacation. Frankie and Annette quarrel: she insists that they plan for marriage, the next step in embracing their heterosexual destiny and becoming Dad and Mom (in a split-level house in the suburbs, naturally), but he is too happy surfing, skydiving, and drag racing with his buddies; that is, he refuses to give up the gang for the girl. They separate, flirt with others, complain about each other to their friends, snipe at each other at the teen hangout, and walk forlornly on the beach. Meanwhile, evil adults hope to exploit the teenagers' attractiveness for the interest of big business, or else they scheme to salt peter their heterosexual passion. Over-the-hill juvenile delinquent Eric Von Zipper (played by Harvey Lembeck) and his gang of Ratz side with the adults (perhaps because some of them are nearly fifty years old), or generally make mischief. The climax comes in the form of a cartoonish teenagers versus adults and Ratz brawl or car chase. Frankie and Annette save the day, reconcile without resolving their disagreement, sing a duet, and head for home.

Like the juvenile delinquents of a few years before, beach movie teenagers are irredeemably middle class, affluent, and white (except for the leads, Italian-American Frankie and Annette). People of color sometimes entertain at the teen hangout, and the working class is represented only by the Ratz. Though they are presumably on vacation with the permission of nuclear family Mom and Dad, adult supervision is absent. Only in *Pajama Party* does a parent appear, the dotty Aunt Wendy who seems to need supervision herself. The cast is presumably in college or the last year of high school. Only in *Ski Party* does a classroom appear, and the teacher is Annette in cameo, lecturing on how sexually frustrated college boys are. No one ever worries about paying for the beach house rental, dinner at the teen canteen, or various amusements; no one ever pulls out a wallet. The teenagers have none of the responsibilities of adulthood and all of its freedoms. They are living in their own arcadia, their own surreal world of spies and saboteurs, drag races and skydiving contests, musclemen hanging from helicopters, and gorillas riding surfboards. There are martians, mermaids, witch doctors, dime store Indians, bumbling crooks, anthropologists, and a girl whose gyrating hips cause volcanoes to erupt. Every now and then Frankie mugs at the camera and asks "Can you believe this?"

The teenage boys in juvenile delinquent and monster movies had only a few minutes to bare their muscles and demonstrate their strength, power, and masculinity, but in the beach movies, their muscles were bare most of the time. Arkoff thought that he was providing cheesecake, reasoning that boys bought the movie tickets, and all boys everywhere wanted to see girls in swimsuits; thus, "the girls looked delicious and the boys [were] funloving."[3] However, his directors, Don Weis, Alan Rafkin, and especially William Asher, actively resisted his hetero-male gaze. Though there are many bikini girls, the AIP beaches are also crowded with lithe, muscular swimsuit boys; bulges are displayed as prominently as cleavage. John Ashley is dragged along the beach, the camera zooming in to capture the curve of his thighs, the tight muscles of his legs and calves, and, rather surprisingly, his front. Tommy Kirk wears a purple swimsuit so tight and revealing that one can't imagine it passed the censors. Frankie doesn't bulge, but he is constantly shirtless, bedding down among his chums or standing tall and iconic beside his surfboard, his smooth, toned body preternaturally bright. *Fireball 500* (1966), has no beach or swimming pool scene, and only counts as a beach movie because it stars Frankie, Annette, and Harvey Lembeck. Nevertheless Frankie spends a long scene shirtless, being interrogated by the police in his hotel room. He never thinks to get dressed, though the officers stare at him, and one cheekily inserts his business card under Frankie's pendant, against his bare chest, like someone might insert a card into a woman's bosom.

Beach movies from other studios are not nearly as eager to expose male muscles. *For Those Who Think Young* favors the male physique,[4] but *Where the Boys Are, Beach Ball, Palm Springs Weekend,* and many others pair girls in bikinis with boys who are fully clothed.

The swimming pool scene in *C'mon, Let's Live a Little* features six mostly naked girls and one boy. We might speculate that the much greater success of the AIP movies is not due to superior scripts, songs, or acting, but to giving all prospective ticket buyers something to look at.

Though the strength, power, and masculinity of the beach boy is well established, his girl-craziness is not. The AIP beach paradise was far removed from adult civilization and its heteronormative mandate. The boys luxuriate in the homoerotic bonds of the East Side Kids and Frankie Darro in the 1940s, and the juvenile delinquent gangs in the 1950s. Though they dutifully hook up with girls—or at least ogle them—they spend most of each movie competing or cooperating with each other. They always appear in tightly intimate groups, thighs brushing, hands on shoulders, arms casually around waists; their friendships are warm, intimate, rich, and fulfilling. By contrast, the girls are as calculating, unimaginative, and cruel as they were in the teen idol songs, cold shouldering their boyfriends at the slightest offense, pretending to be in love but dropping them easily and without remorse when someone more attractive appears. The central problem of every movie is, why would a boy choose the agonies of hetero-romance over the warmth of his same-sex buddies? The Disney comedy *That Darn Cat* (dir. Robert Stevenson, 1965) worries that he won't. High schooler Patti (Hayley Mills) is sick of her boyfriend Canoe's (Tom Lowell) obsession with biceps and bikinis on the beach:

PATTI: Couldn't we just once see a nice quiet movie where boy meets girl, they have problems which aren't too weird, fall in love and live happily ever after?

CANOE: Why would you wanna see a lot of unhealthy stuff like that?

PATTI: I dunno. It's just that it would be different.

CANOE: You go with me to the drive-in Thursday night, and next week I'll take you to one of those happily-ever-after clambakes. . . . Where's the thing playing?

PATTI: Oh, who knows? Maybe they don't even make movies like that anymore.

CANOE: Sure, and you know why? People don't wanna be depressed by all that slop.[5]

Since beach movies usually star failing teen idols, they try to pull the boy away from his buddies with the standard teen idol pitch. Hetero-romance, they say, is the unique domain of teenagers, a marker of teenage identity. In *Pajama Party,* Donna Loren sings that the pairing off of a boy and a girl is simply "the way it's done when you're very young." Adult men are either blankly uncomprehending or hostile, though sometimes they can revisit their old heterosexual desires under the tutelage of an attentive woman. In *Beach Party* (dir. William Asher, AIP, 1963), Professor Robert O. Sutwell (Bob Cummings) is researching a book about the teens' "primitive tribal" sexual practices, but his assistant (Dorothy Malone), dismayed by his own lack of heterosexual interest, snippily advises him to "read it"; in the end she convinces him to kiss her. In *Bikini Beach* (dir. William Asher, AIP, 1964), the natting, prissy (e.g., gay) Harvey Huntington Honeywagon III (Keenan Wynn) plans to write a series of articles excoriating the teens' "abnormal preoccupation with sex," until a hip schoolteacher on vacation (Martha Hyer) convinces him to kiss her.

The beach movies also promote the teen idol pitch that the goal of life is to find *the one,* with its end in organization-man job, wife, kids, possibly Caroline and John-John scampering on the White House lawn, and a barrier against the chaos outside. In *Fireball 500* (dir. William Asher, AIP, 1966), Frankie prefers race-car driving to girls, arguing that he wants to be free, but Annette doublespeaks the pitch: "If you do good work at some job, save some money, have a family, a nice home, and can live in it as you please, you *have* freedom." Freedom must be constrained within heteronormative marriage and nuclear family, or else something unnamable will strike. As we have seen, "homosexuality" was modeled not as same-sex love or gender inversion but as social irresponsibility, a rejection of the man-as-breadwinner ethic.[6] For that reason, juvenile delinquents, Beatniks, carefree AIP beach teens, and anyone else who favored buddy bonds over hetero-romance must be converted or punished. In *Beach Blanket Bingo* (dir. William Asher, AIP, 1965), the teens note with disapproval an aging Buster Keaton (as an Indian) chasing a bikini-clad blonde, but den mother Big Drop (Don Rickles) defends him: "It's just good, clean fun. Keeps him out of pool halls." Heterosexual practice allows the Indian to avoid pool halls, where homoerotic bonds are forged and the marriage/family mandate forgotten.

Frankie initially refuses to submit to Annette's proposed hetero-normative trajectory, putting himself in danger of "pool halls," homo-erotic bonds, and a membership in the Mattachine Society. The wacky machinations of the plot serve to convince him to submit, and kiss Annette or sing about the joy of finding *the one,* but three other beach movie regulars, John Ashley, Tommy Kirk, and Dwayne Hick-man, fail to submit, or submit only after ninety minutes of nonstop "encouragement" from their girls, thus underscoring the fragility of the very heteronormative pose that the beach movies try to present as thundering destiny.

BEACH MOVIE REGULARS

John Ashley

After bolstering many AIP juvenile delinquent and a few monster movies (see Chapter 3), John Ashley was ready to graduate to the beach. He usually played Frankie's best buddy, physically position-ing himself directly behind Frankie and slightly to his right, with a full-body press whenever possible, or at least a hand firmly attached to shoulder. When the gang gathered in a clump to leer at a girl, John usually forgot and ogled Frankie instead, sometimes with obvious erotic interest. Certainly he did not intend for his characters to be taken as gay; in 1963 and 1964, actors would play gay not by affect-ing erotic interest, but by adopting a flamboyantly feminine posture. Yet signs of homoerotic attraction appear frequently in performances without the actor's explicit awareness. They arise unconsciously from scene dynamics and the process of creating a character, and Ashley's characters always seem to be informed by an unstated but intense attraction to a chum.

As in the juvenile delinquent movies, Ashley's beach movies seem to underscore an attempt to position him beyond the constricted boy-in-search-of-the-one dynamic of the teen idol pitch. When the rest of the gang pairs off into boy-girl couples to neck and swoon in the moonlight, Ashley sits by himself, or sits with a girl just talking, as if romance is the furthest thing from his mind. When the rest of the gang pairs off into boy-girl couples to dance at the teen hangout, Ashley sits alone with Frankie, or sometimes with Annette. When Frankie shows up, he is never jealous, he never suspects for an instant that Ashley might be making time with his girl, because obviously there is nothing to fear, Ashley is not the making-time-with-girls kind. If the beach movies were revised for today's audiences, certainly Ashley would be cast as the token gay guy, a witty, asexual confidant.

Ashley's biggest beach movie role, in *Beach Blanket Bingo* (dir. William Asher, AIP, 1965), is structured around the problem of his character's (Steve) attraction to Frankie (Frankie), leading ultimately to "salvation" in the arms of a girl. An instructor at Big Drop's Skydiving School, he meets Frankie and Annette (Dee Dee) for the first time when they sign up for lessons. With no assumption of long-standing friendship, his gaze firmly fixed upon Frankie becomes all the more aggressively erotic, and his big-brotherly interest in Annette all the more confusing. But Ashley is very overtly coded as the not-making-time-with-girls kind. When he visits the teen hangout with fellow skydiving instructor Deborah Walley (Bonnie), his current real-life wife, they express no physical affection, behaving exactly like colleagues having a drink after work. Only gradually do we realize that Walley is carrying an unrequited torch for him. Like Sandra Dee in *Gidget,* she tries to snare him by making him jealous, sexually assaulting Frankie on a solo flight (literally grabbing at his pants) and then accusing *him* of the assault. Ashley responds with no romantic jealously at all, simply big-brotherly concern, and the viewer remains convinced that he considers her merely a co-worker and friend.

Now Frankie angrily rebukes Ashley for his lack of romantic interest in Walley, seemingly a minor matter when one has just been accused of a crime. "If you really care for her," he exclaims, "You should let her know, and knock off the silly games!" But if Ashley were interested, why would he feign lack of interest? He has offered none of the standard movie strategies for postponing the kiss to the third reel—fear of rejection, being hurt in the past, being afraid of rejection, and so on. He is simply not interested in Walley. What "silly games" has he been engaging in? Perhaps Frankie is referring to Ashley's constant gazing at buddies, failing to gaze at girls, refusing to accede to his heterosexual destiny, deviations that subjected Ozzie and Harriet, Jim and Margaret, and Ward and June to endless sleepless nights (here labeled not dangerous but merely silly). In effect, he is trivializing Ashley's interest in him, their intimacy in other beach movies, and their newborn friendship here. No wonder Ashley becomes livid with rage, much more upset than the situation warrants (the accusation of assault is long forgotten). He yells "Nobody makes a monkey out of me!" and stomps off. Again, Frankie could not be making a monkey of him (i.e., making him appear foolish) by merely offering advice about winning Deborah. One is made foolish by unrequited or rejected romantic overtures.

A later scene finds Ashley grudgingly accepting his heterosexual destiny. The villains of beach movies are mean, bullying, and petty, but never murderous; the worst violence character Eric Von Zipper (Harvey Lembeck) threatens is a punch in the nose. Yet Frankie fears that Ashley is upset enough to sabotage the parachutes before the big skidiving finale. Since everything in beach movies must be conveyed by hint and innuendo, Frankie circumambulates, transforming his own concern into Annette's.

FRANKIE: My girl's worried. Any reason she should be?
STEVE: No reason at all. [Eyes him up and down] Or for you, either.

It is unclear what he thinks Ashley's motive for murder might be. Surely not jealousy over Walley, since Frankie has established very clearly that he is not interested. But if we understand that Frankie has simultaneously rejected and brought out into the open the carefully unstated relationship that they have enjoyed over the course of four movies, then a murderous rage becomes comprehensible. Ashley's up-and-down evaluation, a mirror of his frequent wide-eyed ogling, replays his attraction to Frankie, but then he dismisses it with a concluding "or for you, either."

At the jump, Frankie and Annette wait too long to open their chutes, so they hit water "as hard as concrete," and are knocked unconscious. Ashley, who is flying the airplane, heroically dives into the water after them, but he is allowed to pull only Annette to safety. The gang has already surfed out to retrieve Frankie, this prohibiting Ashley from engaging in a buddy rescue that might deepen their emotional connection. He has no time for "silly games" anymore. Instead, he kisses Walley in the surf (one assumes: it's a blurry, distant shot).

When he retired from the AIP teen movie circuit, Ashley divorced Deborah Walley and moved to the Philippines, where he partnered with Eddie Romero to star in and coproduce sleazy, past-midnight drive-in pictures with names like *Beast of Blood* and *Brides of Blood*.

Oddly, in spite of aggressively hetero-male gazes, with Ashley as the stalwart (but fully clothed) hero rescuing bikini-clad and topless babes from monsters, then engaging in steamy, fully-nude sex with them, he still manages to bond heavily with male chums, who prove the key to his salvation or require saving from the monster in the denouement. In the late 1970s he retired from acting to produce such beefcake-laden series as *The Quest, The A-Team,* and *Walker, Texas Ranger.*[7]

Dwayne Hickman

The blond, affable, thirty-one-year-old had graduated from *The Many Loves of Dobie Gillis* (see Chapter 2) and won his first major movie deal, starring with Jane Fonda and Michael Callan in *Cat Ballou* (1965) when sometime-AIP director Alan Rafkin found something inspiring in him, and sent him back to adolescence in *Ski Party* (1965). He and Frankie Avalon play college roommates unable to get laid. At the drive-in movie, their dates sit together in the backseat, and then refuse good-night kisses, stating that "they just don't feel that way." Perhaps the girls' reluctance to commit to a kiss stems from Dwayne and Frankie's obvious emotional investment with each other. They live together, sleep together, participate in exactly the same sports and activities, and they enjoy a physical intimacy unparalleled since the days when Frankie Darro held hands with Mantan Moreland. They are constantly rubbing shoulders, grabbing arms, and brushing knees. This stage business does not appear in either of the actors' buddy-bonding scenes with others, nor can it be explained by an off-camera intimacy. In his autobiography, Dwayne Hickman devotes many pages to his warm friendships with Bob Denver and Michael Callan, but devotes only a scant paragraph or two to Frankie Avalon.[8] Most likely it is their very lack of off-camera intimacy, as well as the absence of all but the most subtle sexual ambiguity in their private lives, that allows the two to imbue their interactions with an astonishingly open homoeroticism, usually in the form of a joke. In an early scene, they are running abreast at track practice, when Frankie reaches down and, for no apparent reason, takes Dwayne's hand. Later, on a ski lift, they are clinging together (in fear of heights), and an onlooker, mistaking their fear for affection, exclaims "I've heard of two guys being close friends, but this is ridiculous!"

When the boys hear that the ski club is planning a trip to a mountain resort, and that some of the club members are *girls,* they gleefully sign on, even though they can't ski, figuring that they will learn when they arrive. However, the beginner's lessons are for girls only, so, in the tradition of *Some Like It Hot* (which is referenced frequently), they don dresses and wigs, affect British accents, and become Jane and Nora. Next come the usual slapstick near discovery, and hearts-to-hearts over hot chocolate in the girls' dorm, but, unexpectedly, blond pretty boy Aron Kinkaid falls for Dwayne-in-drag, and even more unexpectedly, Dwayne falls back. In *Some Like It Hot,* Jack Lemmon (Jerry/Daphne) tried to discourage the smitten Joe E. Brown, but Dwayne seems to invite Freddie's (Aron) attention, and the two become an "item." Returning from a date, Dwayne exclaims breathlessly "We're pinned!" (e.g., pre-engaged). I've never met anyone like him!" Few boys would pin their "girls" without expecting a kiss (or more), so we must assume that two have become intimate, or else Dwayne has admitted the ruse, or both. Seething with jealousy, Frankie objects:

TODD: He can't [pin you]! He's a boy, and you're a boy!
CRAIG (Dwayne): We'll work it out.

Without another word, Frankie bundles Dwayne out of the room and into a cab, and orders the cabbie to drive them to his parents' beach house in Malibu, 834 miles away. Dwayne halfheartedly protests that he was only kidding, but Frankie refuses to be dissuaded. They are leaving Colorado, and the boy who pinned Dwayne, far behind.

If Dwayne was really kidding, what precisely was the joke? That he was in love with a boy, or that he had found someone besides Frankie? Since Frankie has overreacted so hysterically, expending an enormous amount of time and money simply to get Dwayne away from Aron, it seems that he fears both: he might lose Dwayne to another boy, and he might be forced to acknowledge that he and Dwayne are already "pinned," romantic partners closeted by a facade of girl-crazy camaraderie.

The audience is not privy to the fifteen or twenty hours of backseat discussions en route to Malibu, but when the boys finally arrive, their behavior is as cool and forced as any romantic partners who have just broken up. Unwilling to kick Dwayne out onto the street, Frankie invites him to "take any of the bedrooms on the second floor," implicitly excluding him from his own bedroom, but Dwayne declines the offer: he'd rather sleep on the beach. They say no more, and don't even glance at each other as they part company forever. In a concluding coda, the gang follows them all the way from Colorado, and as they gyrate in swimsuits, both Frankie and Dwayne pair up with girls. Heteronormativity wins again, though one can't help noticing that the boys are still refusing to look at each other.

Filming began immediately on *How to Stuff a Wild Bikini* (dir. William Asher, AIP, 1965), which has no homoromantic partners but an enormous number of sexual outsiders, to be redeemed through heterosexual practice (or not). Gang leader Eric Von Zipper wonders why South Dakota Slim, hired muscle in two earlier beach movies, is unavailable. His replacement, North Dakota Pete, explains that he was "the sissy of the family" (with a limp wrist gesture to clarify), and is now "the social director of a suicide club" (e.g., dead). A happier outcome occurs when advertising executive "Peachy Keane" played by Mickey Rooney, looking for a swimsuit model he's hired, asks a beach boy, "Have you seen a girl in a leopard bikini?" He lisps, "Certainly not!" while Mickey gapes in astonishment: a gay person in Malibu! But, like the adult naysayers, the boy soon "sees the light," mugging approvingly at the camera as a girl swoops down for a kiss.

With two gay jokes, more than in any other beach movie, director William Asher probably was wise to ensure that Dwayne and Frankie's characters are strangers and never share a scene. Frankie, seen only in cameo, is in the Naval Reserves in the South Pacific. Though busily groping at the native girls, he hires a witch doctor, played by Buster Keaton, to magically ensure that no other guy "makes time" with his girlfriend Annette. The witch doctor responds by conjuring up a leggy siren, Cassandra (Beverly Adams), so stunning that they fall all over each other in tongue-lolling lust. But Dwayne, playing a male model (currently the "all-American boy" for a series of motorcycle advertisements), fails to give her a second glance:

CASSANDRA: [To Dwayne] You're gorgeous!

RICKY: [Not impressed] Beautiful, maybe, but not gorgeous. [Walks away]

Overhearing, Mickey Rooney gasps "That boy's sick!" thus structurally linking him with the lisping boy as unable or unwilling to experience "healthy" heterosexual desire.

Cassandra becomes one of the few girls in beach movies "suffering" from sexual ambiguity: "I'm not like other girls," she explains, "I'm not all I seem to be." She means that she is a magical creature, but surely the viewer can infer other potential meanings, especially when she passive-aggressively trips or knocks things over whenever a boy tries to get intimate. Mickey Rooney takes her to a psychiatrist, who concludes that she is unconsciously sabotaging her romances because she suffers from "male-o-phobia" (that is, fear of men, presumed one of the root causes of lesbian desire in the 1960s). As a cure, he advises her to repeat "I'm a normal girl" over and over.

Meanwhile, Dwayne (Ricky) meets and starts seeing Annette (Dee Dee), but only as a friend, explaining that he's "not the marrying kind," 1960's code for "gay." Though he does invite her back to his posh beach house (Annette exclaims "You must do very well here!"), they are interrupted prior to the kiss by a series of mishaps: a possessive seagull, a crashing Oriental fixture, hired muscle, thus sabotaging the romance as surely as Beverly's (Cassandra) pratfalls. Is the witch doctor really trying to prohibit Dwayne from making time, one wonders, or is Dwayne also unconsciously trying to avoid heterosexual practice?

Beach movie structure requires those seemingly bereft of heterosexual desire to eventually "see the light," and since Annette is spoken for, surely Dwayne and Beverly will hook up. At the end of the movie, the two do note a heterosexual attraction, but en route to Dwayne's beach house (for more sabotage, one assumes), Beverly suddenly vanishes. Her bikini remains for a moment, suspended in midair without her, and then fades away. Dwayne looks at the camera and groans "This isn't my week!" but he has managed to play the game, pretend to be girl-crazy, without ever having to kiss a girl.

Dwayne and Frankie's final AIP pairing, the James Bond spoof *Dr. Goldfoot and the Bikini Machine* (dir. Norman Taurog, 1965), offers far less cheesecake than the title suggests. The mad scientist played by Vincent Price, does send an army of bikini-clad female robots out to seduce millionaires into signing away their fortunes, but they are shown mostly in trench coats, with only two brief inspections to ensure the audience that they are indeed wearing bikinis underneath.[9]

Secret agent Craig (Frankie) stumbles across the plan when one of the robots mistakes him for trust-fund baby Todd (Dwayne) (the two have switched character names since *Ski Party,* an in joke that causes constant, presumably hilarious mishaps). He rushes off to warn the real trust-fund baby that his new wife is not all that she seems. The two eject the faux bikini babe without regrets, and spend the rest of the night together, drinking, story swapping, and gazing at each other with the eye-bulging intensity of love at first sight.

Dwayne has no motive for further involvement in the case, and one would assume a foppish, self-involved rich kid too apathetic or skittish for a world-saving mission. Nevertheless, he spends the rest of the movie at Frankie's side, usually with his hand firmly attached to his shoulder, (like the women so bedazzled by James Bond that they cannot bear to be parted for a moment). Together they try to convince the secret agent organization, SIC (pronounced "sick"), of Dr. Goldfoot's threat. Rebuffed, they sneak into Dr. Goldfoot's castle together to look for evidence. They are captured and thrown into the dungeon where Dr. Goldfoot straps Frankie to a pit-and-pendulum (a send-up of the 1961 movie) while Dwayne is chained to a wall and forced to watch, a reflection, deliberately or not, of the common adventure motif of the hero tied up and watching helplessly while his girlfriend is threatened.

Dwayne manages to free himself, subdue the henchmen, and mount a daring (if humorous) rescue. It would seem more logical for Frankie, the secret agent accustomed to dangerous missions, to rescue Dwayne, who is just along for the ride. Yet forcing Dwayne to act underscores his growth as a hero in training, and also cleverly accentuates the pair's deepening affection. Dwayne clearly mounts the rescue because he cares about Frankie, but Frankie as rescuer might be just doing his job.

They flee the castle with Dr. Goldfoot in hot pursuit, zooming around in a series of colorful vehicles up and down the hills of San Francisco, across the Golden Gate Bridge and into Marin County, and then into the bay, with the usual fruit-cart collisions and pedestrian chaos. Although the scenes are played for laughs, stage business underscores a reading of the pair as more than newfound friends. Logic would again dictate that the experienced Frankie take charge of the escape, but Dwayne maintains his rescuer role, commandeering and driving the vehicles, while Frankie keeps his arms wrapped tightly around Dwayne's waist. Perhaps safety dictates such a position while they are riding on a moped, but why does he keep his arms around Dwayne when they have switched to a roomy speedboat? Clearly, he is not being protective, nor is he particularly afraid; maybe he is parodying the girls who cling to James Bond during climactic chase scenes, but the effect is to present his feelings for Dwayne as rather aggressively romantic.

In the heat of the chase, Dr. Goldfoot drives his vehicle off a cliff and (seemingly) dies, so the crisis is averted. Dwayne and Frankie walk off together, arms around each other's waists, and Dwayne suggests that they recuperate with a "vacation in Paris." Surely it is no coincidence that he specifies Paris, a city emblematic of romance, so the "vacation" becomes code for "honeymoon." He is careful to note that it is "my treat," thus establishing that he will continue to be in charge. Frankie has spent most of his tenure at AIP with a woman, usually Annette, in charge, cajoling him away from his same-sex buddies toward a staid heterosexual destiny. Perhaps with a man in charge he has found what he wanted all along. In the last scene, Frankie and Dwayne are sitting in first-class airplane seats, en route to a romantic holiday in Paris, and gay actor Tommy Kirk took on the job of promoting heterosexual destiny for the rest of the franchise.

Tommy Kirk

In the fall of 1964, with Frankie Avalon busy with *I'll Take Sweden,* AIP hired Tommy Kirk to appear with his frequent costar Annette, in *Pajama Party* (dir. Don Weis, AIP, 1964). Tommy was not yet out (he would be outed by his boyfriend's irate mother in the spring of 1965, and fired off the set of *The Monkey's Uncle*),[10] yet *Pajama Party* was more aggressive in promoting the teen idol pitch than any of Frankie Avalon's performances. Kirk plays Go-Go, "the stupidest guy on Mars," sent on a reconnaissance mission to Earth (because he's so stupid, he won't give away any secrets if captured). He materializes on the estate of dotty Aunt Wendy (Elsa Lanchester), who immediately dresses him in an extra-bulging swimsuit and sends him out to meet girls. But he's so stupid, so heterosexually unaware, that he treats boys and girls exactly the same. Mistaking a panicked flight for a friendly greeting, he chases both Swedish bombshell Helga (Bobbi Shaw) and her Native American buddy (played by

Buster Keaton), across the estate grounds. Don Rickles, watching from Mars, quips "He'll probably catch the Indian."

Meanwhile, Annette is despondent because her boyfriend Big Lunk (Jody McCrea), a muscular sports enthusiast, does not seem at all interested in girls. He keeps rejecting her romantic overtures and ditching her to play on an all-male volleyball team. His more girl-crazy teammates complain that they can't practice all the time, they need girls too, but Jody does not understand:

TEAMMATE: What about love, romance, cool lips, and moonlight?

BIG LUNK: Sounds great! I never tried playing volleyball in the moonlight!

Obviously, we will be seeing two conversions, as both Tommy and Jody must "see the light" and acquire the proper level of heterosexual horniness. Tommy acquiesces immediately when he meets Annette and realizes that she is *the one.* Within a few minutes, they are singing:

As a matter of fact, it's easy to see—it's really nothing new
It's a natural act, as plain as can be—it's why there's me and you.

Big Lunk's (McCrea) conversion is somewhat more problematic: he must be convinced that hetero-romance is superior to buddy bonding. Bobbi Shaw tries to Swedish sexpot him into heterosexual practice, but he skittishly wards off her hugs and kisses. Then, she tries a different tactic: she challenges him to an arm-wrestling match, and wins. Jody is so impressed at this "masculine" trait that he agrees to date her, thus managing to remain a "man's man" while still following the heteronormative mandate of pairing with a girl.

But we're not finished. In a running gag, a preteen boy (played by ten-year-old Kerry Kolmar) spies on the teenagers smooching, grimaces, and exclaims "Mush!" This is a common reaction among children of the period, as the myth of the pubescent "discovery" of the other sex required them to be oblivious to or disgusted by heterosexual practice. At the denouement, at a gigantic poolside pajama party, Kerry is spying as usual, when a young girl sneaks up and kisses him on the cheek. He grins widely and exclaims "Say, that's not bad!" the only instance of a child acquiescing to heterosexual destiny in any of the beach movies.

Yet we're *still* not finished. Beach movie adults frequently "see the light" and become heterosexual, but only when they were originally hostile. Those who nurture heterosexual practice, like Big Bang (Don Rickles), need not ogle any girls of their own. Elderly matchmaker (Elsa Lanchester) Wendy could certainly be excused from expressing heterosexual desire, but nevertheless at the party she feels left out: "For every man there is a woman, but what have I got?" Then she notices that the audience is a "man" and exclaims excitedly "You! Come on, let's have a swim!"

Why does *Pajama Party* go much further than the other beach movies, hooking up not only teenagers, but children and maiden aunts? We must look at two scenes that seem incomprehensible based on the plotline. In the first, Annette gets up in the middle of the night, goes to Tommy's room, and finds him reporting back to his superiors on Mars, while Jody stands beside him, frozen in a defensive posture. Why is Jody there in the first place? Surely he has his own room in Aunt Wendy's mansion. Perhaps he stumbled across Tommy by accident and had to be magically frozen, but why then are we not shown the scene? One would expect it to be ripe with comedic possibility, and besides, the two have not interacted before. One suspects that the two interact only minimally because they must not compare rationales for their blindness to heterosexual desire. A bedtime heart-to-heart would suggest a third reason. Tommy and Jody *cannot* become intimates, as no off-camera girl-craziness can "prove" that they are nevertheless heterosexual.[11]

In the second scene, Tommy leaves the pajama party to investigate a robbery in progress at the mansion, and he asks Jody to accompany him. After some minor slapstick fighting, Tommy saves the day by magically transporting the robbers back to Mars.

BIG LUNK (McCrea): I don't understand any of this.

GO-GO (Kirk): You don't have to. [Smiling, misty-eyed] Come on, let's get back to the party.

They have just fought comedy villains. Neither was in any real danger, nor did they rescue each other from any threat. Yet Tommy's eyes are shining, he is smiling beatifically, and his voice is hoarse with an emotion unaccounted for in the script. The boys have somehow acquired an emotional connection, an intensity in their interaction that belies the myth of the supremacy of heterosexual bonds. No wonder the rest of the cast worked double-time to ensure that every man found a woman, every boy teenager a girl teenager, every boy a girl.

Tommy was busy in 1965, filming not only *The Monkey's Uncle* but also *Village of the Giants* (1965), a movie about giant teenagers dancing half-naked in the town square; *It's a Bikini World* (released 1967), which features Bobby Pickett in a swimsuit (but not singing "Monster Mash"); and *The Ghost in the Invisible Bikini* (dir. Don Weis, AIP, released 1966). In *Ghost,* he aggressively resists the teen idol pitch. He plays an heir of the deceased Boris Karloff, visiting the ancestral mansion to claim his inheritance along with Deborah Walley, Aron Kincaid, and a gaggle of their teenage friends gyrating in swimsuits. Evil lawyer Basil Rathbone and his henchmen plot to spook the legitimate heirs away or else do them in, and Susan Hart, the titular ghost in the invisible bikini, works behind the protoplasm to protect them. There is a nod to the quest for *the one* when Tommy and Walley flirt, briefly and chastely, but a greater emphasis on oblique references to same-sex desire. Kincaid, last seen getting engaged to Dwayne Hickman in *Ski Party,* displays no interest in girls, in spite of an opening quip meant to establish his girl-craziness.

EVIL LAWYER (Rathbone): [To Kincaid] I'd like you to meet my daughter.

GIRL: He'd like to meet *anyone's* daughter.

He wouldn't like to meet anyone's daughter; he spends the movie rejecting female advances, especially those of the leering Sinistra (Quinn O'Hara), even when he hasn't yet discovered that she intends to kill him. However, he jumps into bed with new acquaintance Tommy, explaining rather unconvincingly that he's unnerved by all the spooky happenings. During the night, Tommy gets up for a moment, and a monster (looking something like the Michelin Man) replaces him in bed. Kincaid reaches over to take "his" hand, gets the monster's hand instead, and shrinks back, gibbering in horror a la Lou Costello. But why did he want to take Tommy's hand in the first place? The gag only works if Kincaid feels comfortable expressing an unusually romantic intimacy unaccounted for in the script.[12]

The next day Tommy and Kincaid team up to investigate the skull-duggery. Their unaccounted-for physical intimacy is retained: they cling to wrists and shoulders, touch hands, hug each other in moments of stress, and ultimately subdue the evil Rathbone together, while facing every horror movie cliché in the book, including a mummy, a gorilla, a séance, secret passages, revolving doors, and eyes peering down from portraits. As the closing credits roll, Kincaid is shown dancing with a girl, Tommy kisses Deborah Walley, though the two have not interacted since their first shy flirtation over an hour of screen time before. This egregious attempt to provide a "happy," that is, heterosexual, ending actually backfires, as audiences may feel cheated that the two boys who solved the mystery must separate to share the spotlight with two girls who did nothing at all (one lacking even a character name). Dismissing the homoromantic bond as trivial and meaningless, after it has formed the emotional ground for the action in the last half of the movie, can only underscore its importance.

THE LAST OF THE BEACH MOVIES

Like juvenile delinquent and monster movies, beach movies were a fad for only three or four years, the time it takes to negotiate high school. Spoofs appeared on *The Monkees, The Beverly Hillbillies,* and even *Petticoat Junction,* and high schooler Tuesday Weld got laughs in *Lord Love a Duck* (1966) by admitting that her biggest goal in life was to star in a beach movie. AIP's stable of fading teen idols incorporated beefcake and cheesecake ticket-draws and occasional songs into drag-racing or spy spoofs, foregrounding the homoerotic lure of the buddy more and more obviously as the teen idol pitch faded into a distant memory. In *Fireball 500* (1966), Frankie Avalon (Dave) locks eyes with fellow racer Fabian, (Leander), postures suggestively, and says "Sonny-boy, I'm gonna climb all over you!" no doubt "really" referring to besting him in the big race. He spy spoofs again in *The Million Eyes of Sumuru* (1967), but this time partnered with gay actor George Nader instead of Dwayne Hickman.

In 1967, the Tony Curtis vehicle *Don't Make Waves* had a beach but no teenagers, *Thunder Alley* teenagers but no beach, and *Catalina Caper* a depressed-looking Tommy Kirk slipping out of character every time he is in the background of a scene for intense-looking talks with costar Peter Duryea. The last of the beach movies, *C'mon, Let's Live a Little* (dir. David Butler, Paramount, 1967), stars faded teen idol Bobby Vee as a handsome, country-fried freshman (Jesse) who fights a subversive plot to promote "free speech" at his college. In an early scene, he goes swimming at the dean's house (so it will count as a beach movie), in a pool occupied by a dozen bikini-clad girls and one boy, fellow faded teen idol Eddie Hodges (Eddie) in a ridiculous 1920's bathing costume. But ensuring a strictly hetero-male gaze does not effectively erase same-sex desire. Bobby rescues Eddie from drowning, and the next day Eddie obligingly saves him, karate chopping away some Southerner-bashing bullies. Each has saved the other's life, doubling the meet-cute requirement of romance. "Meet-cute" is a convention of romantic movies, whereby the couple has a "cute" first meeting. They may bump into each other, knock packages out of each other's hands, or save each other from some minor threat. They flirt voraciously and make plans to get together later. But then, inexplicably forlorn even though he is dating the dean's daughter and has just found an instant best friend, Bobby returns to his dorm room and sings:

> What fool this mortal be,
> Who looks but cannot see,
> Who listens but cannot hear,
> And his heart is full of fear.

Usually, such lyrics would refer to someone blind to the wonders of heterosexual desire, but Bobby has had no trouble noticing girls, he hears them fine, he is not afraid of them, and he is not shy about expressing his interest. Besides, his fear references the last scene, with *Eddie.* Is he critiquing his attempt to hide his homoromantic attraction beneath buddy-bonding camaraderie? Sure enough, while trying to foil the evil free-speech advocates, Bobby and Eddie suffer through enough misunderstandings, quarrels, and reconciliations to fuel any number of romantic comedies. In the end, Bobby kisses the dean's daughter, and Eddie, who never expresses interest in anyone else through the movie, pretends to be delighted with "best buddy" scraps.[13] The Summer of Love arrived with heterosexual practice still celebrated as the teenager's ultimate goal in life, but intense homoromantic partnerships lurked behind every buddy-bonding facade.

Chapter 7

Easy Rider:
The Love Generation

By the late 1950s, teenagers were getting older: 1.7 million graduated from high school in 1960, and 2.6 million in 1966. More of them
were going to college, or to Vietnam (400,000 by mid-1967) or to
Canada to avoid Vietnam (40,000 by 1970), or putting flowers in their
hair and lying on the grass at Golden Gate Park. Frankie quarreling
with Annette or Bobby Van finding the meaning of life in the eyes of
the dean's daughter did not seem all that relevant anymore. Certainly
most teenagers were unable to turn on, tune in, drop out and start
communes in Tucumcari (a famous commune). They were still underage, after all, alone in their rooms, doing homework while downstairs Mom and Dad watched, e.g., *The Jackie Gleason Show*. Still,
they took hip high school classes in Current Events, where mock
elections saw Humphrey triumph in 1968, and McGovern in 1972 (in
spite of Nixon's victories at the adult polls), they read *Time* magazine,
and they knew things—about the environment, politics, racism, sexism,
and sex—that made them feel wiser than the teenagers of just a few years
before. Perhaps they were wiser about some things. After all, they could
borrow or steal *Human Sexual Response, The Sensuous Woman, The
Sensuous Man,* and *Everything You Always Wanted to Know About Sex
but Were Afraid to Ask,* while in 1958 their older brothers and sisters had
to read between the lines in Pat Boone's *'Twixt Twelve and Twenty,*[1] or
raid Mom's nightstand for the steamy novel *Peyton Place.*

Many books have been written about how heterosexual sex changed,
from guilt in the 1920s to a guilty pleasure in the 1950s, to a necessity
by 1972.[2] The sexual revolution did not mean ménage à trois, wife
swapping, openly promiscuous heterosexual activity, and certainly
not the freedom to love someone of the same sex; it meant that sexual
acts rather than finding *the one* had become the key to adult identity,

doi:10.1300/5484_07

the essential ground of a normal, happy, well-adjusted adulthood. In 1958, those who engaged in premarital heterosexual relations were feared monstrous; now the monsters were those who refrained. The pitch had been sold, Pat Boone had triumphed, and every boy's pubescent discovery of girls was now framed in teen culture as universal and inevitable, so commonplace as to not be worthy of comment. But the discovery involved acts far more intimate than dating, pinning, or even necking in a parked car at a lover's lane: becoming a teenage boy meant the first glimpse of a bra, the first glimpse of a naked breast, the first touch of a naked breast, the act of heterosexual coitus itself. Thus, Leonard Whiting in *Romeo and Juliet* (1968) and Richard Benjamin in *Goodbye, Columbus* (1969) discovered *the one* not through gazing or kissing, but through bedding. In 1971, thirteen-year-old Mark Lester married his girlfriend in *Melody,* and in *Summer of '42,* fifteen-year-old Gary Grimes had his "first time" to a lushly romantic score and a tagline extolling boy-adult woman sex as universal experience: "In every man's life there is a summer of '42." In 1973, future teen idol Robby Benson discovered girls through bedroom exploits twice, in *Jeremy.*

Though teenagers of the Love Generation, (roughly 1967 to 1973), knew more about heterosexual coitus than their beach-movie-watching siblings, and in fact were inundated with cultural objects extolling the breast or the bedroom as the meaning of life, they heard nothing at all about same-sex desire, about same-sex love, about gay people, or about the burgeoning homophile movement. Unless they happened upon Gore Vidal's *The City and the Pillar* or Truman Capote's *Other Voices, Other Rooms* in a very large library, they would remain as lost as Darryl Hickman playing in *Dobie Gillis* for half a decade with a lesbian costar, playing gay in all but the name in three beach movies, yet never letting the possibility of same-sex desire intrude upon his conscious thought. Gay men, or at least mincing, lisping sorts of people walking pink poodles, began to filter into the American mass media near the end of the decade. This was when *Midnight Cowboy* (1969), which won three Oscars for its brilliant portrayal of despicable pink poodle walkers, and *Boys in the Band* (1970) achieved box office success with a gaggle of mincing, lisping, self-loathing sorts of people who wish desperately to be "normal" but can't quite manage it. Television held out until 1972, when the card-carrying gay Peter Panama swished onto a summer replacement series called *The Corner*

Bar and Hal Holbrook confided his "homosexuality" to horrified son
Scott Jacoby in *That Certain Summer.* Yet it was still possible, indeed
inevitable, for teenagers to grow up in Chattanooga and Baton Rouge,
and even on the corner of Christopher and Gay, 'round the corner
from the Stonewall, and never know that any boy had ever loved a
boy, that any girl had ever loved a girl, even once since the world began. They still had to depend on the unspoken, the implied, the glimmers of love rumbling around the subtexts of their dark robotic stories
and songs.

THE BIKER-HIPPIES

In July 1966, three years almost to the day after *Beach Party,* AIP
released *The Wild Angels,* with Henry Fonda's son Peter as a lean,
tough, and kind of stupid motorcycle gang member who springs
buddy Bruce Dern from a hospital bed, only to find that he *needed* to
be there and will die shortly. Then he goes through all sorts of biker
mishaps to get him buried in his home town. Peter's alienation, elo-
quence, and scruffy sexual allure pleased audiences in a summer otherwise devoted to such square fare as Cary Grant in *Walk, Don't Run,*
Doris Day in *The Glass Bottom Boat,* and Fred MacMurray in *Follow
Me, Boys. The Wild Angels* grossed $7 million on a budget of just
$360,000. So, like the beach movies in 1963, a host of imitators
roared through the rapidly failing drive-ins and brand-new multi-
plexes at the mall: In 1967, *The Born Losers, Devils' Angels, The
Hellcats,* and *The Wild Rebels*; in 1968, *Angels from Hell, The Glory
Stompers, The Savage Seven,* and *The Young Angels*; in 1969, *The Cycle Savages, Hell's Angels '69, Naked Angels,* and *Satan's Sadists.*
The genre probably reached its nadir in 1971 when bikers started
turning into *Werewolves on Wheels* after a run-in with some Satanic
monks.

AIP's *Riot on Sunset Strip,* released in April 1967, was about another outlaw subculture, called "love children" in the movie but "hippies" by midsummer. The cover story of *Time* magazine offered "The
Hippies: Philosophy of a Subculture" (July 7) and Harry Reasoner
hosted the TV special *The Hippie Temptation* on CBS (August 22).
Goofier than the bikers, requiring fewer props but more drugs, hippies did not remain confined to teenage movies. Soon they were

popping up in Disney movies *(The Love Bug)*, in Hollywood musicals *(Sweet Charity)*, on TV sitcoms *(The Beverly Hillbillies)*, and even on Saturday morning kids' TV *(The Banana Splits Adventure Hour)*. Though the real-life hippie subculture was dead by 1970, comic or tragic hippies pop up in mass media to this day to inspire a quick dazed-and-confused laugh.[3]

In teenage culture, bikers and hippies were more or less identical. While the Nixon-era straights (that is, non–biker-hippies) were busily transforming cities into suburbs, staunching the flow of communism, conquering outer space, and promoting the American Way, biker-hippies sat around idly all day, dancing, singing, kissing, brawling, resisting the nuclear family nine-to-five organization-man cubicle. The straights were savagely gender-polarized crew-cut boys in thin ties and narrow collars carefully matched with bouffant-haired girls in pillbox hats and baby-doll dresses. They promoted the myth that true love unites yin and yang, hard, straight-edged masculine boys and soft, curvy-edged feminine girls. However, among the biker-hippies both boys and girls were soft, curvy-edged, and feminine, and had long hair, beads, medallions, fringes, sashes, and curves. Adults and stand-up comedians complained endlessly that you couldn't tell them apart. The straights rigidly compartmentalized their relationships by age, sex, and status, with meticulously defined, instantly recognizable pals and gals, boyfriends and girlfriends, best friends and best girls, husbands and wives, co-workers and next-door neighbors. The biker-hippies moved in amorphous, unwieldy packs, pal and gal, neighbor and spouse all intermingling and chaotic like the juvenile delinquent gangs of the 1950s.

Biker-hippies were descended from the juvenile delinquents of the 1950s, but the biker-hippies evaded the clash between gang and girl by introducing lots of girls into the gang. Now each male gang member had a girl hanging on his back, kissing him, cuddling with him, sleeping with him, or looking bored in the corner. But the most important, most essential relationships in biker-hippiedom remained between men. In *The Wild Angels*, Nancy Sinatra (Mike) complains that boyfriend Peter Fonda (Heavenly Blues) has been insufficiently attentive to her needs since his buddy died: "You've changed . . . it's like you went with him. I know he was your friend and all, but what about *me*?" Oozing with contempt, Peter snaps "What about you?" Girlfriends come and go, but best buddies are forever—his loyalty makes him stay behind to attend to the burial while Nancy and the other bikers ride out of his life.

Similarly, though reviewers insist that *Hell's Angels on Wheels* (1967) is about new gang member Poet (Jack Nicholson) and gang leader (Buddy) Adam Roarke battling over some girl. In fact, Adam is nonchalant about the girl's other loves, literally pushing her into Jack's arms. The crisis, a fight resulting in Adam's death, occurs when *Jack* rejects him.

The biker-hippie boys are open and excessive in their same-sex interactions, hanging on each other as assiduously as the girls, hugging, sitting cuddled against each other, kissing—both the straights and each other, even grinding their crotches together. Only the straights display any homophobic skittishness. In *Hell's Angels on Wheels,* for instance, Jack Nicholson starts out as a straight gas station attendant. As he is drawn more deeply into the biker subculture, he permits Adam Roarke to caress his shoulders, chest, and face, and kiss his cheek, but when the gang leader moves in for a full-mouth kiss, Jack moves away, grimacing in disgust. Later he encounters a necking couple, pulls up the boy's face, and starts kissing the girl; the boy tries to kiss Jack, and he leaps away.

In *The Trip* (dir. Roger Corman, AIP, 1967), straight Peter Fonda (as Paul), a TV commercial director, decides to try out LSD, so he visits Bruce Dern (as John), his buddy in *The Wild Angels,* here playing a very well-to-do older man in a business suit and beard. They drive to a magnificently furnished, multilevel hippie pad overlooking the ocean, where Bruce twice drags Peter away from flirting with girls and leads him to a secluded upstairs chamber. "Where's Bea?" Peter asks, suspicious, naming a wife or girlfriend. Bruce replies that she is conveniently away for the weekend. "You must have absolute confidence and faith in me," he says, as if answering the suspicious banning of girls from the proceedings. "I'm not going to go anywhere. I'm going to be right with you, as long as you need me."

He is right there during the acid trip, touching Peter's face, holding his hand, hugging him. When Peter gets naked during a bad segment and wants to "come down," Bruce dissuades him by clinging tightly to his fully nude body. But eventually Peter begins to suspect that he has a non-drug-related motive, and recoils in homophobic panic. Bruce tries to reassure him.

JOHN (Dern): You're making a whole paranoia thing about this. I'm
your friend . . . friend. Come on, touch me! Friend!

PAUL (Fonda): [Accusing] I know your scene—don't think I don't!
I'm not stupid!

The absence of wife or girlfriend and the request for a touch suggest that Paul is thinking of a gay scene, with Bruce trying to recruit
him into a "deviant" lifestyle. He imagines that he has bashed John's
head in, even in 1967 a clichéd film response to a homoerotic advance. Fleeing, he has a number of picaresque adventures: he sneaks
into a nuclear family home and watches TV with a little girl, tries to
squeeze into a drier at a Laundromat, dreams of cleavage at a hippie
hangout. Eventually, he meets a woman who has sex with him for the
rest of the trip, thus helping substituting hetero-erotic for homoerotic
as his "proper" accompaniment of LSD.

Peter is playing a *straight*. Movies set entirely within the subculture often include characters who are gay defined. In *Werewolves on
Wheels,* only two of the biker gang boys have biker gang girls hanging on their shoulders; the others snuggle by the campfire with one
another. In *Psych-Out* (dir. Richard Rush, AIP, 1968), Jack Nicholson
(Stoney), Adam Roarke (Ben), and Max Julien (Elwood) belong to a
psychedelic band and live together in a Haight-Ashbury hippie commune. The plot mostly involves helping a deaf girl Jenny (Susan
Strassberg) search for her missing brother (Bruce Dern). Jack falls
into monogamous commitment with her, but Adam and Max are interested only in big brothering, since they seem to be romantic partners. They are always together, cozily reclining against each other;
when they climb onto the roof and Adam lies down with his arms behind his head, Max thinks for a moment and then lies down again,
resting his head on Adam's arm.

Many biker-hippies intersplice homoerotic intimacy with scenes
of kissing and grabbing girls, but Adam and Max never express any
heterosexual interest. The hippie pad is full of boy-girl coupling, girls
giving massages to boys, sitting in boys' laps, or reclining against
them, but Adam and Max never once get touched by a girl. Susan
Strassberg's character is an early riser; every morning, she must piece
her footsteps around the piles of hetero couples in blankets, but—
surprise—Adam and Max are already up. We never see their sleeping
arrangements.

Since the gay liberation movement grew out of the hippie movement in 1969 and 1970, it should come as no surprise that real-life hippies often deemed same-sex encounters a harmless example of "doing your own thing."[4] Gay biker-hippies had to stay closeted, however. Peter Fonda and Jack Nicholson both yell out antigay epithets at anyone they are angry with, and in Peter's autobiography, he fails to mention real-life gay people at all.[5] The suggestion of valid, accepted, and normalized same-sex romances does not reflect the conditions of the actual subcultures.

The biker-hippies are presented in an amazingly positive light, as fun loving, exuberant, open-minded, and caring, in sharp contrast to the prissy, narrow-minded, belligerent straights. They are eager to befriend anyone, straight or hip, and they fight only when provoked (and in *Hell's Angels on Wheels,* only in absurdly stylized scenes with slapstick sound effects). Violence is the result of redneck or police bigotry, or bad drug trips as the result of unethical dealers. This world could be made idyllic because it was as far removed from anything teenagers could really experience as Frankie and Annette's Malibu; fifteen-year-olds could hardly buy a motorcycle or head out to Haight-Ashbury. But they could *dream* of freedom from the requirements of heterosexual destiny, job, and wife/kids. In *Hell's Angels on Wheels* (dir. Richard Rush, AIP, 1967), Roarke's girlfriend, played by Sabrina Scharf, significantly named Shill after the person who lures you into parting with your money at a carnival sideshow, insists that all boys must accede to heterosexual destiny, using the same argument that Annette used on Frankie:

SHILL: Don't you have to grow up sometime?
BUDDY: [Dismissively] I can always scrape up enough bread . . .
SHILL: What if someday you want to get married?
BUDDY: I tried that scene, and it stinks!

However, just as the beach movie summers had to end with Frankie and Annette headed back to school and to marriage, the biker-hippie must inevitably find a girl and return to "the straight life," or die. Significantly, the one who resists the most is usually doomed: Roarke in *Hell's Angels on Wheels,* Dern (symbolically) in *The Trip,* Dean Stockwell in *Psych-Out.* The one eager to abandon the biker-hippie lifestyle for the girl gets to live.

EASY RIDER

The most important biker-hippie movie of the decade, *Easy Rider* (dir. Dennis Hopper, Columbia, 1969) is the brainchild of writer, producer, and star Peter Fonda. Yet the movie manages to foreground the homoerotic Eden at the root of the biker-hippie myth. After a big cocaine score in Los Angeles, dealers Wyatt (Peter) and Billy (Dennis) motorcycle across a wasteland of hostile small towns en route to "retirement" in Florida. Wyatt, in skintight black leather pants, "riding one big phallic [symbol] down the road,"[6] calls himself Captain America, and Billy, shaggy and demented, is his Bucky, the doggedly homoromantic hero and sidekick from 1940s' comic books.[7] The redneck straights, of course, code them as gender-transgressive sissy boys, with quips like "nice hair," "nice necklace," "are you a boy or a girl," but only in a redneck café in Louisiana, they are specifically called "queers," and one yokel tells about a time he saw "two males kissin' away!" Oddly, *Easy Rider* distinguishes a lack of interest in girls (Wyatt) and an interest in boys (Billy).

Wyatt is defined by his odd lack of heterosexual practice. At the hippie commune, Billy ogles, grabs, and flirts, but Wyatt does not (he sits next to a girl to eat dinner). When two girls invite them to go skinny-dipping, Billy frolics and cavorts, but the nude Wyatt sits above them, orchestrating but not participating. When they visit a brothel in New Orleans, Billy giggles and chats with his prostitute, presumably planning to have sex (eventually), but Wyatt sits in stony silence. The girl (Karen Black) points out that he's paid for the time, but he protests: "That was for my friend." Still he cannot bring himself to engage in heterosexual sex. "I have an idea!" he says abruptly. "Let's all go outside! We'll all go outside to Mardi Gras!" He drags Billy from his session (the sex has not even started), and they go outside to watch the parade. In the morning, they visit a cemetery, take LSD, and finally initiate sex. At least, Billy does. Wyatt does not. Instead he has a bad trip, with visions of a fey man carrying an umbrella (representing death), and as he hugs a statue of the French goddess of Liberty, he sobs and asks his mother why she abandoned him (according to his biography, Peter was out of character, talking to his real mother, who committed suicide when he was ten years old). Meanwhile, disembodied voices recite the Apostle's Creed.

Why do powerful images associate hetero-sex and death, rather than salvation, and why is he talking to his mother as a substitute for intercourse? Pop psychology of the time still "blamed" an unresolved Oedipus complex for the "sissy" boys who fail to grow up, acknowledge their mortality, and bed girls, seeing in the wife, kids, house, and job only a grave.

Billy, conversely, likes girls a lot, but he also has a strongly exclusionary and arguably erotic relationship with Wyatt. As they ride on their motorcycles, he is always gazing over at Wyatt. At the campfire, he insists that they sit next to each other rather than across from each other. In an opening scene, Billy puts his arm around Wyatt and complains "You're getting a little distant, man!" He also complains when they take on passengers, even girls who promise skinny-dipping, nudity, and probably sex, as if he resents any intrusion into their partnership.

A third person intrudes: Jack Nicholson as Dennis, a *straight,* small-town Texas lawyer and ACLU advocate, living under the shadow of his wealthy parents. He leers at the boys, especially Wyatt in his leather pants, and then invites himself along on their trip. His goal is ostensibly a famous New Orleans brothel, but a different goal is suggested when, in lieu of a motorcycle helmet, he wears a football helmet left over from his high school glory days. His mother dug it out of the trash, he says, and left it on his bed with a note: "Give this to your son someday." That is, he has achieved the job, but not the wife and kids required by the nuclear family model, and going on the road with Wyatt and Billy means that he never will. As the one who most overtly sneers at his heterosexual destiny, he will be the first to die.

After his usual suspicion and hostility, Billy warms up to Dennis, cozying up to him at the campfire instead of taking his usual place next to Wyatt, and talking about government cover-ups. When Dennis asks, "Did you ever listen to bullfrogs . . . in the moonlight," one expects him to invite Billy for some alone time in the woods, but at the last moment he changes his mind. But the flirtation is only minor. The rednecks attack while Billy is off in the woods, urinating, and he rushes to Wyatt's side first, and to Dennis only as an afterthought.

When the hippies suggest that they are subject to redneck disapprobation simply because their hair is long, Dennis disagrees: "You represent freedom." Of course, the biker-hippie lifestyle is doomed; there always must be a job and a girl. Though they cross a wasteland of redneck bigots, twice, at the hippie commune and in New Orleans, they find potential homes, places where "freaks" are accepted. Wyatt makes friends, pitches in, and acts as if he plans to stay on indefinitely; he even meets girls to initiate his heteronormative salvation. Billy pushes him on, rejecting any idea of sharing Wyatt with a community, since he knows that heteronormativity would make his partnership with Wyatt obsolete. When they finally arrive in Florida, Wyatt has nothing to say but "We blew it." They have arrived nowhere, and they are doomed.

THE CLEAN-CUT BOYS

Biker-hippies never dominated the teen culture of the 1960s. Mass media was much more likely to sell clean-cut, gender-polarized, straight boys who never questioned their heterosexual trajectory into college, career, wife, and kids, and "little boxes made of ticky tacky."[8] Their hard, rigid lines suggested straightness as overtly as the teen idol pitch of a decade before, though they might sport long hair, a Nehru jacket, or a love-symbol medallion to hint at youth rebellion. Clean-cut teenage boys appeared everywhere. Future *Animal House* slacker Tim Matheson appeared in *Yours, Mine, and Ours* (1968), a movie in which Lucille Ball and Henry Fonda play parents combining their extensive families, (so Matheson could take his shirt off). Former *Flipper* swimsuit teen Luke Halpin showed up in *If This Is Tuesday, This Must Be Belgium* (1969) evidently just to strut around in tight jeans to demonstrate that, long hair or not, he was still strong, powerful, and masculine. Ex-teen idol Desi Arnaz Jr. divided his time between mugging on his mother's sitcom *Here's Lucy* (1968-1971) and a series of clean-cut teen dramas *(Red Sky at Morning, The Voyage of the Yes, Billy Two Hats)*. Kurt Russell, then a sugary-cute, slightly bewildered-looking, ex-child star, added the requisite clean-cut teen presence to ten movies between 1967 and 1973, including almost every Disney live-action comedy *(The Horse in the Grey Flannel Suit, The One and Only, Genuine, Original Family Band, The Computer Wore Tennis Shoes, The Barefoot Executive, Charley and the Angel)*. Perhaps the most prolific, (and, not coincidentally, the most muscular), clean-cut teen was Jan-Michael Vincent, who spent the late 1960s rushing between six TV movies, a fifteen-episode miniseries (Harold Robbins' *The Survivors*), and the serial *Danger Island* on the Saturday morning *Banana Splits* program.

Since anxiety over the teenage boy's potential failure to "discover" girls had nearly vanished since the days of Ozzie and Harriet, a specific demonstration of the teenage boy's girl-craziness was unnecessary. In *Yours, Mine, and Ours,* Lucille Ball confiscates a girly magazine from her twelve-year-old, and her teenage daughter necks with a boy, but none of the teenage sons in her or Henry Fonda's household express any interest in girls. Desi Arnaz Jr. likewise never has an actual date with a girl on *Here's Lucy,* though his mother constantly wise-cracks about his presumed girl-craziness. In *Voyage of the Yes* (1971), he and Mike Evans (then playing Lionel in *All in the Family*) odd-couple bond during a sailing trip from California to Hawaii neither one mentioning a girl back home. In *Guns in the Heather* (1968), foreign-exchange student played by Kurt Russell, traveling incognito through the Irish countryside while outwitting spies, flirts with a waitress at an inn. His buddy, played by Patrick Dawson exclaims, "You never told me you fancied the ladies!" as if heterosexual interest were uncommonly rare among teenagers. Yet the number-one box-office hit of 1968 that launched a dozen careers, won an uncountable number of awards and critical praises, ranks number seven on the American Film Institute (AFI) list of the top American films of all time, and has defined the 1960s for every generation since, paradoxically makes heterosexual interest itself the only escape from to the constraints of heteronormativity.

Benjamin Braddock

We usually queer movies by looking for same-sex interactions, for longing looks and emotional intimacy between same-sex friends that occur between, around, or in spite of the fade-out boy-girl kiss. But *The Graduate* (dir. Mike Nichols, Embassy Pictures, 1967) has none. Not a single same-sex buddy, not a single masculine glance. The plot centers on Benjamin Braddock (Dustin Hoffman), recent college graduate, track and debate star, and we do see a lot of him: he is naked more often than clothed, and his hard-muscled physique would not look out of place on a *Chippendales* calendar. But there is no one to notice. He lives in a hermetically sealed world of suburban castles with wide lawns and pools, organization-man husbands selling plastic and wives getting drunk, the logical culmination of the nuclear family myth, a glimpse into the future twenty years after the teen idols find *the one* and Frankie and Annette graduate from college.

Benjamin spends most of the movie trapped, staring mutely from behind fish tanks, wet-suit visors, barred windows, wide shots angled to suggest enclosed space, and most famously Mrs. Robinson's legs shaped into a triangular dragnet. There is no escape from his Stepford world, nor even the hope of escape. When he forsakes suburban L.A. for Berkeley, he finds no shaggy-haired, tie-died counterculture, just straights with textbooks (no doubt about marketing plastics) blankly assessing one another as potential husbands or wives. Roger Ebert says "it is clear today that he was utterly unaware of his generation and existed outside time and space."[9]

No one from his generation exists, but Benjamin is profoundly alienated from his parent's generation: "It's like I was playing some kind of game, but the rules don't make any sense to me." He is not a rebel without a cause, made vaguely nauseous by materialism and loveless marriages; several key scenes suggest that he is alienated specifically from his presumed heterosexual destiny. He displays no heterosexual interest: there are no pictures of girls on the walls of his room, he mentions no girls from school, and none at home. It seems quite unlikely that a handsome debate- and track-team champ with a magnificent physique would be deprived of hetero-romance, if he desired it, so one must conclude that he doesn't.

When other clean-cut teenagers of the period fail to display an interest in girls, adults are unconcerned; heterosexual desire is implicit, in the background, beyond conscious worry. The adults are as obsessed with prodding their teenage charge into heterosexual practice as Ozzie and Harriet were a decade before. Benjamin's are always suggesting that he call this or that girl for a date (he always refuses). When Mrs. Robinson first tries to seduce him, he rushes horrified down the stairs, where an oblivious Mr. Robinson sits him down and has a heart-to-heart with him over bourbon, advising heterosexual practice: "You should be having fun with girls! Sow some wild oats!" Benjamin protests that he is not interested in girls, but Mr. Robinson refuses to listen: "You must be quite the lady killer!" No, Ben says, he's not a lady killer at all. Now Mr. Robinson becomes noticeably angry. "You look like you have to beat them off!" he insists.

Later it is Mrs. Robinson's turn. When she can't seduce Benjamin by displaying her body in black lace, she tries to insult him into bed. First she accuses him of being a virgin, that is, not *yet* a man, and then she accuses him of being "inadequate," not man *enough,* that is, gay. Now Benjamin *wants* to be a lady killer; he slams the door and comes toward her. We cut immediately to a beefcake shot of Ben on a float in his family's pool, a can of beer strategically placed on his crotch to simulate an erection. He has demonstrated that he is a man, that is, heterosexual.

Benjamin does not yet dispute the veracity of the nuclear family myth, he is just alienated because the adults did it wrong. They forgot that they majored in art and married for love, so they subsist on brandy and affairs with college boys. Yet Benjamin will get it right. Just as every teen idol song evokes *the one,* and every beach movie ends with Frankie choosing Annette after all, Ben finds a girl, actually the only person his own age in the entire suburb, Elaine, spontaneous, and free, the polar opposite of the cold, calculating, and constrained adults. "You're the first person in a long time," he tells her, "That I could stand to be with." Now that he's met Elaine, everything makes sense, his life means *something.* No matter that she is the daughter of his fling Mrs. Robinson, or that she has plans to marry a Stepford beau at a cold, square church in the suburbs. Ben rushes to the church at the last minute and yells her name over and over until she finally yells back. "It's too late!" Mrs. Robinson snarls. "Not for me!" Elaine responds. She and Ben will not forget that they majored in art or married for love. Never. They will make suburbia deliriously happy and gloriously fulfilling. They fight off oldsters who are literally snarling with rage, flee the church, and jump on a bus (not one of their cars because they're anti-materialist). Fade out to freedom. They have escaped the suburban nuclear family, husband, wife, kids, organization-man job, and house made of ticky tacky—the entire heterosexual trajectory—through heterosexual love!

However, then something remarkable happens. Instead of joyfully planning their future together, or at least congratulating each other on having discovered the meaning of life, Benjamin and Elaine sit somberly, staring out into space, exactly the way Benjamin looked in the first scene when his airplane began its descent into suburban doom. Paul Simon reprises the theme: "Through restless streets I walked alone." Why is he still restless, still alone?

They have just realized that the bus is taking them right back to the suburbs again, where they'll buy a house, and Benjamin will study up on his plastics, and Elaine will sign up for charity drives, and in twenty years he will be a workaholic seducing office girls, and she will be an alcoholic seducing paperboys. *The one* will inevitably become Mrs. Robinson. Heterosexual love cannot serve as an escape. They are still trapped.

TEEN IDOLS

In the early 1960s, the Bobby Vans and Frankie Avalons, singing eternally about being a teenager in love, were overwhelmed by boy bands: The Young Rascals, the Monkees, Herman's Hermits, the Who, and of course the Beatles, with songs that soon strayed far beyond "I Wanna Hold Your Hand" to critique nowhere men, get high, and suggest spending the night together. The teen magazines tried to maintain the autonomy of the earlier teen idols by selecting one boy-band member to promote as particularly dreamy (Davy Jones of the Monkees, Peter Noone of Herman's Hermits), or by waiting for one to strike up a solo career (Michael Jackson from the Jackson 5, David Cassidy from The Partridge Family). Still, the new generation of teen idols did not overwhelm the charts like their predecessors: between 1967 and 1973, only ninety-nine songs by teen-oriented groups or soloists charted, and with a considerably different repertoire. Teen idols still search for *the one* special girl who gives life meaning, and she is still frequently lost, but there is a sharp decline in lying, cheating, deceitful girlfriends (5 percent) and male competitors (6 percent), obliterating every obstacle. Heterosexual romance has become an absolute good. Even adult opposition has practically vanished, appearing in only five songs by Donny Osmond (who at ages twelve and thirteen was a little young even by teen idol standards). The anxiety is over, the pitch no longer as vital.

Most teen idols of the era couldn't (or shouldn't) sing, receiving teen-magazine adulation based solely on their performances in hit TV shows (Mike Cole in *Mod Squad,* David Henesy in *Dark Shadows*), or even struggling, low-rated TV shows (Stefan Angrim in *Land of the Lost,* Sajid Khan, the first South Asian teen idol, in *Maya*). The key to teen magazine promotion was still cuteness, an androgynous stage presence, and minimal or absent heterosexual romance. Jack Wild never falls for any girl in *H. R. Pufnstuf,* nor Stefan Arngrim in *Land of the Lost* or Sajid Khan in *Maya.* Though David Henesy was twice paired with a girl for extended story arcs on the Gothic soap *Dark Shadows,* he treated them as best buddies, and devoted all of his grinning and posturing to adult male relatives and friends.[10]

Sometimes a lack of heterosexual romance is insufficient, and the teen idol must actively pursue same-sex relationships. Sajid Khan accompanied Jay North across India in search of his missing father, for no logical reason except that he rather liked the lanky, blond, ex-Dennis the Menace. Michael Cole bonded with a fellow hippie-cop, Stefan Arngrim with former *Teenage Frankenstein* Gary Conway, and Jack Wild with a seven-foot tall animatronic dragon.

Shoving teen idols into the arms of their male friends and eliminating their hetero-romances may be a toned-down version of *slash,* fan fiction created mostly by heterosexual women that evokes a romance between male characters who are "just friends" or antagonists in the official text: Kirk/Spock from *Star Trek,* Starsky/Hutch from the 1970's cop show, or the contemporary Harry Potter/Draco Malfoy.[11] Critics theorize that slash allows a female fan to explore tenderness and intimacy in a relationship without having to give her idol a girlfriend and thus demolish the fantasy that she is *the one.* Similarly, the teenage girls who presumably comprised 100 percent of the teen idol fan base could watch Sajid and Terry or David Henesy and David Selby to learn about strong emotional bonds without having their dreams of someday becoming Mrs. Teen Idol crushed. The teenage boys, however, learned something else entirely. They learned that same-sex bonds can be strong, intimate, intense, and fulfilling, that Sajid and Jay, David and David could be perfectly delirious in each other's company, that *the one* need not be a girl.

Chapter 8

American Graffiti:
1950's Nostalgia
and Teenage Androgyny

In *Babes in Arms* (1939), Mickey Rooney (imitating President Roosevelt) hears a litany of contemporary political woes, and offers a solution: "Just dance!" In *Saturday Night Fever* (1977), John Travolta (not imitating President Carter) faces the recession, an 8 percent unemployment rate, a skyrocketing poverty rate, the rust belting of the Northeast, and millions of dreams deferred by "Staying Alive" on a flashing checkerboard dance floor. During the economic downturn that ended the Generation of Love, disco, recreational drugs, white leisure suits, and giggly one-night stands staved off despair, at least among young adults and the glitterati. Yet everyone still wanted to save the world, so there were marches, protests, reevaluations, and pride. Miss and Mrs. became Ms.; ethnic minorities got new names and academic departments; and the post-Stonewall Gay Liberation Front became the Gay Rights Movement, a massive, international upswelling of activists, scholars, journalists, and everyday gay people demanding recognition, that they number in the millions—10 percent of every human population—and that they are not monsters.

Though in 1975 Air Force Sergeant Leonard Matlovich got on the cover of *Time* magazine simply by stating "I am a homosexual," an amazing amount of de-monstering happened within just a few years. Between 1973 and 1977, sodomy laws were revoked in fourteen states, a dozen noncloseted gay men and lesbians were elected to public office, antidiscrimination laws were passed in a dozen cities and the state of Pennsylvania, several prominent Christian denominations voted that gay people not abominations in the eyes of God, and the American Psychiatric Association decided they were not in need of straitjackets.

doi:10.1300/5484_08

Mass media moved somewhat more slowly. Popular music still refused to acknowledge the possibility that gay people could exist, even as monsters—Elton John claimed "bisexuality" to his peril in 1976 and didn't revise it to "gay" for twenty years. Though glam rockers could fey it up with eye shadow, long hair, and a Tiny Tim nasal voice, they were still required to sing exclusively about men and women in love: "Tell my wife I love her very much," David Bowie's Major Tom sings to Ground Control in "Space Oddity" (1973), and Alice Cooper topped the charts in the summer of 1975 by singing "Only Women Bleed":

> Man's got his woman to take his seed.
> He's got the power—she's got the need.

Later in the decade, glam was replaced by conventionally masculine, girl-obsessed Eagles, Bruce Springsteen, and Barry Manilow (who never told anyone that he got his start as a pianist for Bette Midler at the Club Baths). The Village People pretended to be Castro clones and sang heavily double-entendre-laden songs like "Y.M.C.A." and "In the Navy," yet in interviews they not only behaved as if no double entendre was intended, they behaved as if none was even possible, since gay people could not exist to provide any meaning.

In the movies, gay characters appeared as reassuring swishes in *Car Wash* (1976) and *The Ritz* (1976). Robby Benson's character committed suicide rather than face life as a gay teenager in *Ode to Billy Joe* (1976); Perry King got cured of his gayness in *A Different Story* (1978); and lots of murderous lesbians and transvestites prowled about with pick-axes for example in *Shivers* (1975), *Don't Open the Door* (1975), *Driller Killer* (1979), and most famously *Dressed to Kill* (1980). *The Rocky Horror Picture Show* (1975) bombed in Topeka but became a midnight movie craze in college towns, with "sweet transvestite" played by Tim Curry exuberantly proclaiming "Don't dream it, be it." On TV, buddies or brothers came out to straight characters, (who were horrified at first but learned tolerance), on *Alice, All in the Family, M*A*S*H, The Mary Tyler Moore Show,* and *The Bob Newhart Show,* until eventually the plot device became a sitcom standard, still in use today. But none of the gay characters, monstrous or tolerance teaching, knew about the Gay Rights Movement, gay communities, gay pride, or even the presence of other gay people on the face of the earth; they may be leering and sniping or conflicted and anguished, but they were always alone.

TEEN DREAMS

During the 1970s, rising print costs and declining newsstand sales made most of the teen magazines fold. Those that survived had to expand their audience to include all money-solvent teenagers, boys as well as girls. Headlines still promised coverage of "The Kind of Girls Elton John Likes To Kiss!!!!" but most articles assumed a general interest in show biz rather than the dream of marrying this or that fave rave. The June 1976 issue of *Tiger Beat,* for instance, asks "What's Next for Willie Aames?" and "Has Leif [Garrett] Been Away Too Long?" Instead of a grinning, swimsuit-clad centerfold, it shows Henry Winkler on a two-page photo tour of his hometown.[1] Both male and female performers are spotlighted, and the letter and advice columns address both boy and girl fans. Every letter promotes the myth of universal heterosexuality—girl fans write something on the lines of "You're such a hottie!!!!!!" while boy fans simply ask "When is your next movie coming out?" But as long as everyone plays the game, the expansion of the market allows boys to buy and read teen magazines without fear, and who can say that not a single "You're such a hottie!!!!!" letter from a boy was ever mailed, or written, or thought of?

To further expand the audience, teen idols began expressing varied and complex interests, not merely an obsession with kissing girls. Suddenly they discussed movies, music, books, and sports. They had parents and siblings. Sometimes they even had same-sex friendships, though they usually described the relationships using the intimate, exclusive rhetoric of the teen idol quest after *the one.* Later in the June 1976 issue of *Tiger Beat,* Paul Michael Glaser discusses David Soul, his costar on *Starsky and Hutch*: "It is a love relationship . . . we started out having a chemistry between us—something that just worked, and we ended up loving each other."[2] He quickly "clarifies" the relationship within a heteronormative model ("He's like the brother I never had"), but not before describing David Soul so ardently that he nearly acknowledges the possibility that boys sometimes fall in love with each other.

The September 1978 issue of *Tiger Beat Star* likewise rhapsodizes over the intimate friendship between Clark Brandon, heavily promoted as a teen idol even though he hadn't done much professionally, and "dental student" Steve Guttenberg. The article fails to mention that Steve is also an actor, with three movies on his resume. Steve has to be presented not as a fellow actor but as an ordinary guy that Clark just happens to like. Which is Steve, best friend or true love? He is presented as extremely girl-crazy, using the friendship primarily to meet and date Clark's female fans. Clark expresses no interest in girls; he seems to have eyes only for Steve. According to the article he courts Steve quite aggressively, always taking the initiative in knocking on his door, asking him out, even inviting him home to meet his mother. The article never suggests that the two are anything other than best friends. Instead, it presents best friends and true loves as exactly the same thing, *the one* who gives life meaning. Sometimes *the one* is a girl, and sometimes a boy.[3]

Most of the teen idols of the 1970s, including Clark Brandon, David Cassidy, Shaun Cassidy, Bobby Sherman, Robby Benson, Leif Garrett, and many less well-remembered, displayed soft, pretty features, feathered hair, and swiveling hips, with only the lead pipe invariably shoved down one leg of their red-fringed jumpsuits offering any hints that they were to be taken as boys. This epicene facade was not an imitation of the adults—the glam rockers were a small and dying breed—instead, it represented a mere intensification of the androgyny visible in teen idols' stage presence since the days of Frankie and Fabian. But when coupled with the new discovery that best buddies were permitted and might even be *the one,* it resulted in an openness to same-sex romance unprecedented in the history of the teen idol.

During his tenure as a mega teen idol, roughly 1977 to 1981, Leif Garrett starred in three movies, *Peter Lundy and the Medicine Hat Stallion* (1977), *Skateboard* (1978), and *Longshot* (1981), but never as a hetero-romantic lead. He ignores girls and lusts after his adult male costars, playing the buddy-bonding scenes with an erotic tension so palpable that it becomes embarrassing. Shaun Cassidy played the youngest of the *Hardy Boys* (1977-1979) as rather uninterested in girls; he does acquire a girlfriend in his single teen idol movie, *Like Normal People* (1979), but he still invests considerably more emotional energy in his male counselor-teacher. Though Lance Kerwin's high school swimming star famously lost his virginity to a Swedish bombshell in *James at 15* (1977-1978), a year later he fell in love quite noticeably with David Soul in *Salem's Lot* (1979).

Jimmy McNichol

Though conventionally masculine, short-haired, with a lanky body-builder physique, Jimmy McNichol was the most active of all the teen idols in opening the possibility of same-sex romance. Indeed, in spite of his wife and children, he was still subject to more "gay rumors" than any of the other teen idols of the 1970s, even Clark Brandon. After guest-star spots on kid-faves such as *Little House on the Prairie* and *Shazam!* his teen idol career was launched when he played Clark Brandon's troubled brother on *The Fitzpatricks* (1977-1978) and displayed his bod and bulge on *The Battle of the Network Stars*. It was not an auspicious beginning, but nevertheless Jimmy soon became *Tiger Beat's* favorite photo subject, surpassing even Leif Garrett by the spring of 1978. Fans liked his muscles, of course, but it seems that they were even more interested in playing the "is he gay?" game, and Jimmy was more than happy to accommodate. That summer he and his sixteen-year-old sister Kristy, star of the weeper *Family,* debuted their first single at Manhattan's infamously omnisexual Studio 54. It was a cover of the Chiffon's 1950's classic "He's So Fine!" (with the actual Chiffons singing backup), about a hot guy who might be gay, and therefore not worth the trouble of flirting with:

> He's a soft spoken guy
> Also seems kinda shy
> Makes me wonder if I
> Should even give him a try.[4]

The song floundered at number seventy, and a subsequent album, *Kristy and Jimmy McNichol,* similarly flopped, though some of the tracks made intriguingly gay-coded duets: "He's a Dancer," "Girl, You Got Me Going," "My Boyfriend's Back." Teen magazines continued to praise Jimmy as the next Leif Garrett, and the network brass couldn't get enough of him. In the fall of 1978 he and Kristy hosted the *ABC All-Star Saturday Preview Special* and sang in *The Carpenters: A Christmas Portrait,* and Jimmy rated his own talk show, *Hollywood*

Teen.[5] In January 1979 he hit the big time with a starring role in a TV movie, *Champions: A Love Story,* evidently scripted just to continue the "is he gay?" game. Jimmy plays an upper-crust sissy-boy ice skater who falls in love with his teammate (Joy Leduc) while they train for the big competition. His father believes that he is gay for selecting an unmanly sport, and he is feminized more by becoming a clone of the upper-crust character Ally McGraw played in *Love Story,* complete with tear-jerking death. In spite of a tiny bit of kissing with Joy Leduc, Jimmy doesn't do much to demonstrate straightness.[6]

In April 1979 Jimmy got his own *Jimmy McNichol Special,* with guests Kristy, Magic Johnson, and up-and-coming teen idol Ricky Schroeder. In the fall of 1979 *California Fever* sent him and frizzy-haired buddy Marc McClure (Jimmy Olsen in the *Superman* movie) to Southern California where they skateboarded, roller-discoed, surfed, started a garage band, and hung out with hunks Lorenzo Lamas and Rex Smith. Interest was beginning to fade: as we have seen, teen idols have a shelf life of only three to five years, so Jimmy tried for relevance with *Blinded by the Light* (1980), about a girl (Kristy) trying to deprogram her gay brother who has fallen in with a Moonie-like cult. In *Smokey Bites the Dust* (1981), Jimmy tried to capitalize on the *Smokey and the Bandit* and *Dukes of Hazzard* craze, zooming down the country-fried roads complete with Southern accent and girlfriend, but ratings were dismal, and the teen magazines had moved on. Perhaps he thought he could spark some new audience interest with *Night Warning* (dir. William Asher, Comworld, 1981), which not only asks "is he gay?" but actually has gay characters.

In *Night Warning* Jimmy plays Billy Lynch, a high school athlete who lived with his Aunt Cheryl (Susan Tyrrell) since his parents died in an accident (that really wasn't an accident) years ago. Aunt Cheryl spends her time eying Billy incestuously and figuring out excuses to give him shirtless massages, but she is not beyond yelling "I need a man!" and grabbing the TV repairman. When he rejects her, she grabs a kitchen knife and stabs him, then claims that he was trying to rape her. Yet Detective Carlson (Bo Svenson) is suspicious: the repairman was gay (perhaps the only gay person in all of American cinema who is not an urban sophisticate), and so unlikely to rape maiden aunts. His lover, Coach Landers (Steve Eastin), has been big brothering Billy after basketball practice, so the detective deduces that Billy committed the crime in a lover's quarrel gone wrong, and Aunt

Cheryl is trying to protect him. But this is no dispassionate investigation: the detective hates "fags," and wishes it were legal to kill them all.

As the investigation progresses, everyone at school assumes that Billy is gay. Even his girlfriend Julie (Julia Duffy), after sweaty sex, asks "How come we haven't . . . more often? Is there something wrong?" meaning "Are you gay?" (evidently gay people have heterosexual sex, just not very often). Billy is horrified by the "accusations," and even assaults one of his accusers, yet in other parts of the film, he is not homophobic. He continues to support Coach Landers, who in fact is the only positively portrayed character in the whole town. There are even hints that the "accusation" may be close to the truth: Billy seems to have much more invested in Coach Landers than an ordinary student-teacher relationship. When Aunt Cheryl tries to kill him (so he won't go away to college and leave her alone), Billy calls Coach Landers, not his girlfriend or some heterosexual buddy, for help.

The question of Billy's sexual identity is not answered by his constant protesting-too-much or by his buddy bond with the coach. Was *Night Warning* a backhanded means of coming out, or a means of acknowledging and rebutting the "is he gay?" rumors, or an attempt to stay in the limelight by writing "is he gay?" in big, bold letters? A more interesting question is why heterosexual desire is always portrayed as oppressive and sinister. Aunt Cheryl opines that "Homosexuals are very, very sick!" as she murders half a dozen people, grabs and fondles Billy, drugs his milk, and finally tries to stab him, and Julie obsesses over Billy almost as blatantly. The movie ends in freeze with Julie hugging Billy and saying "it's okay" in eerie reflection of Aunt Cheryl, as he stares horrified into space, trapped again, just as the teen idol, gay or not, is always trapped behind the mandate to espouse universal heterosexuality.

THE 1950s CRAZE

In February 1972, the anthology series *Love, American Style* aired "Love and the Happy Days," a twenty-minute segment set during comedy writer Garry Marshall's adolescence in the early 1950s, and starring a freckle-faced seventeen-year-old named Ronnie Howard, then well-known for strolling toward the fishin' hole with his dad in

the hayseed *Andy Griffith Show* (1960-1968). When his family buys
one of those newfangled television gizmos, the young Richie Cun-
ningham is allowed to invite one guest for the first-night viewing.
Everyone assumes that he will select long-term best friend Potsie
(nineteen-year-old Anson Williams), but when a snooty girl flirts
with him, Richie gets a vision of post-television breast fondling and
invites her instead. It turns out that she was just using him to see television, but Potsie doesn't resent being rejected for a girl (he would do
the same), and Richie learns a valuable life lesson, that every flirtation does not lead to breast fondling.

The next year, George Lucas penned, produced, and directed
American Graffiti (1973), a movie set during his own adolescence.
He also hired Ronnie Howard to be a recognizable face in a group of
high school buddies saying good-bye on the last night of summer in
1962, before they fly off to separate colleges and separate destinies.
"Where were you in 1962?" the tagline asks, as if referring to the distant past rather than eleven years ago. Contemporary teenagers, in
kindergarten in '62, liked the conflict between hometown friends and
distant-college career goals, something they themselves would be
facing in a few years. Audiences drove *American Graffiti* to gross
$115 million and four Oscar nominations, and started a craze for teen
movies set during the "golden age" after McCarthy and before Vietnam, the era of the juvenile delinquent, the monster mash, the teen
idol, and the beach movie. During this era movies such as *The Lords
of Flatbush* (1974), *Senior Year* (1974), *Summer City* (1977), *American Hot Wax* (1978), *Animal House* (1978), *Grease* (1978), *I Wanna
Hold Your Hand* (1978), *Hometown U.S.A.* (1979), *The Wanderers*
(1979), and many others were made. On TV, *Happy Days* and
Laverne and Shirley dominated prime time, and on the radio, pop
rockers dusted off old Beach Boys classics or else reminisced about
how "late December back in '63" was "a very special time for me."[7]
The decade was littered with nostalgia, for the jazz age after *The
Great Gatsby* (1974), for the Depression after *Paper Moon* (1973),
even for the Korean War with *M*A*S*H* (1972-1983). But the late
1950s and early 1960s were marketed overwhelmingly to teenagers.

Why market the teenagers of yesteryear to teenagers today? Because it was within living memory, when most of the writers, directors, and producers were teenagers themselves, yet far removed from
the sexual ambiguity of the present, where queens kept swishing on

stage to leer and double-entendre at the straights, or else the straights were mistakenly identified as queens, and teen idols made their careers out of hints, innuendos, and "is he gay?" posturing. In late December back in '63, no queens existed to leer and double-entendre. None of Fonzie's friends ever came out of the closet, nor did Laverne and Shirley ever hint that they might be lesbians. In *Grease,* Danny's buddies could lunge at one another's crotches, and in *Animal House,* Otter could give his buddy a dildo (while they were both naked) without anyone for a moment suspecting them of being *that way*—*that way* didn't exist in 1962. Gay, lesbian, bisexual, transsexual, transgendered, queer, nonheterosexual, non-gender-polarized beings absolutely, emphatically, did *not* exist, anywhere. They were not even conjured up in fiction, not even hinted at in folklore. Producers could relax while feeding the teenagers their own fondly recalled or imagined hetero-obsessed, breast-fondling utopia. But even if gay people could be eliminated from the scripts, same-sex love could not, and the cultural texts of the 1950's craze often portray heterosexual desire as silly, trivial, and infantile, while the love of comrades can redeem the world.

In *American Graffiti* (dir. George Lucas, Universal, 1973), everyboy Steve (Ron Howard) and stocky, long-term buddy Curt (Richard Dreyfuss) will part tomorrow morning for different colleges, but they aren't worried about breaking up, since in the standard movie triangulation, Steve is dating Curt's sister Laurie (Cindy Williams), so they will eventually be legitimated as brothers-in-law and spend every summer vacation together for the rest of their lives. Then Steve and Laurie agree to "see other people," code for "break up by Christmas," and Curt slips into a frenzy of inarticulate terror. To triangulate away from Laurie, he forces Steve to drive him around in search of a blonde he saw in a passing T-Bird: "Come on, you've got to catch up to her! . . . I think she said 'I love you!' . . . Someone wants me! Someone roaming the streets *wants me!*"

That is, Steve may not want him anymore, but *someone* does. His friends riff over girls and cars, with the drive-in and drag race scenes and Wolfman Jack smiling benevolently over all, but Curt spends the night feverishly bargaining for love. He tries to join a juvenile delinquent gang called the Pharaohs. He considers not going away at all: "why should I leave friends that I love to find new friends?" Yet in the end, he gets on that DC10 and flies off to his future, while Steve changes his mind, decides to stay in town and marry Laurie after all. The closing credits tell us that Curt is now a writer living in Canada, still resisting the heterosexual trajectory into wife, kids, house, and organization-man job, while Steve is a new Jim Anderson, an insurance agent living in Modesto. We know who to be sorry for.

The 1950s Craze on Television

In 1974, Garry Marshall convinced ABC to use his old *Love, American Style* script as a pilot for a new series called *Happy Days*, set in the late 1950s, but in an archetypal, small-town Milwaukee rather than Los Angeles. Ron Howard reprised his role as Richie, an inexperienced but intensely hetero-horny high school boy, and Anson Williams returned as Potsie, his leering buddy, equally inexperienced but better at fabricating stories about breast fondling at "Inspiration Point." To ensure that their bond did not seem uncomfortably intimate, Donny Most was hired as a third friend, the wisecracking Ralph Malph. Though the plots would revolve around inept and hopefully hilarious attempts to acquire girls, Richie would come from a complete *Father Knows Best*-style nuclear family, with organization-man Dad, housewife Mom, jock older brother, and bratty little sister, a conservative backlash to the prime-time TV trend toward single Moms (e.g., *One Day at a Time, Alice*), singles at work (*The Mary Tyler Moore Show, Taxi*), and people who weren't white (*Good Times, Sanford and Son*). *Happy Days* premiered in the spring of 1974 and lasted for eleven seasons among the top-ten network programs most of the time. It received eight Emmy nominations and six Golden Globes, spawned seven spin-off and crossover series, and produced tie-in products, books, magazines, songs, toys, and games.

In spite of, or perhaps because of the lack of actual gay characters, the boys of *Happy Days* indulge in ample "is he gay?" innuendos beneath a facade of girl-ogling, forging passionate, same-sex friendships, on-screen and off, that make their scripted dates with girls seem tepid and mechanical. One must dig beneath the lame one-liners about fondling breasts, but one needn't dig far. In spite of the hype about hetero-horniness, only 25 percent of the first season's episodes centered on Richie and company's attempts to meet, fondle, kiss, or romance girls, and the percentage declined every year through season number seven, Ron Howard's last.[8]

Most of the enduring popularity of *Happy Days* can be attributed to Fonzie (Henry Winkler), a leather-jacket-clad juvenile delinquent introduced to add conflict to the otherwise tepid plotlines. Fonzie was practically the opposite of Richie, Potsie, and Ralph: impoverished to their middle class, orphaned to their nuclear families, a high school dropout to their frequently discussed college and career plans; and while they were forced to defend their manhood by pretending that they had merely fondled breasts, Fonzie went "all the way." Soon Henry Winkler became the standout star of the series; though he was no teenager, either in the story or in real life, he received most of the fan mail and most of the gushing in teen magazines. Fonzie was systematically domesticated, moving in with the Cunninghams, getting his high school diploma, teaching at the high school, playing father to young cousin Chachi (Scott Baio), teaching racial tolerance and respect for women, eating vegetables, drinking milk, ultimately becoming a moralizing Saturday morning cartoon. Oddly, his bedroom gymnastics did not decrease. As he became domesticated, it actually *increased,* until he became a mythical Priapic figure, sexing dozens of women every night, often two or three at a time, and in the morning snapping his fingers for more. On the rare occasions that a desired woman said "no," he merely smiled and walked away, knowing that she would have a change of heart by the commercial break. He never looked for *the one,* nor did he ask any woman to marry him until late in the season; the act of heterosexual coitus itself had become wholesome and all American, like eating your vegetables and drinking your milk.

But sex can be pursued as a goal separate from human connections, and Fonzie's nightly heterosexual exploits seem to have the approximate emotional impact of an aerobics routine. When the workout is over, he prefers the company of men. One struggles to find a reason why the adult Fonzie wanted to spend all of his time with high school boys, and especially with the impossibly naive Richie, whom he calls "Howdy Doody" after the puppet. Like Sal Mineo for James Dean, or Neal Cassidy for Jack Kerouac, Richie fills an essential void for him, a void that cannot be filled by infinite nights of breast fondling in bedrooms. When Fonzie is injured, it is Richie, not some girl, who rushes to his bedside; when Richie is injured, it is Fonzie, not some girl, who cries. When the alien Mork (Robin Williams) drops in from *Mork and Mindy* to research a report on the 1950s, he hears anecdotes not about girl groping or even about buddy bonding, but about Richie and

Fonzie, while "Isn't It Romantic?" plays in the background. No wonder Fonzie never searched for true love, or ratings started to decline when Richie met steady girlfriend Lori Beth:[9] like Starsky and Hutch, they were one of the 1970's great romantic couples.

Happy Days spearheaded ABC's Tuesday night lineup, a remarkable assortment of comedies and light dramas that regularly topped the ratings through the middle and late 1970s (including, in 1978-1979, *four* of the top-ten network programs). Immediately before or after *Happy Days* came the spin-off *Laverne and Shirley* (1976-1983), set in a blue-collar Italian-accented neighborhood of 1950's Milwaukee, where brassy Laverne (Penny Marshall) and wannabe sophisticate Shirley (Cindy Williams) shared a basement apartment and a bottle-capping job at the local brewery. Alexander Doty has already established that the duo behave as a stereotypic 1950's butch-femme lesbian couple, by design or not, and that the characters (if not the actresses) were aware, on some level, that theirs was a romantic partnership rather than a platonic friendship.[10] But the men of the series were equally adept at wielding a subtext. Carmine (Eddie Mekka), Shirley's sometimes rather tepid boyfriend never expresses any other heterosexual interest. While waiting for his big break as a dancer, singer, or boxer (two out of the three career fields gay coded), he is employed as the boy toy of a wealthy woman named Lucille; that is, he is a skittishly made-for-TV version of a male hustler, who in real life would have a male clientele. Wacky next-door neighbors Lenny (Michael McKean) and Squiggy (David L. Lander) do express heterosexual interest, but with constant smooching sounds, groping gestures, and crass come-ons that seem designed to drive women away while they get on with their long-term monogamous relationship.[11] There is barely a heterosexual person in the presumably heterosexual 1950s.

The rest of the Tuesday night lineup similarly starred heterosexuals who played the "is he gay?" game as eagerly as the teen idols. At 9:00 p.m., *Three's Company* (1977-1984) had young, hetero cooking student Jack Tripper (John Ritter) swishing it up so his narrow-minded landlord will let him share an apartment with two girls. The 9:30 time slot was used as a proving ground for new programs: *Soap* (1977-1981), a soap opera spoof featuring Jody (Billy Crystal) as gay, bi, transvestite, or transsexual (the writers weren't quite sure of the difference); *Taxi* (1978-1983), about New York cabbies, with boxing hopeful Tony (Tony Danza) barely hiding his homoerotic passion for pretty-boy actor Bobby (Jeff Conaway); and *Too Close for Comfort* (1980-1983), about a cartoonist (Ted Knight) overprotecting his two hot daughters, with wacky next-door neighbor (gay actor Jim J. Bullock) allowed to camp unmercifully as long as it was understood that he was *really* heterosexual. The 10:00 p.m. time slot included *Family* (1976-1980), a soap featuring the fey Leif Garrett hitting on the butch Kristy McNichol to demonstrate that both were *really* heterosexual; and *Starsky and Hutch* (1975-1979), with Paul Michael Glaser and David Soul as two cops in love. But no one actually said the word gay (or, on *Soap,* meant it).

THE GAY 1950s

Late in the decade, gay people began to break out of the innuendos and subtexts and be named, albeit in a fearful whisper. On *Happy Days,* Fonzie and his cousin Chachi (Scott Baio) go to a romantic restaurant, where the maitre d' seats them, quipping that "all types" are welcome. Fonzie, the champion of racial and gender equality, bug eyes with horror and cries "He thinks we're a type! Let's get out of here!" In *Grease,* the boys and girls are strictly divided into polar oppositions in dress, costume, tastes, and sex and romance, so at the big dance contest, the coach cautions: "All couples must be boy-girl." He is "really" forbidden the common 1950's practice of heterosexual girls dancing together when no boy has asked, but someone jokes "Too bad, Eugene," naming the school nerd as gay.

Animal House (dir. John Landis, 20th Century Fox, 1978), premiering during the late 1970's antigay backlash (see Chapter 9), is more open and more hostile. The Delta House Fraternity at Faber College consists of "good guys," tolerant, kind, helpful, and homophobic: they accept all pledges "except for real closet cases," and yell "fag," "fruit," and "homo" at any boy who is clumsy, inept, or insufficiently eager to grab at girls' breasts. The evil rival fraternity, called "fags" by the good guys, is decidedly homoerotic. In their initiation ceremony, everyone strips to his underwear, muscles glow in candlelight, and the pledges are thwacked rhythmically on their behinds in imitation of anal sex. But not to worry, the evil "fags" get their comeuppance when Delta House steals all of their girlfriends.

Eight or nine antigay epithets sprinkled through *The Wanderers* (1979) do not diminish the overtly homoromantic tale of buddies brawling their way through their senior year in 1963 in the Bronx. Early in the movie, Joey (John Friedrich), a high school sissy who specializes in paintings of beefy football players, is rescued from a bully beating by the new kid, a solemn, dark-eyed man-mountain named Perry (Tony Ganios, later "Meat" in the *Porky's* franchise). They have a lot in common. Both live in the same apartment building, and both come from dysfunctional families (Joey's bodybuilder dad is abusive, and Perry's mom is crazy). Joey jealously guards his new buddy, refusing to introduce him to the other students, but bringing him home to meet the folks as eagerly as if he were a girlfriend. Dad stares suspiciously and refuses to shake Perry's hand.

Shortly before they are to leave for a bachelor party that will spell the end of the old gang, Perry and Joey lie on single beds pushed together, in their underwear, talking quietly (the script does not explain why they are in bed, half-naked, in the middle of the afternoon). They decide to leave town together after the party. At that moment, Dad bursts in, yells at them, and attacks Perry. Joey defends him, hitting Dad on the head with a beer bottle, and he falls to the floor, unconscious and maybe dead. Now they have to leave right away. The movie ends with them driving down the Jersey Turnpike, agreeing that their final destination will be San Francisco: perhaps because it happens to be at the end of Interstate 80, or perhaps because in 1979 it was famous as a gay mecca. They have "lit out to the territory," finding love with each other.

Among the last of the 1950s craze movies, *Porky's* (dir. Bob Clark, 20th Century Fox, 1982) is hyped as a hetero-horny girlfest about high school boys getting laid in 1950s Florida, but it seems designed for audiences composed entirely of heterosexual women and gay men. There is little cheesecake and no female nudity (except for an unattractive girl's buttocks), but endless shots of muscular male bodies, including frontal and rear nudity, and an opening close-up of an erection through underwear. Indeed, the cast seems much more obsessed by penises than by any female body parts. Pee Wee (Dan Monahan) worries that he's not big enough; Meat (Tony Ganios) is asked "Why do they call you Meat? Because it's so big?"; there are gags involving a ten-gallon novelty condom and a glory-hole set up in the girl's shower. Only the coach engages in heterosexual practice in a scene played for laughs. None of the teenage boys have sex, fall in love with girls, or even kiss girls, though they play many practical jokes in which someone thinks he's going to get laid, (but doesn't). The plot is about male friendship.

Perhaps more interesting is that there are no antigay slurs. Jokes that would be phrased as antigay in *Up the Academy* or *Animal House* are neutral here. The adults do not attempt to seduce the boys or quash their girl-craziness, the butch female coach is ridiculed for being fat and authoritarian, not for being a lesbian. The *other* in *Porky's* is Jewish, the shy, troubled, new kid in town Brian Schwartz (Scott Colomby), but his Jewishness is oddly associated with a lack of girl-craziness. All of the boys befriend Brian except for the hulking redneck Tim (Cyril O'Reilly), who challenges him to a fight. Brian trounces him. Later Tim is assaulted by his father, who believes that any "real man" should be able to best a Jewish boy. What does being Jewish have to do with being a "real man"? Perhaps it is the failure to be sufficiently girl-crazy that actually bugs Tim and his father, and Jewish is code for gay. In the end, Tim rejects his Dad's homophobic "anti-Semitism":

DAD: Looks like I'm gonna make a man of you yet, boy.
TIM: If being a man means being what you are, I'd rather be queer.

Both Tim and his father correlate being Jewish with being "less than a man," that is, gay. After the dressing-down, Tim walks over to side with Brian, in effect selecting "queer" over redneck, and the two buddy bond sufficiently to orchestrate the gang's final prank. But he would be the last of his generation to embrace even a surrogate queerness.

Chapter 9

Real Men and Psycho-Slashers

The glimmering of gay awareness began to falter in 1977 and 1978, when the Save Our Children Campaign (against gay rights in Dade County, Florida) and the Briggs Initiative (against gay teachers in San Francisco) yelled, loudly, in national forums, that gay people were monsters after all. Even the more moderate voices began to realize that gayness did not reside merely in double-entendres or androgynous poses, to be dismissed with a wink when it came time for the fade-out walk into the sunset with a girl. Somewhere out there, real live *homosexuals* (i.e., gay men) did not walk into sunsets with girls, and they hated God and America, and their chief joy was snatching little boys from playgrounds. Thirty little boys were found buried under the floorboards of John Wayne Gacy's house in Chicago in 1978, and twenty more disappeared at the hands of Wayne Williams in Atlanta between 1979 and 1981 (no one seemed to care that both serial killers were heterosexual).

In January 1981, the liberal Baptist Democrats retreated from Capitol Hill, and the ultra-ultra conservative Ronald Reagan tried to produce a real-life version of the circumscript, white, Protestant, heterosexual nuclear family-only world of his childhood or old movies (he couldn't seem to tell them apart). For eight years (plus four more under his successor George Bush), he heated up the Cold War, favored big business, and demonized minorities, immigrants, the poor, single-parent households, single mothers, working mothers, working women, everyone who would have been excluded from the set of *Love Finds Andy Hardy.* The party was over, jubilant nonconformity replaced by obedience. In "Grease" (1978), Frankie Valli assured us that "Conventionality belongs to yesterday," but by 1983, Styx's "Mr. Roboto" confessed:

> I am the modern man, who hides behind a mask
> So no one else can see my true identity.

Between 1975 and 1985, the number of undergraduates majoring in leveraged buyouts nearly doubled, while the number majoring in understanding other people shrank by half.[1] The teen idol's "Is he gay?" question must always be answered "no," and no homoerotic subtext should ever be found. Teenage boys could no longer refuse to take up their briefcases and ply girls with engagement rings, lest they be snatched from playgrounds and buried under floorboards, or else be struck down by God.

Introduced to the mainstream by Tom Brokaw on *The NBC Nightly News* in June 1982, GRID (gay-related immune deficiency) was renamed AIDS by 1984 when it was discovered that anyone could contract it. Yet many people continued to believe that it was caused by marching in gay-pride parades, and that God was striking down those who dared refuse the briefcase, brokerage firm, and the engagement ring. Through the 1980s, conservative pundits, and even some moderates and liberals, yelled that AIDS would end when the *homosexuals* stopped acting like sissies and got jobs and wives.

Although President Reagan seemed unaware that *homosexuals* existed, legislators knew. Gay rights ordinances were repealed in Wichita, St. Louis, and even the ultra-cool college town of Eugene, Oregon. During the 1970s, half of the states in the United States threw out their sodomy laws, but during the 1980s the other half resolutely insisted that gay people were criminals. In 1986, the Supreme Court handed down the momentous *Bowers v. Hardwick* decision, decreeing that they *should be* criminals, indeed that "it is the very act of homosexual sodomy that epitomizes moral degeneracy." As late as 1982, the mass media was presenting nice gay men *(Making Love)*, lesbians *(Personal Best)*, and transvestites *(Victor/Victoria)*, but thereafter they—and especially the gay men—were placed squarely on the losing side of a cosmic battle between the heterosexual (masculine, wholesome, healthy) and the homosexual (feminine, creepy, diseased).

The battle lines were disrupted in the summer of 1985, when Hollywood veteran Rock Hudson revealed that he had AIDS. Most

Americans were stunned. Liberace, perhaps, or even the fey Tony Randall, but Rock Hudson was the antithesis of "homosexual" (feminine, creepy, diseased). He was a two-fisted action hero, a beefcake pinup, a romantic lead, a heartthrob; his triad of on-screen bicker-romances with America's favorite girl next door, Doris Day,[2] defined Kennedy-era heterosexuality for adults as definitively as the beach movies for teenagers. It didn't seem possible that, as Sturken states, "many of our fundamental, conventional images [of heterosexuality] were instilled by someone gay."[3] But there was an even greater problem: if all gay men didn't sashay and all straight men didn't swagger, how were "we" supposed to tell them apart? How could we avoid being snatched from playgrounds or contracting AIDS from a handshake if we couldn't instantly distinguish masculine from feminine, wholesome from creepy, healthy from diseased?

The solution was to suspect everyone, police everyone, interrogate everyone, even ourselves. The realest of real men could sleep with 15,000 women, yet still wonder if a trivial moment of same-sex tenderness or a momentary lapse in girl-ogling *meant something.* Teenage boys were not yet real men, they might easily be snatched from playgrounds, so they must police themselves even more thoroughly for trivial moments of tenderness and momentary lapses in ogling. As a result, mass media teenagers began to reduce every word, gesture, and bit of stage business to a demonstration of their unquestionable straightness.

TEEN IDOLS

The wispy, androgynous, gay-teasing teen idols endured for awhile; Peter Barton played the "is he gay?" game as late as 1983, in *The Powers of Matthew Star.* Yet the new teen idols, and the old ones hoping to survive the Reagan years, sported superbodies by Nautilus (since gay men never went near a gym) and removed the lead pipes out of their pants (since only gay men looked *down there*). The December 1984 issue of *Teen Beat* featured a dozen pecs-and-abs boys (Scott Baio, Robby Benson, Steve Bond, Christopher Collet, Matt Dillon, Ricky Schroeder, Charlie Sheen, John Stamos), but only one androgyne (Prince). Scott Baio, Robby Benson, and Ricky Schroeder were the favorites, centerfolded about a thousand times, shirtless,

flexing, in tight jeans obviously lacking in lead pipes, as if to say
"See, I'm 100 percent real."

In the movies, nude backsides and even frontal shots became even
more blatant signifiers that the teenager was 100 percent real, therefore straight, not requiring the blow-dried hair, stylish costumes, or
feminine affectation of the "homosexual." Between 1975 and 1984,
the number of scenes displaying the privates of male teenage actors
(or adults playing teenagers) nearly tripled, even though the total
number of male nude scenes increased only a little.[4] By the end of the
decade, even shirtless shots came to signify straightness. In *Weekend
at Bernies* (1989), two buddies take a break from their organization-
man jobs to sunbathe, and heterosexual, played by Jonathan Silverman unbuttons his shirt to display some chest, while ambiguously
gay character played by Andrew McCarthy keeps covered up.

Yet demonstrating that they were 100 percent real was not sufficient.
The new teen idols must also eliminate speculation that a stray same-
sex look or touch might *mean something*. Robby Benson spent most of
his 1980's movie career having tear-jerking hugs with men, but only
when they were safely cast as relatives (fathers Jack Lemmon and Paul
Newman, grandfather George Burns), or when he was playing an ethnic minority (Chicano in *Walk Proud,* Hasidic in *The Chosen,* Native
American in *Running Brave*). Since gay men were white urban fancy
boys sipping on wine and acting decadent, the downtrodden must be
straight, and their hugs safely devoid of *meaning*. When Robert
MacNaughton, the big brother in *E.T.*, kicked off a brief teen idol career with the thriller *I Am the Cheese* (1983), he avoided same-sex
looks by trekking through a New England comprised entirely of violent, cruel, bigoted boys and caring, supportive girls (see *Karate Kid*).
Two of the most popular teen-idol movies of the period, *Blue Lagoon*
(1980) and *Paradise* (1982), went even farther, trapping Christopher
Atkins and Willie Aames, respectively, on desert islands, with no other
boys within a thousand miles for them to have same-sex moments with.

Scott Baio

Scott Baio received some glimmers of teen-idol interest as early as
1977 when he was cast as Fonzie's young cousin, Chachi, on *Happy
Days* to give the greaser someone to act paternal with. But in 1982,
when he had grown up and bulked up noticeably, he began four years

of constant promotion as a new, macho, nonandrogynous sort of teen idol. His movies and *After School* specials[5] failed to draw in the crowds, his *Happy Days* spin-off, *Joanie Loves Chachi* (1982), died after seventeen episodes, and his two albums, *Scott Baio* (1982) and *The Boys Are Out Tonight* (1982), bombed. Yet he had the suitably macho-teen-idol affect, so teen magazines published hundreds of articles overbrimming with ecstatic praise, and had him flex for beefcake photos, shirtless, (but not lead piped), in almost every issue.

To ensure that Scott never be subject to "is he gay?" speculation, he was usually placed in roles lacking significant male friendships. He bonds with a girl (Jodie Foster) in *Foxes* and with his big brother (Vincent Bufano) in *Stoned*, and in *Senior Trip* he keeps to himself, merely observing as a classmate is nearly seduced by a gay man (a white urban fancy boy sipping on wine, naturally). Yet when he is paired with a buddy, sparks fly. *The Boy Who Drank Too Much* (1980) is nothing less than a love story about two high school hockey players, the shy, conflicted Buff (Scott) and the handsome, popular Billy (Lance Kerwin, who had just finished falling in love with David Soul in *Salem's Lot*). *Zapped!* (1982), in spite of the gleeful leers on the video box, is not at all about boys leering at girls.

No doubt *Zapped!* looked sufficiently heteronormative on paper. Scott's character, an everyboy named Barney, acquires telekinetic powers and uses them to lift up girls' skirts, thus reinforcing the notion that teenage boys are all obsessed with girls. The director, Robert J. Rosenthal, specialized in leer fests like *The Pom-Pom Girls* (1976), so there would be ample close-ups of "nekkid girls" but no "nekkid" or even shirtless boys, not even in long shots.

In *Zapped!* a magical secret always requires a confidant, so Scott was paired up with fellow ABC teen star Willie Aames (troubled Tommy Bradford on *Eight Is Enough*). The two had never worked together before, but they had an amazing chemistry, with none of the put-downs and passive-aggressive love-hate that characterizes most teen nerd-best friend pairings. When they were together in a scene, their eyes lit up, and everyone else in the room seemed to fade away; they shared a palpable joy that made their girl leering seem trivial by comparison, and their requisite heterosexual romances cold and calculated. Reagan-era audiences did not approve; looks must not *mean* anything. *Zapped!* bombed at the box office, grossing a mere $17 million while that year's *Porky's* grossed $105. So Scott Baio returned to

Happy Days and teen-dream centerfolds, and Willie Aames found work on the soap *The Edge of Night.*

In the fall of 1984, after *Happy Days* ended, CBS hired Scott for *Charles in Charge,* an attempt to draw teenagers away from ABC's *The Fall Guy* (in which Lee Majors played a guy-punching, girl-smooching stuntman). Scott played Charles, a college student working as a live-in nanny for three latchkey kids (wallflower girl, nerd boy, and brat boy), and Willie Aames played his scheming, con-artist buddy (named Buddy). To ensure that they would be accepted as heterosexual in spite of the gender-transgressive job and their own screen looks that *mean*t something, Willie was asked to ooze hetero-horniness, constantly tongue-lolling about girls, and Scott was given a steady girlfriend, Jennifer Runyon. Yet the amazing chemistry remained, even intensified with the lack of bras being zapped off, and within a few episodes Scott was treating Willie as the boyfriend and Jennifer Runyon as the gal pal.[6] Ratings floundered as audiences failed to abandon Lee Majors in favor of college boys grinning at each other, and by the end of the year Charles was sent packing.

A retooled *Charles in Charge* went into first-run syndication in January 1987, with a new, softcore porn-sounding take on the theme song ("I want . . . oooh . . . I want Charles in charge of me!") and a new group of latchkey kids (supermodel girl, wallflower girl, and brat boy). The girls, both in their teens, provided some unstated hetero-erotic tension (Scott Baio actually dated Nicole Eggert, off-camera), and the homoerotic tension was minimized by making Buddy an idiot. This time *Charles* was a hit, regularly topping the syndication charts through 1990 and ensuring Scott Baio a lot of undeniably heterosexual roles in his adult career, while Willie went on to play the costumed superhero Bible Man on evangelical Christian TV.

Ralph Macchio

Ralph Macchio lacked the Nautilus-toned physique that interested the teen magazines, and his movie career in the early 1980s *(Up the Academy, High Powder, The Outsiders)* featured significantly homo-romantic buddy bonding. But he hit the big time with a display of undeniable straightness in *The Karate Kid* (dir. John G. Avildsen, Columbia, 1984), which grossed $90.5 million and ranked number five at the box office in 1984. The first scene is a tease: New Jersey transplant Daniel (Ralph) has met the new boy-next-door, Freddy Fernandez (Israel Juarbe), who looks embarrassingly love-struck and can't seem to stop inviting Daniel to do things, first karate lessons and then a beach party. Yet just as one suspects that *The Karate Kid* will be a gay teenage romance, the rich-kid bully who runs the town (William Zabka) forces Freddy to break up with Daniel for no apparent reason, and he vanishes until the final scene, where he appears as a well wisher in the big karate tournament.

The rest of the movie effectively eliminates moments that might *mean something* by depicting every teenage boy, without exception, as cruel, vicious, violent, and seething with unexplained anti-Daniel hatred (maybe racial prejudice? Daniel is Italian American, and the other boys all blond Aryans studying a goose-stepping, neo-Nazi brand of karate). Every word the boys say, to Daniel, to one another, even to their girlfriends, is a boast, an insult, or a threat. They wear skeleton costumes to the Halloween party to demonstrate their link to the dark side, and their karate uniforms are black to contrast with Daniel's Luke Skywalker white. In contrast, every girl Daniel encounters is an angel, nurturing, supportive, tolerant, and kind. This is heteronormativity run rampant, proof in black and white that same-sex love, friendship, even polite coexistence is utterly impossible. Boys must necessarily stare at one another in contempt; they can find love, friendship, tolerance, and even the freedom to walk across the cafeteria without harassment only in the company of girls.

Sports underdogs are always tutored by loner/outsiders who lack jobs, wives, and other outside interests, so they are sexually suspect, and therefore Mr. Miyagi, the apartment complex janitor who tutors Daniel in karate, might have added a significant homoerotic subtext. The two become best friends. Miyagi gives Daniel a birthday cake and a car, and Daniel helps Miyagi into bed after a drinking binge. The video box shows them face to face, mouth to mouth, gazing at each other as if moving in for a kiss. Miyagi is elderly and Asian (Pat Morita was fifty-two years old but playing about seventy), both movie codes for "asexual." His character is placed among the ethereal, zen-koan spieling "Orientals" (Charlie Chan, Mr. Moto, the elderly caretaker of the Mogwai in *Gremlins,* perhaps Yoda in *The Empire Strikes Back*) who smile as the whitebread hero kisses a girl but never express any romantic interests of their own. Still, no one should worry that a stray look means that Mr. Miyagi wants to snatch Daniel from the playground, so he is shown drinking to the memory of his dead wife, thus "proving" that he is heterosexual.

After *The Karate Kid*, Ralph's baby face and soulful puppy-dog eyes allowed (or forced) him to play teenagers into the 1990s, well past his thirtieth birthday, but his lack of a Nautilus-toned physique meant that he had to work harder than Scott Baio or Robby Benson to eliminate moments that might *mean something*. Usually, he was thrown into worlds so heavily polarized into cruel, violent boys and kind, loving girls that same-sex intimacy seemed absurd. In *Karate Kid II* (1986), both Daniel and Mr. Miyagi fight cruel, violent boys and fall for kind, loving girls. In *Crossroads* (1986), Macchio plays the guitar instead of karate, and his mentor (Joe Seneca) is black and elderly instead of Asian and elderly, but still he encounters nothing but cruel, violent boys, and kind, loving girls. In *Distant Thunder* (1988), en route to a reunion with his white-and-elderly father John Lithgow, Macchio and a kind, loving girl (Kerrie Keane) are kidnapped by her cruel, violent boyfriend (Reb Brown). Not until *My Cousin Vinny* did Macchio bond with a peer, a fellow college student waylaid by a murder charge in Alabama, and then, not coincidentally, neither express even a moment of heterosexual interest, not an ogle at a local girl or a call to a girl back home, or even a *Playboy* tucked away in the luggage: it was 1992, a new era, with a new freedom for boys to exchange looks that might mean something.

TEEN GORE

Teenagers were murdered in Mario Bava's *Bay of Blood* (1971) and Wes Craven's *Last House on the Left* (1972), but John Carpenter's *Halloween* (1978) is the first move to contain all of the archetypal plot devices of teen gore: high schooler Laurie Strode (Jamie Lee Curtis) is stalked by a masked killer with no apparent motive (other than the shock of seeing his sister kissing a boy years ago), who dispatches her friends one by one, leaving her alone to fight back and kill him (but not really). Horror movies rarely make a lot of money, but *Halloween* grossed $47 million and ranked number six at the box office, unleashing a torrent of imitators. *Friday the 13th* (1980) upped the ante by increasing the number and attractiveness of the teenagers and by offing them with grosser special effects, and soon dozens of young starlets and boy toys were being sliced and diced in features like *Prom Night* (1980), *Funhouse* (1981), *Graduation Day* (1981), *Strange Behavior* (1981), *Frightmare* (1982), and the ever-proliferating series: seven *Halloweens* (1978-2002), eleven *Fridays the 13th* (1980-2003), seven *Nightmares on Elm Street* (1984-1994).

The audience for teen gore consisted mostly of teenagers. The adults stayed home to moan, gasp, picket, and published jeremiads about the moral bankruptcy of today's youth. Of course, they used to flock to monster movies when they were teenagers, but then it was good clean fun. Why would kids today enjoy watching people hacked to bits on camera, and by a gleefully unrepentant, wisecracking, psycho-killer, unless they were psycho-killers in training themselves? Op-ed pages attributed the skyrocketing number of real-life serial killers in the United States to teen gore brainwashing, and worried that we were raising a whole generation of Freddies and Jasons. Media scholars countered that the teenagers were harmlessly working through feelings of guilt over their premarital sexual activity by releasing Freddies and Jasons onto couples having sex, and then letting the "last girl," the one who retained her virginity, fight back.[7]

But this hypothesis is usually based solely on an analysis of *Halloween* or *Friday the 13th*. Pycho-slashers actually account for only about a third of the teen gore movies; teenagers were also being harassed and hacked to bits by space aliens, satanic cults, voodoo cults, possessed cars, possessed cousins, possessed dolls, evil hillbillies, and lumbering hairy things.[8] Sexual activity was rather limited. There were always many unpartnered and uninvolved characters, and even the teenagers interested in each other usually had to run for their lives before they had a chance to pant and fondle. In the first seven *Friday the 13th* movies, eighty-six teenagers die, but only six during or after sex. A girl dies immediately after sex in the first *A Nightmare on Elm Street* movie, but her partner survives for another couple of days, and Johnny Depp dies even though he specifically states that he has never been intimate with his girlfriend. No one has sex at all in most *Nightmare* installments, or in *Phantasm* (1979), *Prom Night, Funhouse, Graduation Day,* or *Night of the Creeps* (1986).[9] In *Strange Behavior* (1981), no one even kisses. Dan Shor's (Pete) girlfriend invites him up to her room at the sorority house and sits on the bed expectantly, but he sits on a chair, and the scene ends.

Even boy-girl romance is minimized in many teen gore movies. *Phantasm* has none; Michael Baldwin braves the sinister mausoleum to rescue not a girlfriend, but boyfriend Reggie Bannister, and when a demonic "Lady in Lavender" bares her breasts to get his attention, he whispers "Don't fear" and moves on. In the climax of *Strange Behavior,* the person strapped to the chair in the mad scientist's lab is not Daniel Shor's girlfriend, but his father. In *976-Evil* (1988), Patrick O'Bryan keeps rescuing and being rescued by tabloid journalist Jim Metzler instead of a girl, and in the denouement he persuades Stephen Geoffreys to stop being a pawn of absolute evil by evoking a buddy-bonding moment from their past.[10]

Though the psycho-killers and sundry nasties are usually coded as gay, transvestite, transsexual, pedophile, mother-obsessed or otherwise sexually "abnormal" to the gender-polarized heterosexual-macho real man,[11] they are not punishing heterosexual romance or sexual activity, but the condition of being a teenager, a powerful, disruptive, and uncivilized force. Heteronormative civilization requires all emotion and relationship to be shaped into boy-girl pairs, boyfriend/girlfriend or husband/wife. The psycho-killers have avoided or been deprived of boy-girl pairing, so they are outcasts and loners, deprived of any human relationship except that of slayer-slain. The teenagers, however, are equally unrestrained by heterosexual destiny; though they sometimes pair off for girl-boy romps, more often they travel in unwieldy groups, and searches and rescues are conducted on behalf of friends rather than romantic partners. In *A Nightmare on Elm Street,* Nancy (Heather Langenkamp) has a boyfriend snatched by the dream-psycho Freddie Krueger, but when she confronts him, she yells "I want my mother and my friends back!" not "I want my boyfriend back!" Ironically, the teens have not succumbed to heteronormativity, yet they are not loner/losers . . . and the psycho-killer is angry.

Several characteristics of the teen gore movies suggest a structural resistance to heterosexual destiny. They are as evenhanded as AIP's beach franchise in depicting both male and female bodies, and many actually emphasize the male. Nick Corre, Johnny Depp, Mark Patton, John Shepherd, and others are underwear-clad far more often, and with far more exposure, than their female counterparts. The tightly muscled Vincent Van Patton spends about a third of *Hell Night* dressed only in boxers, while his girlfriend is fully clothed or hidden under the covers of the bed.[12] Lee Montgomery bares his chest continuously for the first thirty minutes of *Night Shadows* (1983), even when it would be inappropriate in real life: in a bar, while renting a room from an old lady, at the doctor's office (where he is told "You can put your shirt back on," but doesn't); evidently director Bud Cardos thought he would sell more tickets that way. *976-Evil* offers Stephen Geoffreys shirtless, Patrick O'Bryan naked while having sex with a fully clothed girl, and a strip poker game in which four male players have stripped to their underwear while the single female player has removed nothing. David Naughton has three full-frontal nude scenes in *An American Werewolf in London*, and Jenny Agutter none, and *Strange Behavior* has no female nudity but an extended shot of Daniel Shor's nude backside. (In the DVD commentary twenty years later, Shor jokes "This is the scene that cemented my popularity in West Hollywood.")

Though no self-identified gay or lesbian person appear in any of the teen gore movies of the 1980s, the genre is surprisingly free of antigay hostility. Most movie teenagers in the 1980s ruminate endlessly on how much they hate gay people, sprinkling their dialogue with so many "fags" and "homos" that one loses count (See Chapter 10), but *An American Werewolf in London* and *976-Evil* contain only one yelp of "faggot" apiece, *Christine* a single "queer," and *Friday the 13th, Halloween, Nightmare on Elm Street, Hell Night, Prom Night, Graduation Day, Funhouse, Strange Behavior,* and *Phantasm* no antigay slurs at all.[13] A jock in *Nightmare on Elm Street 2* (1985) does denigrate the coach for frequenting "one of those queer S&M bars downtown," but when Jesse (Mark Patton) visits, it turns out to be a straight bar, with lots of leather-punk girls and guys pawing each other. In *Society* (1989), Bill (Billy Warlock) first suspects that his parents are space aliens when he overhears them planning a bisexual orgy at his sister's upcoming birthday party, but he is more horrified by the incest than by the hint of same-sex activity.

In addition to not denigrating gay people, many teen gore movies make same-sex friendships as valid as boy-girl romances, sometimes more important, often the key to survival. In *Hell Night,* Peter Barton (Jeff) and Vince Van Patton (Seth) cling to each other as assiduously as boy-girl couples in other flicks, and Peter investigates a suspicious noise twice, once with Marti (played by Linda Blair) clutching fearfully at his back, and then with Seth in exactly the same position. Moreover, when Seth escapes from the psycho-slashers in the haunted house, he hightails it back to town; when no one believes him, he steals a gun, hijacks a car, and rushes back to save not his girlfriend (already deceased) but his buddy. In *An American Werewolf in London*, the dead Jack (Griffin Dunne) keeps reappearing to David (David Naughton), explaining "I missed you." In *Night Shadows*, Wings Houser cradles dying Lee Montgomery in his arms and tells him how much he loves him. They have been heterosexualized into brothers (even though they look nothing alike), but in *Night of the Creeps* (1986), Jason Lively cradles creep-slain buddy Steve Marshall and sobs with no heteronormative recourse.

In *Fright Night* (dir. Tom Holland, Columbia, 1985), there is no significant homoerotic interaction between fresh-faced young horror-movie buff Charley (William Ragsdale) and his Peter Lorre-like friend, Evil Eddie (future gay-porn star Stephen Geoffries), unless one counts an obsession with insulting each other's penises (Charley calls Eddie "pencil dick"). Nor is the vampire Jerry (Chris Sarendon) explicitly gay: he bites lots of women, and tries to transform a very young Amanda Bearse into his lost love. But when Jerry wants to bite Eddie, he seems to intuit the boys implicit gayness and couches his invitation in undeniably homoerotic terms: "You don't have to be afraid of me. I know what it's like to be different. They won't pick on you anymore, or beat you up—I'll see to that. All you have to do is take my hand."

Sobbing, obviously thinking that he has found a boyfriend, Eddie throws himself against Jerry's chest. Instead of a kiss, he gets bitten. Later, a vampire himself, Eddie tries to bite obviously gay horror movie host played by Roddy McDowall. When he is staked instead, he transforms from vampire to an amazingly muscular nude teenager, perhaps hoping that McDowall will be sufficiently turned on to unstake him.

Christine

In *Christine* (dir. John Carpenter, Columbia, 1983), no explanation—other than love at first sight—is offered to explain why high school jock Dennis (John Stockwell) keeps ignoring the girls throwing themselves at him to spend time with supernerd Arnie (Keith Gordon, his extremely handsome features poorly hidden by horn-rimmed glasses). Yet we get a clue when Dennis announces that it's their senior year, "Time to get you laid!" Arnie protests: "You need a girl to get laid!" Dennis hesitates, a sly half smile on his face, as if he knows different. His getting-Arnie-laid plans are stymied when Arnie buys the evil car Christine and is transformed from nerd into a pale, handsome James Dean in leather jacket and tight pants. Now he has no time for his old boyfriend. "I hardly see him anymore!" Dennis complains. Finally, after blowing him off several times, Arnie agrees to a movie date. Dennis rushes to his house, only to be told that Arnie is not home. Dennis drives home disconsolate, and the car radio plays Del Shannon's "Runaway":

> As I walk along, I wonder what went wrong
> With our love, a love that was so strong.
> And as I still walk on, I think of the things we've done
> Together, while our hearts were young.

The choice of songs is no accident: Dennis is obviously heartbroken over a lost love. In the next scene, in the school library, his buddies are pushing him to approach a girl. Do they think it's time to move on, or are they being heteronormative bullies, trying to force heterosexual practice onto him? Other than this single (rejected) advance, Dennis never kisses, fondles, ogles, asks out, or otherwise expresses interest in girls. To not read Dennis as Arnie's ex-boyfriend requires ignoring so many plot elements that one suspects director John Carpenter intended it (it does not appear in the original Stephen King novel).

Next, Dennis is playing football. Arnie stands on the sidelines, waits for Dennis to stand nearby to catch the ball, and then kisses his girlfriend, Leigh (Alexandra Paul), as if trying to flaunt his new relationship. Dennis is so distracted that he allows himself to be tackled, and he is severely wounded. He spends the next forty minutes of air time in a hospital bed, while Arnie busily falls under Christine's spell, using her powers to mow down his enemies. Dennis recuperates sufficiently for their big New Year's Eve date. He wants to drink "to us," but instead Arnie insists that they drink to "Death to all the shitheads!"

Now Dennis realizes that the car has an evil influence on Arnie, so he teams up with Leigh to kill it. Heteronormative film structure indicates that every boy-girl pair will inevitably fall in love, but this one does not (they hug, in a brotherly-sisterly fashion). During the extended fight scene, Dennis and Leigh manage to kill the car, but Arnie is killed, too. "A real hero would have saved Arnie," Dennis moans, faithful to his friend—to his ex-boyfriend?—to the final fade-out.

Most teen gore movies were produced between 1978 and 1983, in the early days of the antigay backlash, when one could still be faithful to ex-boyfriends as long as no one tried to define the relationship or give it a name. Later in the 1980s, such relationships would be named and spoken, but with a fear heretofore reserved for Freddy, Jason, and other nightmares.

Chapter 10

The Brat Pack:
Teen Nerds and Operators

During the early 1980s, Hollywood put dozens of young men on display, more at the same moment than ever before in history, a core of twenty-three plus innumerable minor lights, space fillers, imitators, and wannabes. To a great extent 1980's teen culture, its movies, music, fashions, and fads, derived from this group, dubbed the Brat Pack after Frank Sinatra's hell-raising Vegas Rat Pack.[1] They were amazingly homogenous, all masculine, athletic, attractive, at least marginally talented, heterosexual (not one publicly gay, and very few the subject of gay rumors), white, or closet Hispanic, and amazingly affluent: Matt Dillon was the son of a stockbroker, Tom Cruise Mapother IV the son of an electrical engineer, and the others sons of architects, actors, filmmakers, college professors, and politicians. Only Patrick Dempsey, son of an insurance agent and a secretary, might be considered vaguely middle class. They mugged for the camera or trod the boards while still in diapers, attended fancy prep schools, and studied drama at University of Southern California or New York University. They were very lucky: their big-screen debuts came not after years of walk-on parts and yogurt commercials, but when a talent scout visited their high school, or one of Daddy's friends agreed to an audition, or when they happened to be visiting a celebrity buddy on the set and the director yelled "Get me that boy!"

Between 1983 and 1989, Brat Packers played 277 roles in 228 movies, usually set in a here-and-now suburbia where a boy could find or lose a girl amid product-placed props and a kicky soundtracks lifted directly from the Top-40 chart. Even their action-adventure movies usually involved Russian paratroopers in Colorado rather than a snake cult in India, and the science fiction was set on the local shopping promenade rather than in a galaxy far, far away. They painstakingly reproduced Reagan's privileged, glossy vision, with mansions masquerading as middle-class homes, supermodel babes and hunks with $100 haircuts masquerading as high school geeks. They had cardiologist dads, charity-volunteer moms, sport cars in every garage, Perrier in every refrigerator, Ivy League recruiters in spite of poor grades, future careers in law, medicine, or public relations. Except for a few contented servants and forays into mean streets for comic effect (as in *Risky Business* and *Adventures in Babysitting*), not a word suggested that this was not the universal American experience. But there was one very significant difference: when the Nelsons, Andersons, and Cleavers first built their nuclear family dream houses, they could safely pretend that everyone on earth was heterosexual. The Brat Packers and their audiences knew that gay people existed, not only in hair salons in San Francisco, but maybe even in our town, at our school, on our team, *among us*. And they were outraged.

Most of the Brat Packers spent their formative years at the height of the Leif Garrett era, surrounded by androgynous, jeans-bulging pop stars, and when they came to Hollywood, they rebelled with a vengeance. Some allowed *Teen Beat* a few photo shoots,[2] but most refused to be identified as teen idols at all. To demonstrate that they were real men, they rejected gold lamé, teased hair, girlish squeaks, and lead pipes. They appeared shirtless and in underwear as often as the scripts allowed, they refused projects with gay characters,[3] they ensured that every movie faded out with a boy-girl clench, and they had their real-life heterosexual exploits celebrated in every movie magazine and checkout-counter tabloid. Yet they could not produce a world strictly divided into brutish, violent boys and kind, sympathetic girls, like the teen idols did: they were a pack, a team, and they had to have friends. How could they display intimate, emotionally intense same-sex bonds and still assure each other—and the audience—that they were undeniably straight? Fade-out boy-girl clenches were insufficient, since they left many unguarded moments in many scenes that might mean something. The solution was to displace gayness onto a homoerotic *other,* a sinister, threatening figure, male but unnaturally feminine, usually an adult, an ethnic minority or white urban fancy boy alien to Reagan's America, who could be defeated, reviled, or proved mythological, thus leaving the Brat Packers free to fall in love with one another.

BUDDY DRAMAS

Brat Packers played in ninety-three dramas of all types, including crime capers, costume dramas, hostage standoffs, father-son reconciliations, even diseases-of-the-week. About a quarter (23 percent) of dramas were about finding *the one (About Last Night, Crazy Moon, Rooftops)*, but a significant 18 percent were about buddies charting the waters of adolescence or young adulthood together (even though the fade-out was still a boy-girl clench). Since buddy dramas necessarily included many moments that might mean something, the Brat Packers had to be especially vigilant about rejecting the homoerotic other, demonstrating that intimate same-sex relationships had no connection whatsoever to being gay.

In *Less Than Zero* (dir. Marek Kanievska, 20th Century Fox, 1985), a college freshman played by Andrew McCarthy returns to L.A. for Christmas to find that his lifelong best friend played by Robert Downey Jr. has been snatched from the playground to an underworld of drugs and "homosexuality" (presented as the same thing). Downey leaves a sleazy motel room, his eyes wide with horror over the things he has seen or done. Later the camera pans through a party full of decadent-looking fancy boys (all blond, like the evil California beach boys in *Karate Kid*) and then long shots of Downey going down on a trick in the bedroom. Andrew McCarthy—another blond, but straight, as attested by his many moaning sex scenes with Jami Gertz—comes rushing in like the cavalry, fights his way through the fancy boys, and drags Downey bodily out of the apartment. They drive into open country, away from Los Angeles with its decadent lifestyles, where their deep, abiding love for each other may cure Downey of his addiction to cocaine and guys. It's a little too late— Downey dies—but not before same-sex love is evoked as the remedy for gayness.

The Breakfast Club (dir. John Hughes, Universal, 1985), a movie about high schoolers from five different cliques sentenced to an all-day detention, begins with a montage of still shots to establish that we are in a wondrously "normal," archetypal Middle America (the suburban Chicago of most John Hughes films). One of the shots is a warning scrawled on Judd Nelson's (Bender) locker: "Open this locker and you die, fag!" Though the students criticize their principal for reducing them to "the simplest terms and the most convenient definition," they are amazingly eager to reduce their archenemies, gay people, to the simplest terms and most convenient definition. Nelson taunts the jock, played by Emilio Estivez (Andy), who's on the wrestling team, for "wearing tights" and "rolling around on the floor with other guys," i.e., for being gay, but then he pretends to be gay himself, batting his eyes and saying "You're pretty sexy when you're angry." Estivez deflects the implication by simply transferring it to Nelson, calling him a "faggot." He cannot devise a more complex defense because at the moment he is somewhat vulnerable: after all, he does roll around on the floor with other guys, and the misdeed that got him Saturday detention was taping up a guy's butt, a symbolic sexual assault. His undeniable straightness will not be established until he hooks up with a female detainee played by Ally Sheedy (Allison), so the movie can end with double discoveries of *the one* (Estivez-Sheedy and Nelson-Molly Ringwald (Claire)), double boy-girl kissing scenes, while the music swells.

There are five people in *The Breakfast Club* detention, so baby-faced science geek Anthony Michael Hall will not be able to demonstrate his straightness by finding *the one*. He doesn't discuss past experiences with girls (except when he invents a story about heterosexual exploits in Niagara Falls to avoid being ridiculed as a virgin), hide a *Playboy* in his backpack, or even sketch bare breasts into his science-geek notebook. Instead, he develops an intensely physical attraction to Emilio Estivez. His eyes pop out when he sees Estivez for the first time, and he spends his detention moving closer and closer to the handsome jock until they are sitting side by side and talking about their newfound friendship. When Estivez strips down to a muscle shirt, the stoned Hall makes "woo-woo" sounds of erotic interest. The lack of girl-craziness and interest in boys makes Hall's character seem rather obviously gay, giving the Brat Packers only one recourse: though he never disrobes, Hall is subject to innumerable close-ups. When the other students are shot in torso, he receives full body shots. The camera lingers on his face, chest, and shoulders, and even his crotch (once apparently aroused). No nudity is required to demonstrate that Hall is 100 percent real, and therefore undeniably straight. Judd Nelson's locker is safe, there are no "fags" in Brat Pack world, or, the teenage audience can conclude, in their own.

St. Elmo's Fire (Columbia, 1985) contains no antigay slurs or explorations of a seedy "homosexual" underworld, no doubt because it was written and directed by the openly gay Joel Schumacher. However, it still manages to reject the homoerotic other. As a group of recent Georgetown graduates settle down to their yuppie careers, they assume that the whole world is straight. "There are several quintessential moments in a man's life," law student Emilio Estivez (Kirby) tells his roommate, played by Andrew McCarthy (Kevin). The four he lists all assume that every man everywhere is heterosexual: "Losing his virginity, getting married, becoming a father, and having the right girl smile at you." Virtually every scene in the movie has a boy-girl couple falling in or out of love, except when the friends get together to discuss boy-girl couples falling in or out of love.

At first, McCarthy, playing an aspiring journalist struggling with writer's block, seems to be a holdout. He doesn't discuss how wonderful it is to be heterosexual; he even blasphemes the institution of marriage that everyone else considers the ultimate in human happiness. His male friends don't speculate that he might be gay; actually, they don't seem to notice: when Judd Nelson's character (Alec) discovers that McCarthy has been "entertaining" in his bedroom, he assumes that it is a heterosexual tryst ("Is it the fat chick?"). But his female friends notice, speculate, and define. Demi Moore's character (Jules) invites him to view her new apartment, all redone in pink, and hints "I knew you'd like it—you have such *sensitivity*." She hints again: "I want you to meet my decorator, Ron . . . he's so *fabulous*." When McCarthy doesn't take the bait, she tries to out him with another tactic: "You're the only guy at school who never made a pass at me." In 2001, Georgetown had an undergraduate male enrollment of 5,716, so even if it was half that in 1985, she would have been *very* busy, but the homoerotic other is always alone, the only gay person in his school, college, neighborhood, city, or universe. McCarthy still doesn't bite, so she gets to the point: "You've got a problem! You're gay, and in love with Alec [Estivez]!"[4]

McCarthy responds to the "accusation" with an extremely powerful metaphor, telling Moore that she has "fallen into an abyss," as if mistaking a straight guy for gay negates the fundamental principles by which the universe operates and threatens to plunge the world into chaos. Of course, that is exactly what he thinks—to be a man means to be heterosexual, then to propose the existence of gay men is like suggesting that $2 + 2 = 5$. But nevertheless, McCarthy spends most of his future scenes agonizing over the possibility. He asks a female friend played by Ally Sheedy, "Do you think my attachment to Alec [Estivez] is unnatural?" that is, threatening to plunge us all into chaos. He even asks Anna Maria Horsford, (playing a prostitute, Naomi, who plies her trade on a street corner he frequently passes and the only African American in the movie). She thinks he is gay: "I never see you with a girl, and you look real strange!" He responds "I happen to be in love with someone, only they don't know it!" McCarthy expects this statement to prove that he is straight; he is in love, and he defines gayness as an inability to fall in love. Any feeling he has for (Alec) Estivez could be nothing but an "unnatural attachment." But the prostitute knows different, and asks "Is this person a he or a she?" Only the outsider, the African-American prostitute, knows that same-sex love exists (though she considers it *real strange*).

"It's a secret," McCarthy tells her. The audience is supposed to be wondering "is he gay?" as they did with Jimmy McNichol five years before. After all, McCarthy is an outsider, the only one of the group who walks alone through deserted streets at night, and the only one on a first-name basis with prostitutes—could he be walking on the wild side as well, going to the all-blond decadent parties of *Less than Zero*? Could his proclamation that [heterosexual] love "stinks" be hiding an "unnatural attachment" rather than a broken heterosexual heart?

Yet it's all a tease, and rather more egregious than Jimmy McNichol's same-sex posturing in *Night Warning*. When Ally Sheedy visits McCarthy's apartment, evidently for the first time although they are close friends, she exclaims "I've wandered into a woman trap!" McCarthy bought a coffin under the weird misimpression that women would find it sexy, and keeps a wallful of fake awards to impress women with. But instead of revealing these details in the first scene, director Schumacher holds off for an hour and ten minutes, leaving the question open until McCarthy reveals that the person he's in love with is a *she*, Ally Sheedy herself, forbidden only because she's dating Judd Nelson! A night of giggly, sweaty, apartment-demolishing sex follows, with McCarthy delivering the only seminude shots of the movie to emphasize that he is 100 percent real, with no *unnatural* attachments. In the morning his writer's block has vanished, and his newspaper loves his new article on "The Meaning of Life" (not surprisingly, the meaning is: heterosexual romance). The homoerotic other is evoked only to be dismissed as a mere misunderstanding;

though Ron the fabulous decorator might be gay, but none of *us*, none of the Brat Packers, none of the teenagers in the audience.

However, Sheedy wanted sex, not a relationship. A few days later she dumps McCarthy in the midst of his giggly speech about finding the meaning of life in her eyes. Meanwhile Judd Nelson, incensed that McCarthy has slept with his girl, dumps him as well, off a fire escape to his death (almost). Hetero-passion almost destroys two of McCarthy's most significant friendships. Fortunately, they all manage to reconcile—the movie ends with a group hug and plans to meet for brunch next Sunday. It seems that friends, not *the one,* provides the escape from the iron cage of Reaganomics, as long as all of the friends are undeniably straight.

TEEN NERDS

Thirty-two percent of the ninety-three Brat Packer comedies star a teen *nerd,* a handsome, intelligent, likeable, and wealthy high school or college boy who is nonetheless ostracized by the other students, except for a flamboyantly feminine and equally ostracized best friend. He is desperately in love with a cheerleader-type girl who invariably first appears with her hair blowing in slow motion in the wind (hence she will be called h.b.i.s.m. girl), but she ignores him to hang on the arm of a jock so boorish, violent, possessive, and thoroughly disagreeable that one can't imagine anyone wanting to spend more than thirty seconds with him. After many humorous plot complications, the teen nerd gains the respect of the jock and his disagreeable cronies, whereupon the h.b.i.s.m. girl melts into his arms, or else he settles for the attractive, intelligent, likeable, wealthy, girl next door who supported him all along. Sometimes, an especially clever script made a few minor changes: in *Real Genius* (1985), the jock was replaced by an obnoxious college professor, and the h.b.i.s.m. girl by a supermodel with a genius fetish; in *Weird Science* (1985), the jock was replaced by an obnoxious big brother, and the h.b.i.s.m. girl by a cyber-supermodel; in *Lucas* (1986), the jock was not obnoxious and even befriended the teen nerd. The major players—teen nerd, buddy, jock, h.b.i.s.m. girl, and girl next door—were always identifiable, reenacting a 1980's morality play about evoking and dismissing the homoerotic other.

The reason for the teen nerd's ostracization is never explained in the script, but always extremely clear: he is the homoerotic other. The jocks constantly "accuse" him and his best buddy of being gay, and in spite of his incessant longing for the h.b.i.s.m. girl, he is haunted by the suspicion that his intelligence, lack of athletic prowess, or some other despicable trait does indeed signify gayness. In *Teen Wolf* (dir. Rod Daniel, Atlantic, 1985), Michael J. Fox tries to tell his flamboyantly feminine best buddy, played by Jerry Levine, that he intermittently "werewolfs out." As he stumbles and hesitates about his "problem," Levine stops him cold: "Are you gonna tell me you're a fag? Because if you're gonna tell me you're a fag, I don't think I can handle it."[5] Fox quickly dissuades his fear: "I'm not a fag, I'm a werewolf!" and Levine handles this much less horrifying revelation with panache. In *Lucas* (dir. David Seltzer, 20th Century Fox, 1986), locker room jocks assume that Corey Haim is gay because he has a small penis, so he turns the accusation around, making *small* a signifier of straightness, like the teen idols who remove the lead pipe from their pants: "I don't get semi-erect around other males like some of you fellows do. . . . You can tell the *fags* in a warm shower by who has the longest dong."

In *Three O'Clock High* (dir. Phil Joanou, Universal, 1987), somewhat long-in-the-tooth teen nerd Casey Siemaszko (Jerry) is assigned to interview transfer student Richard Tyson (Buddy) for the school newspaper. He says "hello" while they're both standing at the urinals in the restroom, and Tyson, though a hulking, leather-jacket-clad bruiser, shrinks back in horror: "You're a fag!" Though Siemaszko immediately protests that he is straight, Tyson is not convinced, and schedules him for an after-school gay-bashing. Siemaszko tries to avoid the assault by hiring regular school bully Scott Tiler (Bruce) as his bodyguard (it worked for Chris Makepeace in 1980), but Tiler misunderstands the proposition, growling "If you're a fag. . . ."

Heterosexual desire alone, however ardent, cannot redeem the teen nerd. In *Sixteen Candles* (1984), Anthony Michael Hall asks h.b.i.s.m. girl Molly Ringwald for a date, but she refuses because "You're totally a fag." (It never occurs to her that a gay man would not want a date.) Nor will heterosexual practice: in *Lucas*, Corey Haim dates his h.b.i.s.m. girl in full view of the jocks but is derided as the homoerotic other anyway. In *Three O'Clock High*, Siemaszko smooches with the h.b.i.s.m girl, plus the Goth girl next door who had a crush on him all along, and even the big-breasted English teacher who orgasmed over his class speech, and yet he is still scheduled for a gay-bashing after school. Redemption must come through a spectacle of death and resurrection. The short, scrawny Corey Haim nearly kills himself on the football team; Casey Siemaszko shows up for the fistfight with the towering bully while the whole school watches. The homoerotic other must die so a new, undeniably straight teenager can be born.

Since the teen nerd is constantly accused of being gay, he must constantly police his relationship with his best buddy, always a "weirdo" with feminine costume, hairstyle, and leisure interests, often with no interest in girls, or else with minor instances of girl-ogling subsidiary to his intense, inexplicable loyalty to the nerd. In *Weird Science* (dir. John Hughes, Universal, 1985), policing comes during the denouement: the crisis over, Anthony Michael Hall (Gary) walks off into the sunset with his arm around buddy, played by Ilan-Mitchell Smith (Wyatt), reflecting the standard boy-girl clench, he jokes: "I wouldn't want to date you . . . you're not my type."[6]

In *Better Off Dead* (dir. Savage Steve Holland, Warner Brothers, 1985), nerd John Cusack (Lane) and best buddy Curtis Armstrong (Charles)[7] are sitting together at the big dance, when a jock named Stalin jokingly says "You've got my vote for the cutest couple!" Armstrong starts laughing hysterically; in the next scene, later that night, he is still laughing. Then he vanishes from the movie for thirty-six minutes of screen time, (the entire nerd-h.b.i.s.m. girl courtship), reappearing only during the climactic skiing contest.[8] Clearly, the jock has hit a sensitive nerve, bringing their homoromance painfully close to the surface.

Revenge of the Nerds (dir. Jeff Kanew, 20th Century Fox, 1984) is perhaps the only teen nerd movie to include a gay teenager among "us" (though no one ever says the word). The nerds who band together to form their own fraternity, Tri-Lambda,[9] have various "flaws" that might get them accused of gayness: intelligence, a deficient fashion sense (they wear pocket protectors, horn-rimmed glasses, plaid shirts, high-water pants and white socks), a deficient knowledge of pop music, prepubescence, a braying laugh, Asian ethnicity. Yet no one notices because Lamar, played by Larry B. Scott, really is gay (and black). Though the other nerds accept him, and he is instrumental in their triumph over the boorish-jock fraternity (he wins an athletic competition with a javelin specially designed for his limp wrist), they still frequently demonstrate disgust or discomfort at a gay person in their midst. When they are trying to affiliate with a national fraternity, they tell the director that "our chapter will be open to all races and creeds." Lamar swishes in "And sexual orientations!" His fratmates glare at him in disgust. Though they obviously know that Scott is gay, and their fraternity really will be open to people of all sexual orientations, they still must register their disapproval. At the big party, none of the nerds have dates except Scott; "But it's with a *guy*!" Curtis Armstrong complains. Obviously he knows that a gay man would date a guy, but still he must register his disgust.

By becoming the homoerotic other, Lamar is isolating and restricting same-sex desire. Since he is the only gay person in the world (except for his date at the dance), all of the dozens of "deficiencies" that nerds and jocks have identified as signifiers of gayness really mean nothing; jock accusations have no affect. The Tri Lams can relax with the knowledge that even with intelligence, interest in classical music, musical ability, poor fashion sense, braying laughs, and prepubescence, they are all undeniably straight. In fact, they are more proficient at heterosexual practice than the jocks: when asked why he is so good in bed, Robert Carradine's character observes "Jocks think only about sports. Nerds think only about sex."

One Crazy Summer (dir. Savage Steve Holland, Warner Brothers, 1986) contains a rare example of a homoerotic other portrayed positively. On vacation in Nantucket, John Cusack's character, Hoops, is torn between girl-next-door whose grandfather's house is set to be demolished by an evil contractor, and h.b.i.s.m. girl, who is dating the evil contractor's evil son. He befriends Curtis Armstrong, playing Ack Ack, a sensitive, poetic, nonviolent (i.e., gay) boy who can't abide the militaristic career his ex-Marine father has planned out for him, and twin brothers who look nothing alike played by Bobcat Goldthwait (as Egg) and Tom Villard. None of them display any heterosexual interest. When a gaggle of bikini babes asks Cusack and his buddies for help moving their boat, a very difficult job with no reward but the opportunity to ogle, only Cusack double-takes and gulps a feverishly horney assent. His buddies gripe and complain, and refuse a boat ride in payment. However, they are quite open about expressing same-sex interest. When Armstrong's father kicks him out of the house for being too sissified, Goldthwait (for some reason not gay actor Tom Villard) wraps an arm around him and says "I understand,"

and Armstrong lays his head on his shoulder. One expects them to kiss in a moment.

Patrick Dempsey

After a few bit parts, twenty-one-year-old Patrick Dempsey landed a starring role in the bedding-the-babysitter movie *Meatballs III* (1987). As a summer camp nerd upset because he is "still a virgin" at age fourteen, Sally Kellerman, as the ghost of a porn star, helps him score with the boss's wife. Next, Dempsey Stars in *Can't Buy Me Love* (1987), a movie about a high school nerd who pays the h.b.i.s.m. girl to pose as his girlfriend for a month and ends up the object of her affection. It grossed an amazing $31 million at the box office. Dempsey had found his angle: henceforth he would play teen nerds who need not wrest the h.b.i.s.m. girl from her jock boyfriend, who is instead supremely attractive to her, to all teenage girls, in fact to all women (but never to boys or men). Trying to appear sufficiently nerdish for the angle to work, the nationally ranked athlete wore especially geeky costumes and weirdified his hair, so that when his clothes came off, his physique would be a surprise.

Dempsey's characters were usually virgins, approaching a heterosexual encounter as a tabula rasa, yet amazingly proficient, with a talent for heterosexual practice that rivaled any well-seasoned adult lothario. This juxtaposition of innocence and experience, enthusiasm and expertise, is not uncommon in teen nerd movies. In *Gotcha!* (1985), for instance, Anthony Edwards' character is on vacation in Paris and loses his virginity in a midafternoon quickie with a stranger (who of course becomes *the one*), afterward he worries that he was inept, but she purrs that he was "great." But Dempsey presents it as the ordinary teenage condition. Just as the teen idol pitch of the 1950s made heterosexual romance unique to teenagers, lost or abandoned by the adults, now all teenage boys possess a natural expertise at positions and procedures that the adults have long forgotten how to perform.

In the Mood (dir. Phil Alden Robinson, Lorimar, 1987) is the "famous" true story of Sonny Wisecarver, a fifteen-year-old who married an older woman in 1944. He and his wife were arrested and sent to jail. The marriage was annulled. A few months after Wisecarver was released he ran off with an older, married woman, and again arrested. As

Wisecarver, Dempsey's physicality is constantly on display; his enthusiasm, expertise, and even his measurements constantly under discussion. Nurses at the hospital keep giving him "sponge jobs"; at his trial, his mother notes that "he is a little big for his age," compelling the judge to send the bailiff out with a ruler to check; in bed, one of his women friends dreamily notes that he is "disguised as Clark Kent," that is, Superman. Though Dempsey is supremely attractive to all girls and women without exception, no teenage boys exist, and the adult men in his life are all much nastier than the brats in *Karate Kid:* his uncaring father ("Life's a bitch, and then you die"), his first wife's abusive ex-boyfriend, and Uncle Clete, whose job involves slaughtering bunnies (perhaps if any nice guys existed, they, too, would find Wisecarver supremely attractive). One would expect that the profundity of Dempsey's heterosexual interest and the lack of potential objects of homo-romantic affection would exclude him from the need to demonstrate his undeniable straightness, but he covers all the bases and rejects a homoerotic other anyway. Arrested for marrying too young and thrown in prison, he yells "I want my wife!" Another prisoner simpers "I'll be your wife!" The narrating Dempsey sums up: "Jail is bad."

In the Mood grossed less than $1 million, but Dempsey was back the next year as a teen nerd supremely desirable to women in *Some Girls* (dir. Michael Hoffman, MGM, 1988). Playing a college student, Dempsey opens the movie facing the camera with the confessional "I like girls!" as if this were an unusual trait, before narrating the tale of his Christmas in a brooding mansion near Quebec City, where his girlfriend, her two sisters, and her grandmother (thinking that he is her dead husband) all try to seduce him. Only the girlfriend succeeds, though he gets a kiss from the grandmother, when she reappears after her death as a glamorous ghost from the flapper era. Meanwhile, as it was in *In the Mood,* Dempsey's physicality is constantly on display and under discussion. He appears in boxer shorts and with frontal and rear nudity, to demonstrate that he is 100 percent real, to demonstrate that all teenagers are Superman inside. This time the men in his world are not irredeemably nasty, just eccentric, and there is no rejection of the homoerotic other, perhaps because *Some Girls* was not intended for a primarily teenage market.

Dempsey took a break to fall in love with Michael Biehn in the independent film *In a Shallow Grave* (1988), one of the few gay roles of any Brat Packer. Then he raced back to his angle in *Loverboy* (dir. Joan Micklin Silver, Tri-Star, 1989), about a pizza delivery boy who offers special services to the suburban housewives who order "extra anchovies": dancing, talking, being attentive and romantic, and sometimes sex. Again, he is supremely attractive to every woman he meets, but under constant threat of extortion, manipulation, or abuse from the men, mostly jealous bodybuilder husbands, but also his sarcastic boss and uncaring father. There is a rejection of the homoerotic other, when Dempsey's parents worry that his constant late-night fraternizing means that he is gay.

The supremely attractive to women angle only seemed funny or interesting when Dempsey was able to play teen nerds, scrawny, quirky, and virginal. Yet he was getting too old, too married, and the physique under the geeky costumes was becoming too familiar to produce any surprises. So in *Happy Together* (1990) and *Run* (1991), his teenage characters fall in love with just one girl, and afterward Dempsey moved on to adult roles as mobsters, the young John F. Kennedy, and the biblical prophet Jeremiah.

TEEN OPERATORS

Like the teen nerd, the teen operator must wrest the h.b.i.s.m. girl from the arms of her jock boyfriend, but he is not unattractive or socially inept; he lacks only athletic prowess, so he uses his Reagan-era entrepreneurial skills to wow the girl or to buy out the competition. He still, however, must demonstrate his undeniable straightness by evoking and rejecting a homoerotic other. *Risky Business* (dir. Paul Brickman, Warner Brothers, 1983) probably invented the genre; since the twenty-one-year-old Tom Cruise was being acclaimed as one of the most beautiful men in the world, he could hardly play a teen nerd effectively. So he plays Joel Goodson, a wealthy, white, heterosexual high school senior from a ritzy Chicago suburb whose "normal teenage" urges are stymied only by the belief that girls will ruin his chances for economic prosperity. In the opening sequence, Tom recounts a dream laden heavy with symbolism: he encounters "this girl, this incredible girl" in the shower, but en route to coitus he loses her in the steam, and the scene switches to a classroom, where he has missed his college boards. "I've just made a terrible mistake!" he moans. "I'll never get into college. My life is ruined."

In waking life, Tom tries to keep busy with his Future Enterpriser projects, but it's hard to ignore his "normal teenage urges" among his sex-obsessed buddies, the soulful, androgynous Bronson Pinchot, (Barry), and the sleazy, fast-talking Curtis Armstrong (Miles). To make matters worse, when his parents go out of town for the weekend, his buddies talk him into letting them use the upstairs bedrooms for their own dalliances, resulting in hours of ecstatic groans while he is trying to study. Tom knows that he is attractive: he stands in tight jeans with his hands outlining an unrepentant bulge, or in one of the most famous scenes in movie history, slides across the floor in his underwear and then grinds his crotch into the couch while his buns wiggle in the air. But he still can't risk a date, at least not with a girl his own age who might jeopardize his chances of getting into Princeton. So Anderson, in jest, calls a downtown Chicago escort service.

Before he can acquiesce to his heterosexual destiny, Tom must define and eliminate the homoerotic other. The first "escort" to arrive at his house is a middle-aged black transvestite (Jackie) played by Bruce A. Young. It is important that Anderson made the call: although he did not specifically intend to arrange for a transvestite, he allows his buddy to reject the possibility of same-sex desire as monstrous, "unnatural," as nonwhite, and as belonging to the city, not the suburbs. Thus he simultaneously rejects any possibility of same-sex desire in their own friendships (even the androgynous Bronson Pinchot turns out to like girls—a lot). At first Tom refuses to open the door, but when the transvestite reduces the matter to economics ("You should get what you pay for"), he relents and lets her come in long enough to call a cab. Upon leaving, she gives him another phone number: "It's what you want. It's what every white boy off the Lake wants." That is, boys who are nonwhite and on the Lake (that is, urban) may be gay, but white suburban Brat Packers are always straight.

Homoerotic potential expelled, Tom goes up to his room and prepares to masturbate. Again we see him as an object of desire, nude in his bed, his muscular torso illuminated in ruddy light, his hand under the covers just beginning to jerk. But on a whim he gets up again and calls the number. Rebecca DeMornay plays a young, white, female prostitute (Lana) who appears magically in a rushing wind, a h.b.i.s.m. girl with no jock. The camera zooms in on a picture of Tom as a little boy, and then fades out to a scene of his entry into adulthood through heterosexual orgasm. As DeMornay throws back her head in ecstasy,

Tom appears to be trying a rear entry, reflecting the earlier scenes in which he has offered his buttocks to the camera, and to the audience. The music swells. The wind rushes faster.

The problems start in the morning when Tom is astonished to discover that call girls get *paid* for their efforts: evidently he has never really considered the conjunction of sex and money before. A lightbulb flashes over his head, and he spends the day strategizing how to combine his entrepreneurial skill with "natural teenage" horniness. DeMornay invites her prostitute friends (all of the supermodel variety) to the house, and Tom talks all of his straight male friends into buying sex with them. His sales pitch sometimes involves pure economics: if attaining manhood requires nothing more than a heterosexual orgasm, why bother dating a girl for weeks or months, only to find that she won't "go all the way," when a prostitute's services are quick, easy, and guaranteed? At other times, he implies that boys who do not buy the service might be gay: "All I'm saying is, walk like a man!" Either way, the house fills up with eager clients, and a visiting representative from Princeton is so impressed that he offers Tom admission.[10] Homerotic demons expelled, heterosexual horniness has not ruined Tom's economic aspirations at all. Quite the contrary, it has made him rich.

Campus Man (dir. Ron Casden, Paramount/RKO, 1987) similarly rejects the homoerotic other while exuberantly combining capitalism and sex. Needing tuition money, Arizona State business student John Dye (Todd) gets the idea of producing a calendar with pictures of men, notably swimming-team hunk Brett (Steve Lyon). In discussing the potential market with the Dean, he mentions female students, widows, housewives, high school girls, and then, as if to test the reaction, "men." As the Dean stares in horror, Dye haltingly backtracks: "men, who . . . ah . . . may be students of physical culture." Obviously they both know what he is really talking about, but he has broken the cardinal rule of the Brat Packers: *none of us* can possibly be gay.

He needn't worry: though droves of students line up to buy the calendar, they are all exclusively women. Nevertheless, Dye must constantly defend himself from the allegations that he is gay or marketing his calendar to gay men; since no one can ever say the word gay, the allegations occur mostly in the form of horrified looks or euphemisms. He first gets the idea for the calendar while visiting h.b.i.s.m. girl, played by Kim Delaney (as Dayna). Seeing a beefcake photo of

Brett on her dorm room wall, he has an epiphany: "Brett's looks . . . girls *like* him for this!" and runs off. Delaney's roommate wants to know what happened.

DAYNA: I don't know. He saw a picture of Brett and went berserk.

ROOMMATE: Typical! A little stress, they break down, and the [in a disgusted voice] *latent tendencies* finally come out.

She can't say "gay," so she must denigrate Dye with "tendencies." Similarly, when rednecks confiscate one of his calendar samples and ask "what are you, some kinda funny boy?" Dye defends himself by pointing out that the athletes on the calendar are all "he-men." That is, he can't be gay, because none of the pictures swish.

Although the possibility that anyone in the world might be gay is rejected assiduously and continuously, the movie seems to invite the gay male gaze. There are no cheesecake shots of girls, but dozens of half-naked boys, including close-ups of butts and crotches. No heterosexual sex occurs, except for a single kiss. Though he ends up falling in love with Delaney, Steve Lyon is extremely physical in his interactions with Dye, always hugging him, touching him, sitting on the bed next to him; and he is so devoted to his friend that he endures the controversy and gets kicked off the diving team. Dye, for all of his ogling girls, pasting pictures of girls on his dorm room wall, and flirting with Delaney, never falls in love, kisses, or dates a girl. The movie ends as he moves on from calendars to promoting loan shark Cactus Jack (Miles O'Keefe) as a male model, "the surprise look of the 80's." Though "not gay," he has become an expert on the male physique, and exploits it as expertly as Tom Cruise exploited high school horniness in *Risky Business.*

The apotheosis of the "not gay" teen operator is probably Andrew McCarthy (Larry) in *Weekend at Bernie's* (dir. Ted Kotcheff, 20th Century Fox, 1989). McCarthy plays a young accountant who goes unabashedly wild over his handsome co-worker, played by Jonathan Silverman (Richard), grinning at him, putting his hand on his back or shoulder, inviting him to "the beach" (a rooftop kiddie pool), and pressing against him on a love seat in a otherwise empty living room. The opening sequence has the duo walking together through a bright, shiny Manhattan like a couple in love. He demonstrates that he is heterosexual by screaming "Ohhh!!!!! Would you look at that!!!!!"

every time he glimpses at a woman, yet he never actually flirts with, kisses, or dates any of them (in one scene, Silverman knocks on his bedroom door and he opens it nude, implying that he is in the middle of a heterosexual liaison, but no other person is shown, and he could easily be pretending). Meanwhile Silverman demonstrates that he is heterosexual by unbuttoning his shirt to show off his chest, wearing a wedding ring (though he is single), and grinning at co-worker Catherine Mary Stewart (Gwen). McCarthy accepts the competition good-naturedly, and even offers Silverman the use of his apartment for the end-of-date smooching.

When the "couple" is invited to boss Bernie's house in the Hamptons for the weekend (hence the title), the "not gay" innuendos become more pronounced. One of Bernie's friends is a fey, elderly book reviewer, who demonstrates that he is not gay by rejecting a gay-themed book (about whether Sherlock Holmes and Dr. Watson were secretly married). He swishes up to Silverman, places a hand on his shoulder, and leers "Like a drink?" Silverman freezes in deer-caught-in-the-headlights horror, but McCarthy, not at all uncomfortable, butts in: "I'd love some champaign, thanks!" McCarthy is trying to defuse the situation by pretending it was not a same-sex flirtation, just friendliness, but his nonchalance suggests that he is not entirely unfamiliar with being "cruised." The next scene shows McCarthy opening the door nude, sleeping with a girl (or pretending to); perhaps he is moving on (or pretending to) after Silverman has demonstrated that he would object violently to any attempt to redefine their relationship as openly romantic.

Eventually the boys figure out that Bernie stole money from the company and planned to pin the crime on them, then kill them and make it look like a murder-suicide. They find the note he intended to use as proof: "Richard Parker [Jonathan Silverman] and I stole this money from the company to pay for my sex-change operation. Now he tells me he loves someone else. I can't live with that, and neither will he."

"It's not bad enough that he's trying to kill me!" McCarthy moans. "Now he's trying to turn me into a drag queen! Why couldn't he have said that *you* were going to have the operation?" He dislikes the part about being a drag queen (e.g., transsexual) but doesn't mind being posthumously identified as Silverman's lover because they are lovers of a sort, involved in an exuberant but unstated romance that is now doomed exactly because, as the note states, "he loves someone else." At the end of the movie, after the murder attempt and corpse plotlines have been settled, Stewart invites Silverman, now her boyfriend, back to her apartment to rest up. She invites McCarthy, too, and he is about to accept, but Silverman behind her back mouths an absolute "No!" Rejected again, he "decides" to spend the rest of the weekend at Bernie's, where, he claims, he might encounter some girls.

Michael J. Fox

On television, Brat Packer series about groups of angst-ridden buddies, exuberant romances, or teen nerds either didn't get made or dive-bombed after a few episodes. The "teen operator" character became a sitcom staple of the 1980s, usually as the eldest son in a nuclear or single-parent family: Ricky Schroeder on *Silver Spoons* (1982-1987), Malcolm Jamal-Warner on *The Cosby Show* (1984-1992), Jason Bateman on *It's Your Move* (1984-1985) and *The Hogan Family* (1986-1991), Rob Stone on *Mr. Belvedere* (1985-1990), Kirk Cameron on *Growing Pains* (1985-1992). Not coincidentally, most of them vanished in the early 1990s, when Brat Packers graduated into adulthood and most of the upcoming teen hunks were being grabbed up by specialized teencoms and teensoaps.

Among the first and most successful of the sitcom operators was Michael J. Fox, who played Alex P. Keaton, three-piece-suited son of ex-hippies Meredith Baxter Birney and Michael Gross, on *Family Ties* (1982-1989). Alex was a mugging, disingenuous sort, thoroughly likeable in spite of his yuppie money-grubbing, which paled in comparison to his girl-craziness. From the first lines of the September 1982 pilot episode, he grappled with the central paradox of the operator, a tension between economics and "natural urges." A boy who is obsessed with financial gain can't be dreaming of girls every second, but in those seconds not spent dreaming of girls, how does he demonstrate to himself and to his peers that he is undeniably straight?

The g-word is never spoken in any *Family Ties* episode, since no gay people exist—if any did exist, Alex's ultra-liberal parents would certainly mention gay rights somewhere in their litany of ultra-liberal causes—and though Alex is slim, fastidious, fashion conscious, intelligent, and nonathletic, no obnoxious jock ever accuses him of being gay. However, sometimes he deliberately attempts to play the old "is he gay?" game of the teen idols. In "Ladies' Man" (February 1984, dir. Will Mackenzie), he tries to impress feminist Deena (Tracy Nelson) by putting on an apron and making tea. When Dad expresses his anxiety over this gender transgression by passive-aggressively commenting "nice apron!" Alex responds: "I hope you don't mind that I borrowed yours. . . . Mine's in the wash. I got quiche on it." He refers to the popular contemporary maxim "Real men (i.e., heterosexuals) don't eat quiche."

In the third-season episode "Little Man on Campus" (October 1984, dir. John Pasquin), Alex receives his first low grade, and he suspects that he may be an average student rather than brilliant. He asks his sister Mallory (Justine Bateman) why she fails so many tests.

MALLORY: When I take a test . . . my mind starts wandering.

ALEX: What do you think about?

MALLORY: Boys.

ALEX: [Waits for the howls of laughter to subside] Let's hope it's different with me.

Pretending to be gay as a joke or to acquire girls can only work if the boy does not display any significant same-sex bonds. Therefore, Alex rejects the friendships of the Brat Packers, not even acquiring a sitcom sidekick like Theo Huxtable's Cockroach, Mike Seaver's Boner, or Ricky Stratton's Alfonso. Wacky next-door-neighbor Skippy (Marc Price) appears in about a third of the *Family Ties* episodes, but the potential of a homoromantic relationship with Alex is strategically defused by giving Skippy a crush on Mallory, and therefore a heteronormative motive for hanging around. They become friends anyway, but Alex carefully polices their interactions to ensure that they do not become too intimate, even rejecting the standard sitcom stage business of sitting pressed together on a couch (so they can both be in a close-up). In one episode, the two somehow fall onto the bed together; Skippy nonchalantly continues their conversation, but Alex recoils in horror and jumps away. Since no gay people exist in Alex's world, this rejection has an even greater emotional impact than the anti-fag dialogues of the Brat Packer films, summarily marking even nonsexual friendships as bad, wrong, and disquieting.

A few episodes suggest but immediately reject the possibility of romantic love between Alex and a male friend. In "Best Man"

(November 1984, dir. John Pasquin), Alex's friend Doug (Timothy Busfield), who has appeared in only one previous episode but seems to be his best friend, is engaged. Though he treats Alex and his fiancee as emotional equivalents, hugging them simultaneously and squealing "You're both so cute!" Alex feels threatened by Doug's new relationship and refuses to be his best man. When he understands that he will still be an essential part of Doug's life, he hugs Doug so tightly at the altar that the minister asks, in "jest," which couple is going to be married. But Timothy Busfield would appear on the series only once more, and not as Doug; the relationship could be evoked but not sustained.

In an Emmy-winning two-part episode, "A, My Name is Alex" (March 1987, dir. Will Mackenzie), Alex's friend Greg (Brian McNamara), another best buddy introduced for only a single episode, dies tragically in an auto accident, and Alex is so distraught that he seeks psychiatric help. It turns out that he is not distraught because he loved Greg; he feels guilty because he refused to accompany Greg on the errand that killed him, and he is dealing with his own mortality.

During *Family Ties*, Fox starred in two TV movies. *High School U.S.A.* (dir. Rod Amateau, Hill-Mandelker Films, 1983), filmed before his Alex P. Keaton character had stabilized and before the Brat Packers took control of teen culture, does not reject the homoerotic other. Fox plays a sixteen-year-old slacker and con artist from a single-parent household. Tony Dow, Wally on *Leave It to Beaver* in the late 1950s, plays the principal. He has taken on a parental role.

PRINCIPAL: Down deep in the far, far recesses of your innermost self, I think there may be some potential. But we're never going to find it unless you start caring about something.

JAY-JAY: [Pretending to be offended] Hey, I happen to care very deeply about who becomes [*Playboy*] Playmate of the Year.

The "something" Fox comes to care about is wresting h.b.i.s.m. girl Nancy McKeon (Beth) from the arms of her obnoxious jock boyfriend, Anthony Edwards (Beau). Leader of the wealthy "Prep" clique. Edwards gets his comeuppance and loses his girl during a climactic auto race between his roadster and Michael's clunker (refurbished by a gang of his friends). This is the only movie in all of Fox's opus that gives him a best friend, an African-American genius named

Otto (Todd Bridges, at the time playing straight man to Gary Coleman on *Diff'rent Strokes*). All of the intimacy that Fox fails to express as Alex P. Keaton comes out here: the two are constantly touching arms and shoulders, grabbing wrists, virtually hanging on each other, and they are constantly asking each other out on dates. Otto fails to express any heterosexual interest of his own, but he practically pushes Michael into Nancy McKeon's arms, and then grins appreciatively as they kiss. No doubt the fact being nonwhite excuses Otto from heterosexual practice, and gives them a freedom of intimacy that would be impossible if Fox's best friend were a fellow "white boy off the Lake."

Fox played a teen nerd in his second TV movie, *Poison Ivy* (1985), but his greatest success came as a teen operator in the theatrical release *Back to the Future* (dir. Robert Zemeckis, Universal, 1985), the top-grossing movie of the year. He plays seventeen-year-old small-town boy Marty McFly as a veritable gay icon, with feathered hair and extremely tight jeans, so it is even more important that he reject the homoerotic and demonstrate his undeniable straightness. He has already won his h.b.i.s.m girl, with supermodel Claudia Wells (Jennifer) gazing, oozing, and writing "I love you" in a display of passion as unwarranted by the plot as Annette's plea that she was in love with Tommy Kirk twenty years before. Instead of the flamboyant best buddy traditional to teen nerd comedies, Fox hangs out with the white-haired, goggle-eyed Doc Brown (Christopher Lloyd), and though the martinet school administrator warns against the relationship, making him elderly and eccentric ensures that it is not read as a homoromantic bond (plus, a deleted scene has the Doc reading *Playboy*).

Fox travels back in time thirty years to 1955 and accidentally sabotages his parents' first meeting, obliterating their future marriage and his own existence. To save his life, he must become the best buddy in a teen nerd movie, assisting shy, bullied teenage Dad (Crispin Glover) to win wild-child h.b.i.s.m. Mom (Lea Thompson). But his manipulations lead him to constant suspicion of being *that way*. Teenage Dad is merely made confused and uncomfortable with this new boy's interest, and cries "Why do you keep following me around?" but when teenage Mom flirts with him, Fox jumps away in a panic. The viewer realizes that he is upset because Thompson is his mother, but *she* doesn't know this. The most accessible explanation she has is the old stereotype of gay men being afraid of women. Mom still finds him "a dreamboat," but after forcing a kiss onto him, she reflects "This is all wrong . . . kissing you is like kissing my brother." Of course, she is actually his *mother,* but she is again reflecting the stereotype of gay men as nonsexual beings. Fortunately, like many gay-coded schoolboys before him, he facilitates the romance necessary to ensure his own future existence; then he goes home to kiss his own h.b.i.s.m. girl, ensuring that in spite of everything, no one thinks of him or any teenager, ever, as being *that way.*[11] Teenagers must always be undeniably straight.

Chapter 11

Teencoms and Teensoaps

During the 1990s, liberal Baptist President Clinton let on that he knew that gay people existed, though he admonished them to pretend they were straight in mixed company, and gay men, lesbians, bisexuals, transvestites, transsexuals, or otherwise nonstraight sorts of people began to appear with some frequency in the mass media: RuPaul, Ellen, David Sedaris, k.d. lang, R.E.M., "Not that there's anything wrong with that," Waylon Smithers, *Veronica's Closet, Queer As Folk, The Bird Cage, In and Out, Something About Mary.* But the years after 2000 looked more like 1955, with a retro White House, bombs scrawled with *faggot* being dropped on Afghanistan, gay people being blamed for the 9/11 terrorist attacks, the word "gay" itself becoming all-purpose slang for anything bad, and "don't exist" preferred to "don't ask, don't tell."[1]

In general, depending on the state of the economy, the state of the Middle East, and the blockbuster of the moment, the mass media of the 1990s liked transvestites, lesbians, and gay men to an extent. They were portrayed as wise but asexual gal pals or humorous eccentrics; as long as there was no kissing, the lesbians fell in love with men by the third reel, and the gay men acknowledged that they were really women.[2] Occasionally, gay people were even allowed full humanity, in stories that the heterosexuals gave the highest praise they could think of: "This isn't a gay story." But more often the rule was, it's okay to be gay as long as you help us pretend that gay people do not exist. Ellen DeGeneres made headlines for coming out on prime time in 1997, but then she became a talk show queen by unapologetically never, ever mentioning it. *A Beautiful Mind* (2001) won four Oscars by closeting its subject. *Queer Eye for the Straight Guy* dispatched a van full of stereotypes to teach straight guys how to be fabulous, but when a young fan asked head queer Carson Kressley if he

doi:10.1300/5484_11

were really gay or just pretending, he refused to answer. Of course, Kressley et al. "admit" that they are gay to their adult fans, but children and teenagers *must not* know.

The independent cinema often told stories about gay teenagers: *Beautiful Thing, Come Undone, Get Real, The Incredible True Story of Two Girls in Love, Nico and Dani.* But they were for art house-attending, out-of-the-closet gay and lesbian adults. Real teenagers, unless they had very, very permissive parents or could sneak out to the Castro Theatre, continued to subsist on a diet of media images virtually unchanged since the days of Frankie and Annette, with boys and girls constantly fantasizing about, mooning over, longing for, and scheming to acquire each other. There was a decrease in overt homophobia, with fewer teenagers yelling "fag!" at one another, coupled with an increase in the insistence that there were no gay teenagers. Heterosexual desire defines you, teenagers were told, especially the boys. Without it the very term "teenager" is gibberish.

For this reason, both Ellen the sitcom character and Rosie the talk show host discussed boy-crazy teen years[3] they may have "become" lesbians later, as adults, but at fifteen they were undeniably straight, like every other fifteen-year-old since Adam and Eve awoke in the Garden.[4] For this reason, in *A Dangerous Place* (1995), when preteen Ted Jan Roberts (Ethan) tires of his older brother's girl-craziness and asks "Is that all you think about?" Mom sets him "straight": "He's seventeen! Of course it is!" Seventeen-year-old boys spend 100 percent of their time thinking about girls, with never a momentary lapse, never a moment devoted to thoughts of family, friends, sports, classes, clubs, college, part-time jobs, future jobs, politics, religion, the environment, or social issues, except as a means to the end. Yet this is not a problem, not a fact of life to be grudgingly accepted: Mom's "Of course it is!" is jubilant. She is celebrating her son's girl-craziness as a thing of beauty, a triumph over darkness and chaos.

Gay people sometimes appeared in the cultural products sold to teenagers, but almost always adults, and the very, very, very few gay teenagers were all absolutely complicit with ideological equation of teenage and straight, so they always defined their gayness as *something else:* confusion, blindness, despair, heterosexual desire misplaced in the wrong body, or a nonsexual interest in show tunes and shopping. Thus they proclaimed, perhaps more fervidly even than the heterosexuals, that they themselves did not and could exist.[5] We know the result. The utter absence of gay people in social studies class, the Friday night dance, parental heart-to-hearts, pastors' sermons (gays are monsters), and locker rooms (gays are monsters) meant that mass media took on an immense epistemological significance, and gay teenagers in real life still believed their gayness to be *something else* (confusion, blindness, despair), and straight teenagers believed that it was a good idea to kill gay teenagers, or else brutalize them into suicide.[6]

THE TEENCOM

In the fall of 1987, NBC's Saturday morning lineup premiered *Good Morning Miss Bliss,* about a caring Indianapolis middle school teacher (former Disney teen Hayley Mills) with a classroom full of wisecracking, rambunctious students. Mills quickly tired of being upstaged by the two standout stars, blond pretty boy Zack (Mark-Paul Gosselaar) and weirdo Screech (Dustin Diamond), so after thirteen episodes she walked,[7] abandoning Saturday morning to the Smurfs and Gummi Bears. Two years later, NBC realized that teenagers liked to watch teenagers, not teachers, so it released a retooled version, *Saved by the Bell.* Zack, Screech, and shallow richster Lisa (Lark Voorhies) from the original series joined sullen muscle jock Slater (Mario Lopez), shallow cheerleader Kelly (Tiffani Thiessen), and intellectual-feminist Jesse (Elizabeth Berkley) to form a tight-knit clique of hunks and babes, now at Bayside High in California (so they could wear swimsuits).

Like Brat Packer suburbia, Bayside is squeaky clean and Reaganized. Everyone is attractive, wealthy, masquerading as middle class, white even when portrayed by minority actors,[8] and heterosexual even when portrayed by gay actors. Plots involved mostly demonstrations of undeniable straightness—falling in love with the wrong person, deciding if the kiss meant anything, deciding whether to go steady, having two dates on the same night—with a smattering of minor social problems, like smoking or cheating on a test. *Saved by the Bell* was an immense hit among teenagers, especially young teens who had not yet experienced Baysides of their own. It lasted for four seasons, spawned two spin-off series and two feature films, and gained twenty-five Young Actors Awards nominations. The gang, especially Mark-Paul Goesselaer and Mario Lopez, appeared in innumerable teen magazine pinups, board games, pin-backs, paperback novels, lunchboxes, and articles of clothing.

Soon teencoms were proliferating: between 1991 and 1999, tight-knit groups of hunks and babes hijinked in twenty-one clean-scrubbed generic high schools, usually on the new niche-market cable channels, or in the Saturday morning or early-evening time slots favored by young teens.[9] Nickelodeon offered *Welcome Freshmen* (1991-1993), UPN *Breaker High* (1997-1998), the USA network *U.S.A. High* (1997-1998), and the Disney channel a different series every year. NBC and CBS remained oblivious to the teencom fad, but ABC kicked in with a Friday Night lineup full of "family sitcoms" that heavily emphasized teenage hunks and babes while relegating parents to an occasional "That's not a good idea" proviso.

None of the 1990's teencoms ever featured a gay character, and none ever used the g-word. Yet many of the high school hunks came in pairs, often polarized into white and nonwhite (Zack and Slater on *Saved by the Bell*, Alex and Max on *Breaker High*), affluent and non-affluent (Corey and Shawn on *Boy Meets World*, Murray and Sean on *Clueless*), or nerd and jock (El-Train and Jamal on *City Guys*, Alan and Lewis on *Even Stevens*), and often enjoying emotional bonds much more intimate and intense than any of their knee-jerk heterosexual romances. As a consequence, they had to constantly police the boundaries of their relationships, evoking and rejecting the possibility of homoromance in joke after joke, episode after episode. The studio audience usually responded with laughter as nearly hysterical as Curtis Armstrong's in *Better Off Dead:* they knew exactly what was not being discussed.

Zack on *Saved by the Bell*, gay-coded as blond, pretty, stylish, fashion conscious, wealthy, vain, and somewhat of a manipulator, is constantly the butt of jokes about misdirected or misinterpreted same-sex desire, but only when Slater, otherwise his constant companion, is not around. In "Running Zack" (November 1990, dir. Don Barnhart), Zack has just qualified to be on the track team so Bayside can beat Valley High, and the competitive Principal Belding (Dennis Haskins) hugs him and cries "I love you!" Seeing the suspicious looks from passing students, Belding breaks into an arm-clasp and backtracks to "I like you!" There are more suspicious looks, so he backs off altogether and shakes Zack's hand: "Uh. . . . I mean, good job, son." The audience goes wild. Similarly, in "Breaking Up Is Hard to Undo" (December 1990, dir. Don Barnhart), there's a knock on Zack's bedroom door. He thinks it's his girlfriend, so he opens it with his arms wide and an exclamation of "I love you!" Screech walks in, waits for the audience howls to die down a bit and then tells a mortified Zack "I love you, too . . . but only as a friend." An adult authority figure or the school weirdo could participate in such a "joke," but Slater never could, lest he draw attention to their unstated romance.

Boy Meets World's Corey (Ben Savage) is also the butt of jokes about mistaken or misdirected same-sex desire, again when his partner, the pretty, stylish, gay-coded Shawn (Rider Strong) is absent. Though the secret in "Dangerous Secret" (November 1996, dir. Jeff McCracken) is "officially" an abusive father, the episode includes two gay misdirections, suggesting that there is more than one "dangerous secret" in Philadelphia. First, Corey tries to impress his girlfriend Topanga by feigning interest in romantic poetry, especially Shelley's "sensual imagery." Topanga points out that Shelley was "a guy," whereupon Corey throws the book down with an "Ewww" of disgust. Audience howls. Next, Corey asks his older brother Eric (Will Friedle) about his "first time." Eric says "Remember Mitchell Davis?" Stunned, Corey stops him: "There's an unexpected surprise. Why don't you tell me about your second time?" But instead, Eric tells about how Mitchell Davis convinced him to take the training wheels off his bicycle before he was ready, a parable about waiting for sex. Yet he also evades the question of his first sexual experience. His knowing smile suggests that it may indeed have been with Mitchell Davis, but he switched to the bicycle story (or transformed the sex story into a metaphor) after determining that Corey would respond badly.

However, *Boy Meets World* did not depend entirely upon misdirection. In "Learning to Fly" (April 1997, dir. Jeff McCracken), Topanga finds Corey and Shawn hugging, and cries "Stop it! You're both boys!" A flashback reveals another same-sex hug when they were kindergarteners, and Topanga again crying "Stop it! You're both boys!" Evidently she has spent her life policing Corey's actions and thoughts to ensure that he "remains" heterosexual. After all, it was Topanga who pointed out that the poet Shelley was "a guy," and therefore his imagery inappropriate for a (straight) guy to enjoy. At Topanga's instigation, Corey must constantly, and consciously, explain that he is in love with her but not with Shawn. In "The Happiest

Show on Earth" (May 1996, dir. Jeff McCracken), in the midst of a conversation, Corey suddenly feels the need to tell Shawn: "When I see Topanga, I want to hold her, hug her, kiss her. When I see you, I have no desire to do any of those things." This is a nonsequiter. Shawn has never intimated that he *expects* Corey to hold, hug, or kiss him. Shawn remains placid, waiting for the audience howls to die down before he goes on to his next line. Really, there is no way he could react without foregrounding the possibility that their relationship is indeed romantic.

In its first home on ABC (1996-2000), *Sabrina the Teenage Witch* evoked same-sex desire more often and more openly than any other teencom, perhaps because the cast included an extraordinary number of gay, gay-friendly, and camp-friendly actors, writers, and directors; Nate Richert (Harvey, Sabrina's sometime boyfriend) was spotted dancing at the Rage in West Hollywood, and Jenna Leigh Green (Libby, her bratty nemesis) spoke at UCLA during National Coming Out Week in 2000.[10] In the first episode (September 1996), Sabrina's aunts explain to her new teacher that they are "sisters, not an alternate couple." In "Dream Date" (November 1996, dir. Gail Mancuso), Sabrina needs a date for the big dance, and as she walks down the hall looking for prospects, she casually asks "I wonder if that guy is taken?" Harvey tells her "Yeah, by *that* guy," thus making history by marking the first gay romantic couple in any teencom.

During the next season, Sabrina "becomes" gay for an episode. In "Sabrina the Teenage Boy" (October 1997, dir. Peter Baldwin), she transforms herself into a boy named Jack to find out what guys talk about when they are alone. Jack has retained Sabrina's desire for boys, becoming the heteronormative explanation that gay men are really women. More interesting are the reactions of the guys. When Jack accidentally exclaims that a baseball player is "hot," Harvey stares in horror at this evidence that his new friend is gay, and Jack must quickly redeem himself by explaining that he meant player's athletic prowess. But when the spell starts to fail, giving "Jack" makeup, Harvey tells him "Your mascara is running. It doesn't bother me, but the guys will razz [harass] you." He has become considerably more homophobic since last season,[11] but he finds transvestites more acceptable than gay men, perhaps because makeup does not require a recognition of his own unstated same-sex interests.

Since Sabrina and Harvey are best friends, the program has no hunk duos in the tradition of *Saved by the Bell* or *Boy Meets World* until the fall of 1999, when muscle-jock Brad (Jon Huertas, who has played gay in several movies and television programs, including MTV's *Undressed*), moves to town and falls into love-at-first-sight with Harvey. Though the scripts have them heterosexually buddy bonding over talk of sports and girls, their sizzling on-screen chemistry leaves little doubt that their attraction is both physical and intensely romantic. They spend the rest of the season joyously making plans to be together tonight, tomorrow night, every night, while Brad and Sabrina snipe jealously at each other, and each devises schemes to get Harvey out of the other's clutches.

In the next season, not coincidentally the beginning of the amazingly retro White House, *Sabrina the Teenage Witch* moved from ABC to the Warner Brothers network, the writers were all replaced, along with Harvey, Brad, and most of the rest of the cast, and plotlines became downright homophobic. Now in college, Sabrina goes to see *The Rocky Horror Picture Show*, which is *about* the freedom to "be it" rather than "dream it," and she is horrified by a man in the audience *wearing garters*. Her co-worker relates a story about how he went to New Orleans, met a girl, and discovered while they were kissing that she was really a *dude*. He's laughing, not at all offended or upset by the memory, but Sabrina grimaces in disgust. Kissing a *dude*? She was never so homophobic in high school, but times had changed.

THE TEENSOAP

The earliest teenage soap opera was *Never Too Young* (1965-1966), a sort of angst-ridden *Beach Blanket Bingo* starring Tony Dow's biceps (the former *Leave It to Beaver* big brother must have wondered why the scripts called for him to appear shirtless in nearly every scene, even at the coffee house hangout or at a party where everyone else was fully clothed). Yet teen hunks didn't sell to the adults, and most teenagers were in school during the daytime, so *Never Too Young* folded after a season, and for the next twenty years teenagers were rare in television drama. Cute kids generally vanished for a few months and returned as law school graduates. Then Fox discovered that the main attraction of its *21 Jump Street* (1987-1990), a show about cops going undercover as high school students, was the teen angst rather than the cop action. So, Fox premiered *Beverly Hills 90210* (1990-2000), a show about the a tight-knit group of babes and hunks at Beverly Hills High. Teenage audiences were ecstatic, marketing tie-ins flew off the shelves, and the teensoap was born. It was identical to the teencom except that the audience was a bit older, so the problems were worse and the sex more explicit. Soon *Party of Five* (1994-2000) appeared on Fox, *My So-Called Life* (1994-1995) on ABC, the teensoap-fantasy hybrid *Buffy the Vampire Slayer* (1997-2003) on UPN, and *Felicity* (1998-2002), *Dawson's Creek* (1998-2003), *Smallville* (2001-), and half a dozen others on the teen-oriented WB.

The teensoapers occupied the same world as their teencom counterparts. With few exceptions, they were all white, wealthy, nonreligious Protestants, with spectacular physiques and vague but socially relevant career goals. Like the teencoms, plotlines centered on hetero-romance, with the social problems upgraded to alcoholism, drug abuse, child abuse, violence in schools, illiteracy, and homelessness. "Homosexuality" occasionally appeared as one of the social problems. Out-and-proud gay people never appeared; they were always not asking and not telling, since an accidental outing meant loss of job, home, family, and friends. They were almost always adults, thus reaffirming the ideological position that teenagers are always undeniably straight. The crowded *Beverly Hills 90210* zip code saw eighty-six regular and recurring characters, but only one eventually outed herself: Steve's mother (Christina Belford), an adult. On *Party of Five,* the gay characters did not belong to the party; the first was outed violin teacher Mitchell Anderson, and the other, nanny Wilson Cruz, evidently introduced just so the two could date.[12] On *Felicity,* the gang of undeniably straight college students hung out at a coffee house run by the swishy adult Javier (Ian Gomez). *Grosse Pointe* (2001-2002), a spoof about producing a teensoap, featured a predatory older "homosexual" (Michael Hitchcock) who kept hitting on the undeniably straight boys in the cast.

Occasionally, one of the teensoap gang is outed, but only when they have grown up, become adults, or at least college students instead of teenagers. On *Party of Five,* college girl Julia (Neve Campbell), not one of the high schoolers, has a "sexual identity crisis," thinking that she is in love with a visiting lesbian poet before deciding that she is straight.[13] The first gay person appears on *Beverly Hills 90210* in the fourth season (1993-1994), when the gang is all in college: Steve (Ian Ziering) accidentally outs his fraternity president, evidently so he can defend him during the subsequent harassment and attempt to boot him out of office. Thereafter Beverly Hills remains as exuberantly gay-free as *7th Heaven* until the eighth season (1997-1998), when the gang has long since graduated from college, and started their socially relevant careers, and can safely reconcile a gay teenager with his bigoted parents or a gay community center employee with his bigoted supervisor. On *Buffy the Vampire Slayer*, Willow (Alyson Hannigan) spends three seasons heterosexualizing with boys; only in the fourth season (1999-2000), no longer a high schooler, does she bend in for an off-camera same-sex kiss. Writer/director Josh Whedan refused to say "lesbian," indicating that he disapproved of labels (other than heterosexual). No doubt he really feared admitting that lesbians exist, and preferred to pretend that no other girl had ever kissed a girl in all the history of the world. Not until "Tabula Rasa" in the sixth season (November 2001), did Willow finally get to out herself, and even then in a tentative, highly qualified fashion. Instead of "I'm gay," Willow says "I *think* I'm *kinda* gay."

Though Willow's friends were blasé about her kinda gay identity, most teensoap characters are not so tolerant: they may champion the civil rights of outed adults, but with a kinda gay peer, they regress to the shrill homophobia of the Brat Pack. On *Buffy the Vampire Slayer*, a second-season episode titled "Phases" (January 1998, dir. Bruce Seth Green), has ghoulie-fighter Xander (Nicholas Brendon) interrogating Larry (Larry Bagby), a high school football jock whom he suspects of being a werewolf. "It's over!" Xander exclaims. "I know what you do at night!" First Larry thinks that Xander wants to blackmail him, and then he starts to cry: he knows it's terrible, he hates himself but he can't help it. Xander is an expert on supernatural compulsions, so he puts a comforting hand on Larry's shoulder, and offers Buffy and the gang's help to find a cure. Larry brightens. But suddenly Xander—and the viewer—realizes that he's not talking about being a werewolf at all, but about his homosexuality! So Larry thinks that being gay is a monstrous compulsion; its victims can be blackmailed, but maybe Buffy has a cure.

It seems impossible that any teenager today would even have access to myths discredited long before he or she was born, but maybe

Sunnydale has been swallowed up by a time vortex and it's really 1948. Xander certainly acts like it. Instead of sending the boy to the nearest queer youth club, he stares in horror and rushes off. Later, back at headquarters, Buffy asks "So, was Larry the werewolf?" Ashen-faced, Xander stammers, "No, he wasn't. Now drop it! Just drop it!" Fifteen years after *Teen Wolf,* "fags" are still much scarier than werewolves.

Even the gay teenagers can be remarkably homophobic. For the first half of the first season of *Dawson's Creek,* Jack (Kerr Smith) was the boyfriend of a girl named Joey (Katie Holmes). Then came "That Is the Question" (February 1999), in which, according to the episode guide, their romance is destroyed by "rumor and innuendo." In this case, the rumors and innuendos are true, and Jack finally admits that he "doesn't like labels." For the rest of the series, he plays the conflicted, confused, self-hating, and depressed nonlabel-liking person, like the only gay student in *Fame* (1980), who told us: "never being happy isn't the same as being sad." Girls are constantly trying to get Jack into bed to prove that all teenage boys are heterosexual once they meet someone with the proper sexual prowess, but he fights them off, sometimes literally. He mopes around constantly, talking about how he will have to spend the rest of his life alone, but whenever his straight friends try to push him into the gay community, he resists. Even two years after his accidental outing, he is still bitterly homophobic. In the fourth-season episode "Self-Reliance" (December 2000, dir. David Petrarca), Joey drags him to a bowling night with the local Gay-Straight Coalition, but he's wildly uncomfortable among so many gay and straight people: what if someone thinks that *he* is gay or straight? Out-and-proud Matt approaches him.

MATT: Hey, you're the gay football player!

JACK: I'm just not comfortable with labels like that.

MATT: [Sarcastically] Which label bothers you more, gay or football player?

Two episodes later, in "The Te of Pacey" (January 2001, dir. Harry Winer), when Matt accuses Jack of "self-loathing" (which seems quite accurate), straight buddy Jen (Michelle Williams) advises him to be "nice" and give Jack time to adjust; it takes awhile to accept something so horrific as being gay. Yet she doesn't need time to try to demonstrate that Jack is really heterosexual: she gets drunk and throws herself into his bed (it doesn't work). Later in the season Jack does manage a same-sex kiss, which producer Paul Stupin recalls as making him "cringe a bit" along with other "low points," of the season Dawson dating a stripper and Andie stealing a copy of the PSATs.[14] Eventually, after hundreds of pep talks from desperately well-wishing straight characters, Jack begins dating, and saying gay instead of "not liking labels." In the 2002 series finale, he settles down with a closeted police officer named Deputy Doug.

As the 1990's teensoaps ended in 2002 or 2003, new groups of swimsuit-clad babes and hunks arose to take their place in *Everwood, The O.C., One Tree Hill, Summerland.* They were always exuberantly gay-free, but of course, at this writing, the casts are still in high school. No doubt when they reach college, they will accidentally out a fraternity president, but until then they continue to present the teenage condition as always undeniably straight.

THE REAL WORLD

In 1992, MTV hired seven extremely attractive but otherwise heterogeneous college students (or at least people of college age) to share a large house for six months, filming their every move and hoping they would fight or kiss. They did, and an edited version with the boring parts cut out, *The Real World,* has appeared every year since, fourteen seasons to date, each set in a different big city with a different set of extremely attractive young adults. Though heterosexual hookups in the hot tub are the mainstay of the series, fighting is popular as well, so in six seasons (New York, San Francisco, Miami, Hawaii, New Orleans, and Paris) MTV shoved gay men into lofts with heterosexual rednecks, hoping that there would be bigotry and yelling (in New Orleans, contrary to expectations, the redneck and the gay guy became close friends). Only one season (Chicago) featured a bisexual woman, and one (Boston) a lesbian, who decided that she was bisexual halfway through.

Selection of participants is not random. No doubt many gay people apply to be on the series, but those selected seem particularly eager to be yes-men and Uncle Toms. Pride in being gay is absolutely forbidden; the gay housemates must be conflicted, upset, and willing to take the most horrifying abuse without comment. In *Hawaii* (1999), when Justin protests homophobic jokes, housemates accuse him of being "heterophobic." He "doesn't get along" with the other housemates (that is, he won't lie back and take the abuse), so he leaves halfway through the season. Other gay housemates maintain the campaign of teenage misinformation by presenting their gayness—or standing by without protest while others present it—as confusion, conflict, sickness, sin, heterosexual desire in the wrong body, shopping and show tunes, innate straightness somehow deferred. In the actual house they may have qualified, explained, or argued, but MTV chooses to broadcast statements that sound like fifty-year-old pop psychology articles (perhaps *Buffy the Vampire Slayer*'s Larry has been watching MTV). Even the official *Real World* Web site promotes the old-fashioned idea everyone that is born straight, but some people decide to turn gay: in *San Francisco* (1994), the homophobe Puck "does not respect the way Pedro chooses to live his life." That is, Pedro chose to become gay, but Puck thinks he would be better off going back to straight. In *Boston* (1997), Genesis has decided to become a lesbian, but as the show progresses, she wonders if her decision was "too hasty," so she experiments with dating boys and finally decides to become bisexual instead.

THE INCREDIBLE SHRINKING TEENAGER

Brat Packers were young adults playing college students or high school seniors, rarely juniors, and never sophomores, freshmen, or eighth graders. But in the 1990s, mass media teenagers, and the actors who portrayed them, suddenly became fourteen or fifteen years old, or even younger. The average age of the actors praised in the September 1985 issue of *Teen Set* was 19.8, but ten years later, in the August 1995 issue of the comparable *Bop,* the average age dropped to 16.8.[15] Teen magazines ignoring *Baywatch* hunks David Charvet and Kelly Slater to endlessly display the pubescent cleavage of thirteen-year-old Jeremy Jackson, and the heartthrob of *Boy Meets World* was not seventeen-year-old Will Friedle (who rated a total of two pinups in *Teen Beat*), but Rider Strong, aged fourteen. Jonathan Taylor Thomas began receiving a thousand times more fan mail than anyone else on the *Home Improvement* cast around 1994, when he was twelve years old. At the movies, older teenagers all but disappeared from the box office toppers, replaced by twelve or thirteen year olds like James Jason Richter in *Free Willy* (1993), Brad Renfro in *The Client* (1994), Devon Sawa in *Casper* (1995), and Sam Huntington in *Jungle 2 Jungle* (1997).[16] Even when the main characters were older teenagers, a few hetero-horny junior high schoolers were hired to grin, ogle, and discuss bras in the background, demonstrating that the "discovery" of girls occurred at puberty or before. In *Toy Soldiers* (1991), as a sixteen-year-old cadet (Sean Astin), confiscates a *Playboy* magazine from a fourteen-year-old classmate, and gushes "Some things never change!" Though four main virginity-obsessed buddies in *American Pie* (1999) are all young adults playing high school seniors, a thirteen-year-old (Eli Marienthal) spies on heterosexual coitus with his computer cam, and then in "real life" by hiding in the closet; "This is like the coolest thing I've ever seen!" he exclaims.

Teenage girls, however, remained in their late teens. The central couple of *Boy Meets World,* played by Ben Savage and Danielle Fishel, were both thirteen and going steady when the show began, but when *Home Improvement*'s Randy got his first steady girlfriend in a March 1994 episode, Jonathan Taylor Thomas was twelve, and the actress Anndi McAffee fifteen. On an October 1994 episode of *Baywatch,* Hobie (Jeremy Jackson, one week past his fourteenth birthday), dated a girl played by twenty-four-year-old future *Playboy* centerfold Charisma Carpenter. Feature films had a similar shrinkage, with thirteen- and fourteen-year-old protagonists gazing at super-models in their mid-twenties. In *The Sandlot* (dir. David Mickey Evans, 20th Century Fox, 1993), the eleven-year-old Chauncey Leopardi, swimming at a public pool, groans with painful horniness as the life-guard dabs herself with suntan oil, then exclaims "I can't take this no more!" He jumps into the deep end and fakes drowning so she will give him mouth-to-mouth, and then, grinning, he steals an open-mouthed kiss. The other boys cheer. "He had kissed a woman," the adult narrator says approvingly. "And he had kissed her long and good." But the most egregious shrinkage comes in *Max Keeble's Big Move* (dir. Tim Hill, Buena Vista, 2001) in which "teen" nerd Max (Alex D. Linz) is twelve years old but looks about six, with a childlike physique, a baby face, a soprano voice, and tiny hands that make telephone receivers, apples, and cookies look enormous. Towering over him is the h.b.i.s.m. girl, a seventeen-year-old Miss Junior America 1999 named Brooke Smith.

This decrease in age of the teenage boys but not the teenage girls has several important ideological functions. Since the advent of heterosexual desire has been pushed back to puberty or before, it maintains the MTV myth that being gay is an adult "lifestyle choice," a derailment of the undeniable straightness of children and adolescents. Also, in an industry dominated by the heterosexual male gaze, it maintains the myth of universal heterosexual desire. The "typical" teenage girl could easily pass for adult, and thus is "obviously" desirable, but the "typical" teenage boy, barely pubescent, is "obviously" undesirable. Perhaps most important, it relieves older teenage boys of the need to spend every minute of every scene obsessing over girls. As long as they can demonstrate their masculinity with adequately muscular physiques, they need not display any interest in girls at all, their "discovery" of girls presumably accomplished years ago in junior high. Thus they can pursue other interests without any fear of being labeled gay.

On the TV series *Weird Science* (1994-1997), high schooler Wyatt (played by Michael Manasseri) is aggressively girl-crazy (so he and buddy Gary, John Mallory Asher, build a cyber-babe), but older brother (played by Lee Tergeson) Chett, a macho-stud military school graduate, never once talks to or talks about a girl. On *Even Stevens* (2000-2003), junior high schooler Louis (Shia LaBeouf) has a steady girlfriend, but his bodybuilding older brother, played by former male model Nick Spano, displays not the least heterosexual interest, not even in the form of a bikini-babe pinup tacked to his bedroom wall.[17] On Fox's *Malcolm in the Middle* (2000-), fourteen- to sixteen-year-old whiz-kid Malcolm (Frankie Muniz) Frankie Muniz spends most episodes falling in and out of love with various h.b.i.s.m. girls, leaving his older brother, sixteen- to eighteen-year-old muscle-jock Justin Berfield (Reese), to display so little interest that many fans speculate that the character (or Berfield himself) is preparing for a "very special" coming-out episode.

At the movies, drooling younger boys similarly give older boys carte blanche to pursue goals other than girls, even romance one another. In *Dazed and Confused* (dir. Richard Linklater, Gramercy Pictures, 1993), set on the last day of school in 1976, the new ninth graders have long hair, pretty, androgynous faces, and high-pitched voices that suggest prepubescence, but positively ooze with hetero-horni-ness. "At the party tonight," Carl (Esteban Powell) exclaims, "There's going to be a girl with tits *this big*! Two handfuls!" Hirshfelder (Jeremy Fox) attends the party and necks with a girl; called away, he complains "I was getting there! I had my hand up under her sweater!" Mitch (Wiley Wiggins) is the most successful because Pink Floyd (Jason London) and the other older teens take an interest in him, teach-ing him how to drink beer, cruise in cars, and seduce an h.b.i.s.m. girl (never tell her you like her, say you have your own car, and so on). He kisses her first on a car hood, and then on a blanket under the stars, and they probably have sex, too, since he stumbles home at dawn with a big grin on his face, virginity lost.

In contrast, the new high school seniors are amazingly nonchalant about their girl-craziness, with two very brief kissing scenes, a single ogling scene, no flirtation, no sex, and a single allusion to joining the football team because it increases the likelihood of "making it." Instead, they are devoted to the buddy-bonding pursuits of boozing, smoking pot, playing foosball, knocking over mailboxes, and hunting down the new ninth graders to paddle in a homoerotic initiation ritual. Pink Floyd blows off his girlfriend to spend time with his buddies, and many of the others never try to hook up with girls at all; the cli-mactic scene in the deserted football stadium at dawn consists of heart-to-hearts between friends.

Wooderson (Matthew McConaughey), a recent high school drop-out in tight jeans, seems particularly sexually ambiguous; he leers at one girl and makes a date with another, but he also leers at boys, swaggering and half-joking as if he knows more than anyone is say-ing. As Pink and Mitch leave the arcade, alone together, he calls "You boys have fun!" putting a lascivious lilt on "fun" and then chuckling to himself as if he knows they are a romantic couple. But Pink drives Mitch to an outdoor beer kegger, kisses a girl, and then turns his atten-tion to an unabashedly erotic pursuit of Wooderson, who has dropped by just to be sociable. The two end up heart-to-hearting on the de-serted football field, where Wooderson advises him to live by his own rules: "You gotta do what Randall Pink Floyd wants to do . . . the older you do get the more rules they're gonna try to get you to follow." The movie ends with Pink doing what he wants to do, driving off into the dawn with Wooderson beside him, grinning expectantly. The homoromantic subtext would be impossible if the actors had to spend every moment of screen time ogling girls.

CRUEL INTENTIONS

During the 1990s, Brat Pack concern about rejecting a homoerotic other diminished. *Dazed and Confused* contains only one antigay epithet, when older teen Dawson calls younger teen Mitch a "faggot." Yet at the same moment that *Sabrina the Teenage Witch* became homophobic, policing began in earnest. Sometimes only a few antigay epithets were needed to excuse the most intense homoromance, as when Ashton Kutcher (Jesse) and Seann William Scott (Chester) seem desperately in love with each other in *Dude, Where's My Car* (2000), even indulging in a passionate kiss. They need only demonstrate their undeniable straightness by quipping "The Dalai Lama is a *fag.*" In *Cheats* (2002), Trevor Fehrman (Handsome Davis) never expresses any interest in girls except through one ogling joke, and he treats his cheating business partner, Matthew Lawrence (Victor), in explicitly romantic terms, grabbing him, hugging him, even dancing with him at a party. Nevertheless, he proves that he is straight by "accusing" the principal (Mary Tyler Moore) of being a lesbian, and feigning a "teen identity crisis" to score a good grade from a teacher whose sexual identity can never, ever be spoken. In *School of Rock* (2003), one of Jack Black's prep school charges (Brian Falduto, Dewey Finn) lisps that he'd like to be the band's stylist, just so Black can do a horrified double take and thus demonstrate that he is straight.

Yet more often, homoerotic others drawn in boldly retro colors fluttered out of the same fifty-year-old pop psychology books that Larry the Non-Werewolf (from *Buffy*) reads. In *Cruel Intentions* (dir. Roger Kumble, Sony Pictures, 1999), Joshua Jackson plays a self-described "fag" named Blaine Tuttle,[18] (acted with such jaw-dropping hostility that one is amazed that Jackson was simultaneously playing Pacey on *Dawson's Creek* alongside Kerr Smith's gay character). Blaine has fun seducing his straight male classmates and then telling them that now they're fags, too. His latest project, school jock Greg (Eric Mabius), is so traumatized by the encounter that he tries to de-pervert himself by throwing out his Judy Garland CDs. The fact that Judy Garland was last popular among gay men over thirty years ago seems irrelevant to writer/director Roger Kumble.

Happy Campers (dir. Daniel Waters, New Line Cinema, 2001) features an obnoxious gay guy named Pixel (Jordan King), who keeps trying to get into the pants of his fellow summer-camp counselors. They accept him as a harmless eccentric, but when one of the junior high campers comes out to him, he is horrified, probably thinking that everyone is going to accuse him of perverting the boy. "You're not gay, you're twelve!" he cries, insisting that only adults can be gay, twelve-year-old "teenagers" must be undeniably heterosexual. When the boy continues to insist that he is gay, Pixel makes him promise that at least he won't say anything or do anything, that he'll pretend to be heterosexual like everyone else in the world until he turns eighteen.

Until he is no longer a teenager.

Notes

Preface

1. Foucault, Michel. 1984. "What Is an Author?" pp. 101-102 in Paul Rabinow, ed., *The Foucault Reader.* New York: Pantheon, 104.
2. DiStefano, Christine. 1991. *Configurations of Masculinity: A Feminist Perspective on Modern Political Theory.* Ithaca, NY: Cornell University Press, 9.
3. Epstein, Steven. 1996. "A Queer Encounter: Sociology and the Study of Sexuality." pp. 145-167 in Steven Seidman, ed., *Queer Theory/Sociology.* Cambridge, MA: Blackwell, 157.
4. Hennessey, Rosemary. 1995. "Incorporating Queer Theory on the Left." pp. 266-275 in Antonio Callari et al., eds., *Marxism in the Postmodern Age: Confronting the New World Order.* New York: Guilford Press.
5. Turner, Bryan S. 1984. *The Body and Society: Explorations in Social Theory.* Oxford and New York: Blackwell, 30-32.
6. Butler, Judith. 1993. *Bodies That Matter: On the Discursive Limits of "Sex."* New York: Routledge, 49.
7. Derrida, Jacques. 1974. *Of Grammatology.* Trans. Gayatri Spivak. Baltimore: Johns Hopkins UP, 178. Barthes, Roland. 1950, 1993. "The Rhetoric of the Image." pp. 15-27 in A. Gray and J. McGuigan, eds., *Studying Culture.* New York: St. Martin's Press, 20.
8. Bakhtin, Mikhail.1990. *The Dialogic Principle: Four Essays.* Tr. Caryl Emerson. Austin: U. of Texas P, 48.
9. Iser, Wolfgang. 1987. "Representation: A Performative Act." pp. 217-232 in M. Kreuger, ed., *The Aims of Representation: Subject/Text/History.* New York: Columbia UP, 219.
10. Greimas, Algirdas. 1987. *On Meaning: Selected Writings in Semiotic Theory.* Minneapolis: U of Minnesota P.
11. Doty, Alexander. 1993. *Making Things Perfectly Queer: Interpreting Mass Culture.* Minneapolis: U of Minnesota P, 15.
12. Ibid., 3.
13. Foucault, Michel. 1972. *The Archaeology of Knowledge.* Tr. A. M. Sheridan Smith. New York: Pantheon Books, 109.
14. Meyer, Richard. 1991. "Rock Hudson's Body." pp. 259-288 in Diane Fuss, ed., *Inside/Outside: Lesbian Theory, Gay Theory.* New York: Routledge, 283.
15. Butler, *Bodies That Matter,* 126.
16. Weber, Max. 1905, 1958. *The Protestant Ethic and the Spirit of Capitalism.* 1905. Tr. Talcott Parsons. New York: Scribners, 118.

doi:10.1300/5484_12

Chapter 1

1. Or what Van Gennep called "physical puberty" and "social puberty." Van Gennep, Arnold. *The Rites of Passage*. 1908, 1960. Tr. Monika B. Vizedom and Gabrielle L. Caffee. Chicago: U. of Chicago P, 3.

2. Demos, John, and Virginia Demos. 1969. "Adolescence in Historical Perspective." *Journal of Marriage and the Family* 31: 632-638.

3. Ariès, Philippe. 1962. *Centuries of Childhood: A Social History of Family Life*. Tr. Robert Baldick. New York: Knopf.

4. Hanawalt, Barbara A. 1992. "Historical Descriptions and Prescriptions for Adolescence." *Journal of Family History* 17(4): 341-351.

5. Stokvis, Pieter R. 1993. "From Child to Adult: Transition Rites in the Netherlands ca. 1800-1914." *Paedagogica Historica* 29(1): 77-92.

6. Haines, W. Scott. 1992. "The Development of Leisure and the Transformation of Working-Class Adolescence, Paris 1830-1840." *Journal of Family History* 17(4): 451-476.

7. Bakan, David. 1971. "Adolescence in America: From Idea to Social Fact." *Daedalus* 100(4): 979-996; Fox, Vivian C. 1977. "Is Adolescence a Phenomenon of Modern Times?" *Journal of Psychohistory* 5(2): 271-290; Hiner, N. Ray. 1975. "Adolescence in Eighteenth-Century America." *History of Childhood Quarterly* 3(2): 253-280; Kett, Joseph F. 1971. "Adolescence and Youth in Nineteenth-Century America." *Journal of Interdisciplinary History* 2(2): 283-298; Vicinus, Martha. 1994. "The Adolescent Boy: Fin de Siecle Femme Fatale?" *Journal of the History of Sexuality* 5(1): 90-114.

8. Austin, Joe, and Michael Willard. 1998. *Generations of Youth: Youth Cultures and History in Twentieth Century America*. New York: New York UP; Fornas, Johan, and Goran Bolin. 1995. *Youth Culture in Late Modernity*. New York: Sage; McRobbie, Angela. 2000. *Feminism and Youth Culture*. New York: Routledge; Moran, Jeffrey P. 2000. *Teaching Sex: The Shaping of Adolescence in the Twentieth Century*. Cambridge: Harvard UP; Pilkington, H. 1997. "Youth Cultural Studies." *Sociology Review* 7(1): 22-26.

9. Sociologist Talcott Parsons first used the term "youth culture" in 1942. See *Essays in Sociological Theory*. 1964. New York: Free Press.

10. Hall, G. Stanley. 1904. *Adolescence*. New York: Appleton.

11. Erikson, Erik H. 1968. *Identity: Youth and Crisis*. New York: Norton, 1994.

12. Cohen, Eleanor. 1999. "From Solitary Vice to Split Mind: Psychiatric Discourses of Male Sexuality and Coming of Age, 1918-1938." *Australian Historical Studies* 30(112): 79-95; Templin, Lawrence. 1968. "The Pathology of Youth." *Journal of Human Relations* 16(1): 113-127.

13. Hall, Leslie A. 1994. "Feminist Reconfigurations of Heterosexuality in the 1920's." pp. 135-151 in Lucy Bland and Laura Doan, eds., *Sexology in Culture*. Chicago: U. of Chicago P; Haag, Pamela S. 1992. "In Search of 'The Real Thing': Ideologies of Love, Modern Romance, and Women's Sexual Subjectivity in the United States, 1920-40." *Journal of the History of Sexuality* 2(4): 547-577.

14. *Devil on Wheels,* dir. Crain Wilbur (PRC, 1947). Unless otherwise indicated, all quotations are derived from the film as distributed rather than a script.

15. *Junior Prom,* dir. Arthur Dreyfuss (Monogram, 1946).

16. Loughley, John. 1998. *The Other Side of Silence: Men's Lives and Gay Identities, a Twentieth Century History*. New York: Henry Holt, 74-79; Mann, William J. 1999. *Wisecracker: The Life and Times of William Haines, Hollywood's First Openly Gay Star*. New York: Penguin; McClellan, Diana. 2000. *The Girls: Sappho Goes to Hollywood*. New York: St. Martin's; Mann, William J. 2002. *Behind the Screen: How Gays and Lesbians Shaped Hollywood, 1910-1969*. New York: Penguin.

17. Kaiser, Charles. 1997. *The Gay Metropolis: 1940-1996*. New York: Houghton Mifflin, 59.

18. Cooper, Jackie, with Dick Kleiner. 1981. *Please Don't Shoot My Dog: The Autobiography of Jackie Cooper*. New York: Morrow, 200; Coghlan, Frank "Junior." 1993. *They Still Call Me Junior: Autobiography of a Child Star*. Jefferson, NC: McFarland, 123-124; Rooney, Mickey. 1991. *Life Is Too Short*. New York: Villard Books, 199; Gorcey, Leo. 1967. *An Original Dead End Kid Presents: Dead End Yells, Wedding Bells, Cockle Shells and Dizzy Spells*. New York: Vantage Press, 32. For Dick Hogan, see Barrios, Richard. 2002. *Screened Out: Playing Gay in Hollywood from Edison to Stonewall*. New York: Routledge, 209.

19. Terry, Jennifer. 1999. *An American Obsession: Science, Medicine, and Homosexuality in Modern Society*. Chicago: U. of Chicago Press, 189ff.

20. Wylie, Philip. 1942. *Generation of Vipers*.

21. Buhle, Paul, and Dave Wagner. 2002. *Radical Hollywood*. New York: Norton, 349.

22. Kimmel, Michael. 1996. *Manhood in America*. New York: Free Press, 221-260; Corber, Robert J. 1997. *Homosexuality in Cold War America: Resistance and the Crisis of Masculinity*. Durham, NC: Duke UP, 23-30; Terry, Jennifer, *An American Obsession*, 329-342.

23. Sedgwick, Eve Kosofsky. 1990. *Epistemology of the Closet*. Berkeley: U of California P; Morton, Donald. 1993. "The Politics of Queer Theory in the (Post) Modern Movement." *Genders 17:* 121-150; Erni, John Nguyet. 1996. "Eternal Excesses: Toward a Queer Mode of Articulation in Social Theory." *American Literary History 8*: 566-581; Thomas, Calvin. 1997. "Straight with a Twist: Queer Theory and the Subject of Heterosexuality." pp. 83-115 in Thomas Foster et al., eds., *The Gay Nineties: Disciplinary and Interdisciplinary Formations in Queer Studies*. New York: NYU Press.

24. Kimmel, Michael. 1987. "The Contemporary 'Crisis' of Masculinity in Historical Perspective." pp. 121-153 in H. Brod, ed., *The Making of Masculinities: The New Men's Studies*. Boston: Allen & Unwin; Sedgwick, *Epistemology*, 4.

25. Mann, *Wisecracker*, 169-173; McLellan, *The Girls*, 355-358.

26. Kenny Miller does mention going to a gay restaurant with a friend in *Kenny Miller: Surviving Teenage Werewolves, Puppet People and Hollywood*. Jefferson, NC: McFarland, 1999. Tony Curtis jokingly claims that he was hit on by everyone, "Men, women, children. Animals!" In DiStefano, Blasé. 2002. "Tasty Tony: Some Like It Hot. Some Like It Cold. Actor Tony Curtis Likes It Hot and Cold and Everything in Between." *OutSmart* 6.2. Available at <http://www.outsmartmagazine.com/issue/i06-02/>.

27. Hickman, Dwayne, and Joan Roberts Hickman.1994. *Forever Dobie: The Many Lives of Dwayne Hickman*. New York: Carol Publishing, 125.

28. Hadleigh, Boze. 1986. *Conversations with My Elders.* New York: St. Martin's Press; Hadleigh, Boze. 1994. *Hollywood Lesbians.* New York: Barracade Books.

29. Benshoff, Harry. 1997. *Monsters in the Closet: Homosexuality and the Horror Film.* Manchester: Manchester UP, 193.

30. Grant, Julie. 2001. "A Thought a Mother Can Hardly Face: Sissy Boys, Parents, and Professionals in Mid-Twentieth Century America." pp. 117-130 in Alid M. Black, ed., *Modern American Queer History.* Philadelphia: Temple UP.

31. Katz, Jonathan. 1996. *The Invention of Heterosexuality.* New York: Penguin, viii, 111.

32. Dutton, Kenneth R.1995. *The Perfectible Body: The Western Ideal of Male Physical Development.* New York: Continuum, 92.

Chapter 2

1. White, William J. 1958, 2002. *The Organization Man.* Philadelphia: U of Pennsylvania P. Cf. Wilson, Sloan. 1955, 2002. *The Man in the Grey Flannel Suit.* New York: Four Walls Eight Windows; Corber, Robert J. 1997. *Homosexuality in Cold War America: Resistance and the Crisis of Masculinity.* Durham, NC: Duke UP, 45.

2. DeHart, Jane Sherron. 2001. "Containment at Home: Gender, Sexuality, and National Identity in Cold War America." pp. 124-155 in Peter J. Kuznick and James Gilbert, eds., *Rethinking Cold War Culture.* Washington, DC: Smithsonian Institution Press.

3. Clark, Clifford E. 1989. "Ranch-House Suburbia: Ideals and Realities." pp. 172-191 in Larry May, ed., *Recasting America: Culture and Politics in the Age of the Cold War.* Chicago: U of Chicago P.

4. *The Adventures of Ozzie and Harriet* (1952-1964). *Bachelor Father* (1957-1962). *The Betty Hutton Show* (1959-1960). *Blondie* (1957-1958). *The Bob Cummings Show* (1955-1959). *The Donna Reed Show* (1958-1962). *Father Knows Best* (1954-1960). *The Life of Riley* (1953-1958). *The Many Loves of Dobie Gillis* (1959-1963). *Meet Corliss Archer* (1954-1955). *Too Young to Go Steady* (1959-1960). *Leave It to Beaver* (1957-1963) and *Make Room for Daddy* (1953-1965) had teenagers by 1959.

5. Twenty-three seasons, if we count the spin-off *Ozzie's Girls* (1973-1974).

6. See, for instance, Taylor, Ella.1989. *Prime Time Families: Television Culture in Postwar America.* Berkeley: U. of California Press, 26-27. Curtis, Gregory. 1997. "A Defense of the Drama of Quotidian Life: Leave Ozzie and Harriet Alone." *New York Times Magazine* (January 19):40. For a more problematic analysis, see Joslyn, James and Pendleton, John. 1973. "The Adventures Of Ozzie And Harriet." *Journal of Popular Culture* 7(1): 23-41; Holmes, John R. 1989. "The Wizardry of Ozzie: Breaking Character in Early Television." *Journal of Popular Culture* 23(2): 93-102.

7. *Here Come the Nelsons,* dir. Frederick De Cordova (Universal, 1952). Nevertheless, a hint of his later gender transgression occurs when Ricky asks, "Do you think I'll grow up to be like Dad?" and David quips, "No, I think you're more like Mom."

8. But his biographer notes that he was "painfully shy" around girls, often code for "not particularly interested in girls," and that his most intimate companions throughout his life were men. Selvin, Joel. 1990. *Ricky Nelson: Idol for a Generation*. Chicago: Contemporary Books: 46-54; 63; 152.

9. Only slightly more remarkable is a dream sequence in "Tutti-Frutti Ice Cream" (December 1957), in which Harriett sings "Goody Goody" to Ozzie, chiding him for leaving her for another boy!

10. *The Girl Next Door,* dir. Richard Sale (20th Century Fox, 1953). His Dad, Dan Dailey, agrees, but the moment Billy goes upstairs to bed, he changes his tune: "I'd rather have a gal than a pal—anytime!"

11. Denis, Christopher Paul, and Michael Denis. 1992. *Favorite Families of TV.* New York: Citadel, 39.

12. Goldrup, Tom, and Jim Goldrup. 2002. *Growing Up on the Set: Interviews with 39 Former Child Actors of Classic Film and Television.* Jefferson, NC: McFarland; Billy Gray official Web site <http://www.billygray.com/>.

13. I am not aware of any published pro- or antigay statements from Billy Gray. After retiring from acting, he became a motorcycle racer and invented a new type of guitar pick. He has been married and divorced twice.

14. The lyrics never appeared on the show, but they included an odd gender-bending image of a "plastic clown in a wedding gown dancing with Raggedy Anne." Is this an image of a lesbian wedding, or is the clown a transvestite?

15. "Come On-a My House" (1951), words and music by William Saroyan and Ross Bagsadarian.

16. Mathers, Jerry, with Herb Fagen. 1998. *And Jerry Mathers As The Beaver.* New York: Berkeley Press, 90.

17. Ibid., 111.

18. Stephen Talbot, today a documentary filmmaker and the producer of *Frontline* on PBS, reminisces about the series and his later experiences in the counterculture of the 1960s. Available online <http://www.salon.com/aug97/mothers/beaver970822.html>.

19. Sidekicks of any sort were rare in nuclear family sitcoms before the 1980s. Teenagers usually had different best friends in every episode calling for them. Wally on *Leave It to Beaver* may be an exception, but Eddie Haskell was more of a nemesis than a sidekick.

20. Denver, Bob. 1993. *Gilligan, Maynard, and Me.* New York: Citadel Press, 16, 48.

21. The producers originally planned to transform *Dobie Gillis* into an army-humor series, but the ratings proved disastrous, so Dobie and Maynard came home and spent their last two seasons in college.

Chapter 3

1. Robert J. Corber. 1997. *Homosexuality in Cold War America: Resistance and the Crisis of Masculinity.* Durham, NC: Duke UP, 17.

2. Acland, Charles R. 1995. *Youth, Murder, Spectacle: The Cultural Politics of "Youth in Crisis."* Boulder: Westview, 120-123; cf. White, Armond. 1985. "Kidpix." *Film Comment 21*(4): 9-15; Doherty, Thomas. 1988. *Teenagers & Teenpics: The*

Juvenalization of American Movies in the 1950's. Boston: Unwin Hyman; Rapping, Elaine. 1987. "Hollywood's Youth Cult Films." *Cineaste 16*: 14-19.

3. Bloch, Herbert, and Arthur Niederhoffer. 1958. *The Gang: A Study in Adolescent Behavior.* New York: Philosophical Library, 104.

4. Freidenberg, Edgar. 1959. the Vanishing Adolescent. New York: Dell.

5. Manso, Peter. 1994. *Brando: The Biography.* New York: Hyperion, 162-163 et seq. Other biographies that allude to Brando's bisexuality include McCann, Graham. 1993. *Rebel Males: Clift, Brando and Dean.* New York: Rutgers UP, 1993; Schickel, Richard. 2000. *Brando: A Life in Our Times.* New York: Thunder's Mouth Press.

6. Manso, *Brando,* 161; cf. Manso, Peter. 2003. *P'Town: Art, Sex, and Money on the Outer Cape.* New York: Scribner, 31, 65.

7. Schickel, *Brando,* 191; McCann, *Rebel Marks,* 106, 51; Jarman, Derek. 1994. *At Your Own Risk: A Saint's Testament.* New York: Overlook Press, 55.

8. Ramaker, Micha. 2000. *Dirty Pictures: Tom of Finland, Masculinity, and Homosexuality.* New York: St. Martin's Press, 3-4.

9. McCann, *Rebel Males,* 106, 51.

10. *The Wild One,* dir. Laszlo Benedek (Columbia, 1953).

11. Dictionary of Mountain Bike Slang <http://world.std.com/~jimf/biking/slang.html>.

12. Stewart Stern wrote the screenplay based on a previous version by Irving Shulman, but never saw the original treatment by Nicholas Ray, even though Ray won the nomination for "best story" Oscar.

13. See Castiglia, Christopher. 1990. "Rebel Without a Closet." pp. 207-221 in Joseph A. Boone and Michael Cadden, eds., *Engendering Men: The Question of Male Feminist Criticism.* New York: Routledge; Simmons, Jerold. 1995. "The Censoring of *Rebel Without a Cause.*" *Journal of Popular Film and Television 23*(2): 56-63. Critics are still, of course, quite capable of ignoring it: note the complete heterosexualization of the movie in May, Kirse Granat. 2002. *Golden State, Golden Youth: The California Image in Popular Culture, 1955-66.* Chapel Hill: U. of North Carolina P, 68-72.

14. Kashner, Sam, and Jennifer MacNair. 2002. *The Bad and the Beautiful: Hollywood in the Fifties.* New York: Norton, 103.

15. Hadleigh, Boze. 1986. *Conversations with My Elders.* New York: St. Martin's Press, 21; McCann, *Rebel Males,* 151; Jeffers, H. Paul. 2000. *Sal Mineo: His Life, Murder, and Mystery.* New York: Carroll & Graf, 30.

16. Jeffers, *Sal Mineo,* 26.

17. McKuen, Rod. 1967. *Listen to the Warm.* New York: Random House.

18. Afterward his discovery of girls remained intact for *Summer Love* (1958) and two schoolboy small-town romances, before he moved on to adult roles.

19. McGee, Mark Thomas. 1990. *The Rock and Roll Movie Encyclopedia of the 1950's.* Jefferson, NC: McFarland, 1990; cf. Brian's Drive-In, <http://www. brians driveintheater.com/johnashley.html>; and Silver Screen Heroes, <http://www.jcs-group. com/oldwest/silver/oklahomacowboy1926-.html>.

20. William Castle's TV series was an anthology, with no recurring characters, so John Ashley could not have landed a starring role. He probably appeared in the pilot episode, about a young cadet barred from the swim team after an injury, but he is not listed in most episode guides. See Alexander, Sherman G. 2002. "Men of

Annapolis: Good Show?" in *Naval History,* <http://www.usni.org/NavalHistory/Articles02/NHalexander04.htm>.

21. Numbers include "Born to Rock," "Pickin' Up the Wrong Chicken," "The Hangman," "The Net," "Seriously in Love," and "The Cry of the Wild Goose." He seems to have been more popular in Europe than in the United States; a 2-CD collection of his hits was released in 2001 by Hydra.

Chapter 4

1. Arkoff, Samuel Z., with Richard Trubo. 1992. *Flying Through Hollywood by the Seat of My Pants.* New York: Birch Lane Press, 51.

2. Twitchell, James B. 1993. *Dreadful Pleasures: An Anatomy of Modern Horror.* Oxford: Oxford UP.

3. Benshoff, Harry. 1997. *Monsters in the Closet: Homosexuality and the Horror Film.* Manchester: Manchester UP, 144; Berenstein, Rhona J. 1996. *Attack of the Leading Ladies: Gender, Sexuality, and Spectacle in Classic Horror Cinema.* New York: Columbia UP.

4. Lilley, Jessie. 1995. "How to Make a Monster Movie: An Interview with Herman Cohen." *Scarlet Street 17:* 65-71, 108.

5. Biskind, Peter. 1983, 2000. *Seeing Is Believing: How Hollywood Taught Us to Stop Worrying and Love the Fifties.* New York: Henry Holt, 220.

6. Oddly, the film was released in France under the title *Des filles pour Frankenstein* (Girls for Frankenstein). Evidently the creation was produced to acquire dates for Dr. Frankenstein?

7. In 1958, ten of thirty-eight; in 1959, nine of twenty-seven. Source: Warren, Bill. 1997. *Keep Watching the Skies! American Science Fiction Movies of the Fifties.* 2 volumes. Jefferson, NC: McFarland.

8. Watson, Elena M. 1991. *TV Horror Hosts.* Jefferson, NC: McFarland; Skal, David J. 1993. *The Monster Show: A Cultural History of Horror.* New York: Faber & Faber, 229-233; Diehl, Digby. 1996. *Tales from the Crypt: The Official Archive.* New York: St. Martin's Press, 28; Otfinoski, Steve. 2000. *The Golden Age of Novelty Songs.* New York: Broadway Books, 87-95.

9. In real life, Hall's heterosexual interest seems rather more than usually exuberant. He has two screenwriting credits, including *The Magic Spectacles* (1961), about eyeglasses that see under women's clothes. After retiring from his acting career, he became a professional pilot, world traveler, and all-around adventurer. In 2001 he published *The Apsara Jet,* an old-fashioned "men's adventure" novel about jet pilots, drug lords, and "sex-crazed native girls" in Cambodia.

10. Teenage Monster Movies, <http://www.geocities.com/Hollywood/Mansion/5272/index.html>.

Chapter 5

1. As often happens, the name for the phenomenon arose in retrospect. Rick Nelson sang about being a "Teenage Idol" in 1962, and the January 1964 issue of *Teen* magazine has an article about *teenager idols,* but the term *teen idol* was not common until the Bobby Sherman-David Cassidy era in the early 1970s.

2. Or at least they pretended to be. Bobby Vinton was twenty-seven when he hit the charts, Pat Boone twenty-two, Elvis twenty-one, Dion twenty, and Frankie Avalon nineteen. Paul Anka, Fabian, Ricky Nelson, and Bobby Rydell were still in high school when they began, but they continued to pose as "teenagers in love" until they were nearly thirty.

3. On the newsstands between 1959 and 1963: *Dig, Flip, Movie Dream Guys, Movie Teen Illustrated, Record Hop Stars, Seventeen, Sixteen, Teen, Teen Life, Teen Pin-ups, Teenage, Teenager Parade, Teen Screen,* and *Teen World*.

4. Male pop soloists marketed to teenagers, with at least four songs in the American Top 40 between 1956 and 1963: Paul Anka, Frankie Avalon, Pat Boone, Johnny Burnette, Jimmy Clanton, Johnny Crawford, Bobby Darin, James Darren, Dion, Fabian, Ricky Nelson, Gene Pitney, Elvis Presley, Bobby Rydell, Tommy Sands, Del Shannon, John Tillotson, Bobby Vee, Bobby Vinton.

5. The nineteen major teen idols placed 263 songs in the Top-40 between 1956 and 1963, but twenty of them, such as Fabian's "This Friendly World" (1959) and Bobby Darin's "Artificial Flowers" (1960), were about God, country, or social issues, with no allusion to either homo-romance or hetero-romance.

6. Duffet, Mark. 2001. "Caught in a trap? Beyond pop theory's 'butch' construction of male Elvis fans." *Popular Music 20*(3): 395-408.

7. In "Watching Elvis: The Male Rock Star As Object of the Gaze." pp. 124-143 in Joel Foreman, ed., *The Other Fifties: Interrogating Midcentury American Icons.* (Urbana: U. of Illinois Press, 1997), David R. Shumway argues that Elvis juxtaposed masculine and feminine sexual codes deliberately to appeal to both sexes (and, one would assume, all sexual orientations).

8. See Kennedy, Gordon. 1998. *Children of the Sun.* Ojal, CA: Nivaria Press.

9. Fathers may have a Freudian rationale for forbidding their daughters from participating in teenage romance. In Bobby Rydell's "18 Yellow Roses" (1963), the singer receives the flowers and a card indicating that his girl "belongs to another," even though "I always thought you would be true." He insists that he still loves her anyway, and he only hopes that her new boyfriend will treat her properly. Only in the last line do we discover that the singer is her father!

10. Kohler, Frederick. 1957, 2001. *Gidget.* New York: Berkeley, 10.

11. Alfred Hitchcock used the term "maguffin" for a goal or object of desire that propels the action in a movie. The specific nature of the maguffin is irrelevant: it might be stolen microfilm, stolen jewels, or an attempt to assassinate an ambassador. Maltby, Richard. 2003. *Hollywood Cinema.* Oxford: Blackwell, 479.

Chapter 6

1. May, Kirse Granat. 2002. *Golden State, Golden Youth: The California Image in Popular Culture, 1955-66.* Chapel Hill: U. of North Carolina P, 53.

2. Griffin, Annie. 1993. "The Blondest Thing on the Beach." *Sight and Sound 3*(8): 35-36; Morris, Gary. 1993. "Beyond the Beach." *Journal of Popular Film and Television 21*(1): 2-11; Rutsky, R. L. 1999. "Surfing the Other." *Film Quarterly 52*(1): 12; Caine, Andrew, and Gary Morris. 2002. "Beyond the Beach: AIP's Beach Party Movies." *Bright Lights Film Journal,* Vol. 21. <http://www.brightlightsfilm.com/21/21_beach.html>.

3. Arkoff, Samuel Z. with Richard Trulo. 1992. *Flying Through Hollywood by the Seat of My Pants*. New York: Birch Lane Press, 133.

4. Coincidentally, it features an obviously gay couple, Uncle Sid (gay actor Paul Lynde) and Uncle Woody (burlesque comedian Woody Woodbury), who share an apartment, a bedroom, and a pet sheepdog.

5. In the 1997 remake, Christina Ricci has no boyfriend, nor does she express any interest in boys.

6. Cohan, Steven. 1997. *Masked Men: Masculinity and Movies in the Fifties*. Bloomington: Indiana UP, 175.

7. There is little biographical information available. See Weaver, Tom. 1997. *Return of the B Science Fiction and Horror Heroes: The Mutant Melding of Two Volumes of Classic Interviews*. Jefferson, NC: McFarland, 37-46; Ray, Fred Olen. "Remembering John Ashley." <http://www.bmonster.com/scifi15.html>; and the interview with his wife, Jan Ashley, on the *Beast of the Yellow Night* DVD from Ventura Distribution.

8. Hickman, Dwayne, and Joan Roberts Hickman. 1994. *Forever Dobie: The Many Lives of Dwayne Hickman*. New York: Carol Publishing, 58. In real life, both are probably heterosexual. Frankie Avalon has been married to the same woman since 1962, and Dwayne Hickman has been married three times, most recently for twenty years.

9. *The Wild Weird World of Dr. Goldfoot*, which appeared in November 1965, substituted Tommy Kirk and Aron Kincaid for Dwayne and Frankie. In 1966, Fabian tried his hand in an Italian-made sequel, *Dr. Goldfoot and the Sex Bombs*.

10. Valley, Richard. 1993. "Just an Average Joe (Hardy): An Interview with Tommy Kirk." *Scarlet Street 10*: 60-69, 97.

11. I have not been able to establish Jody's sexual identity or marital status. In the 1970s he retired from acting to manage his father's ranch in New Mexico.

12. In Valley, "Just an Average Joe," Tommy Kirk notes that of all the beach movie regulars he worked with, only Aron Kincaid became a friend. They still keep in close contact.

13. Though he topped the charts with "Girls Were Made to Love" in 1962, Eddie Hodges never displayed any heterosexual interest in his movie roles. He did, however, display girl-craziness in several television guest roles. Today he is a mental health counselor in his native Mississippi.

Chapter 7

1. Boone, Pat. *Twixt Twelve and Twenty*. New York: Prentice-Hall, 1958.

2. Allyn, David. 2001. *Make Love, Not War: The Sexual Revolution: An Unfettered History*. New York: Routledge; D'Emilio, John. 1997. *Intimate Matters*. Chicago: U of Chicago P; Radner, Hilary, and Moya Luckett, eds. 1999. *Swinging Single: Representing Sexuality in the 60's*. Minneapolis: U. of Minnesota P.

3. *Dharma and Greg*, about a hippie-establishment romance, aired from 1997 to 2001. The hippie, Dharma (Jenna Elfman), must have been born around 1975, yet still she dotes on tie-die and chakras as if it is eternally 1967.

4. McRuer, Robert. 2001. "Gay Gatherings: Reimagining the Counterculture." pp. 215-240 in Peter Braunstein, ed., *Imagine Nation: The American Counterculture of the 1960's and 70's.* New York: Routledge.

5. Fonda, Peter. 1998. *Don't Tell Dad: A Memoir.* New York: Hyperion Books. He has also never played an openly gay character, or even appeared in any movie with gay characters except for the recent documentary *Laramie Project* (2003).

6. Peter Fonda, speaking in "The Making of Easy Rider" on the *Easy Rider* DVD.

7. They were actually to be called Captain America and Bucky, until Marvel Comics threatened to sue. The characters are allowed to call themselves Captain America and Bucky in jest, as long as these are not *really* their names.

8. From "Little Boxes" (1962) words and music by Malvina Reynolds, a favorite of folksinger Pete Seeger:

> And the boys go into business
> And marry and raise a family
> In boxes made of ticky tacky
> And they all look just the same.

9. Roger Ebert, "The Graduate." *Chicago Sun Times* (1997, March 3).

10. Late in the series, his character David Collins tells his gal pal, "I dreamed about you in your green dress." She replies "Lots of boys dream about me," assuming that he has a heterosexual crush, but actually the green dress foreshadows their upcoming possession by the ghosts of teenagers from the 1840s.

11. Virtually every pop culture friendship or antagonistic relationship has been subject to slashing. There are a few female slash stories, but male slash predominates.

Chapter 8

1. *Tiger Beat Super Special* 1.6 (1976). The Willie Aames quote comes from the Gossip section (p. 49), Leif Garrett from "Leif's Private Room" (p. 61) and Henry Winkler, "Henry's Special Childhood" (p. 66).

2. "Paul Glaser: His Private Feelings About David Soul!" (1976, July). *Tiger Beat,* 12:10-68.

3. Steve Guttenberg is extremely gay-friendly, and therefore probably straight. Clark Brandon was subject to constant gay rumors in the 1970s, but he has never publicly stated a sexual identity.

4. It has also been covered by Jody Miller and Jane Oliver. The Pointer Sisters changed it slightly to "He's So Shy."

5. Sue Reilly, (1978, November 20). "Nifty Kristy McNichol." *People.*

6. Actors in ice-skating movies can rarely play convincing hetero-romance. Teen idol Robby Benson would try the same thing in *Ice Castles,* a few months later, with equally tepid results.

7. The Four Seasons, "December 1963" (1976).

8. Season number one, four of sixteen episodes; Season number two, six of twenty-three; Season number three, five of twenty-four; Season number four, five of

twenty-five; Season number five, six of twenty-seven; Season number six, five of twenty-seven; Season number seven, four of twenty-five. Jokes, casual references, and interaction with girls incidental to the plot are not counted.

9. Fonzie did get a steady girlfriend in Season number ten, long after Richie was gone.

10. Doty, Alexander. 1993. *Making Things Perfectly Queer: Interpreting Mass Culture.* Minneapolis: U of Minnesota P.

11. The homoromantic subtext is parodied in a 1995 episode of *The Nanny,* in which David L. Lander plays the landlord at a gay apartment complex who is celebrating his twentieth anniversary with "Leonard" (i.e., Lenny). This would place the beginning of their relationship in 1975, a year *before Laverne and Shirley* premiered.

Chapter 9

1. Undergraduate business majors: 142,000 in 1975-1976, 237,000 in 1985-1986. Social science majors: 126,000 in 1975-1976, 94,000 in 1985-1986. Source: *Digest of Educational Statistics.* <http://nces.ed.gov/programs/digest/d02/tables/dt252.asp>.

2. *Pillow Talk* (1959), *Lover Come Back* (1961), *Send Me No Flowers* (1964).

3. Sturken, Marita. 1997. *Tangled Memories: The Vietnam War, the AIDS Epidemic, and the Politics of Remembrance.* Berkeley: U of California P, 157.

4. Number of nude scenes featuring male actors playing teenagers: between 1975 and 1979, twenty-two of 317 (7 percent); between 1980 and 1984, sixty-seven of 355 (19 percent). Source: *Movie Buff Checklist* <http://www.hunkvideo.com>.

5. The *After School* specials were sixty-minute drama (rarely comedies), generally shown on television at 4 or 5 p.m., about teenagers facing everyday problems and conflicts.

6. In real life, Baio was rather more hetero-horny than most teen idols, propositioning, rudely or not, most of the women on the set. Guest star Samantha Fox reminisces: "Every time I was about to do a take he'd whisper, 'What's it like when you're taking your clothes off?' I felt like telling him to get lost. Another time he smooched up to me and said, 'I've often wondered what it would be like to kiss you.' I turned round and said, 'You're going to have to wonder, aren't you?' " Quoted on *Sitcoms Online,* <http://www.sitcomsonline.com/charlesincharge.htm>.

7. Rieser, K. 2001. "Masculinity and Monstrosity: Characterization and Identification in the Slasher Film." *Men and Masculinities* 3.4: 370-392; Clover, Carol. 1992. *Men, Women, and Chainsaws: Gender in the Modern Horror Film.* Princeton: Princeton UP; Heba, Gary. 1995. "Everyday Nightmares: The Rhetoric of Social Horror in the Nightmare on Elm Street Series." *Journal of Popular Film and Television 23*(3): 106-15; Sharrett, Christopher. 1996. "The Horror Film in Neoconservative Culture." pp. 253-278 in Barry Keith Grant, ed., *The Dread of Difference: Gender and the Horror Film.* Austin: U of Texas P; Dika, Vera. 1990. *Games of Terror: Halloween, Friday the 13th, and the Films of the Stalker Cycle.* Rutherford, NJ: Fairleigh Dickinson UP.

8. Between 1978 and 1985, seventy-four full-length horror movies starring teenagers were released in the United States. 36 percent (twenty-seven) feature psycho-slashers, and 64 percent (forty-seven) other threats.

9. Excluding characters who are not teenagers and those killed by someone other than the main psycho-killer.

10. But it's a ruse: the moment a sobbing Hoax collapses into his arms, Spike throws him out the window.

11. Women masquerade as men in *Graduation Day* and *Friday the 13th;* a boy masquerades as a girl (or believes he really is a girl) in *Sleepaway Camp,* and an offscreen member of the freak-show family in *Hell Night* is "so hideously deformed" that the gender is not instantly discernable.

12. Tom Simone, director of *Hell Night,* did most of his previous work in gay porn *(Swap Meat, Heavy Equipment, Hot Truckin').*

13. An exception, *Sleepaway Camp* (1984) contains about thirty antigay epithets, plus a scene of the killer as a child traumatized by the sight of two men in bed.

Chapter 10

1. Many scholars and entertainment reporters define the Brat Pack as the much smaller group surrounding the Sheen-Estivez brothers, who got into trouble together, but I am using the term to mean all male actors between the ages of sixteen and twenty-one in 1983 who appeared in five or more feature-length theatrical movies between 1983 and 1989: Matthew Broderick, Nicholas Cage, Tom Cruise, Jon Cryer, John Cusack, Patrick Dempsey, Matt Dillon, Robert Downey Jr., Anthony Edwards, Emilio Estevez, Michael J. Fox, Zack Galligan, Jason Gedrick, Anthony Michael Hall, C. Thomas Howell, Rob Lowe, Ralph Macchio, Andrew McCarthy, Judd Nelson, Sean Penn, Charlie Sheen, Casey Siemaszko, Eric Stolz, Kiefer Sutherland.

2. Matt Dillon and Rob Lowe were the darlings of the *Teen Beat* set, and Ralph Macchio and Michael J. Fox got some attention when they were on television, but one has to search to find an article about Robert Downey Jr., Andrew McCarthy, Charlie Sheen, or Kiefer Sutherland.

3. Near the end of the era, Matthew Broderick played gay in *Torch Song Trilogy* (1988), Patrick Dempsey in *In a Shallow Grave* (1988), and Eric Stoltz bisexual in *Haunted Summer* (1988). A few others played gay in the 1990s and 2000s.

4. A number of 1980's movies feature Emilio Estevez throwing around antigay slurs while bonding with a baby-faced buddy who can't keep his eyes off his muscles. See *Tex* (1982), *The Outsiders* (1983), *That Was Then, This Is Now* (1985), *Wisdom* (1987), and *Young Guns* (1988).

5. The exchange is cut from television broadcasts, but because Jerry is searching for his stash of marijuana as the talk, not because of any fear of offending gay people.

6. Even Hall's military-school bully brother, played by Bill Paxton, fails to call him anything antigay. When he discovers Hall wearing women's underwear, he exclaims "That's a severe behavioral disorder!" but he is just feigning shock to extort hush money from his brother.

7. The short, scruffy-looking Curtis Armstrong was thirty years old in 1983, almost a decade older than the Brat Packers, but he appeared with them in eight movies between 1983 and 1989, usually as a teen nerd's best friend. At the same time he was starring with Bruce Willis and Cybill Shepherd in *Moonlighting* (1985-1989).

8. He also has an eight-second scene earlier on the slopes.

9. Lambda is a gay symbol, of course, and the fraternity logo, three lambdas in a triangle, reflects yet another gay symbol, the pink triangle. But no one points this out in the film. Perhaps it is a coincidence.

10. The original script had Joel losing his Princeton admission, and of course that would make far more sense.

11. In a parody on the animated *Futurama,* delivery boy Fry goes back to the 1950s, discovers that the boy who would become his grandfather was gay, and unwittingly sleeps with his girlfriend, thus becoming his own progenitor.

Chapter 11

1. Stuever, Hank, "The Bomb with a Loaded Message for Gays in America." *Washington Post* (October 27, 2001): C01.

2. On an April 2002 episode of *Will and Grace,* Will's cousin is getting married, and her fiancé asks for advice:

BOB: I need a woman's opinion.
WILL: Sure, I'd be happy to help.

3. Rosie O'Donnell made headlines when she noted that she was attracted to Tom Cruise as a teenager; when asked how she could then be a lesbian, she replied that it was "only a teenage crush," part of what being a teenager means, and irrelevant to her adult identity. Ellen DeGeneres's character Ellen Morgan bonds with her girlfriend's teenage daughter, who has a crush on a boy, by saying "I was a teenager once myself, you know."

4. Adam's apparent age at his creation comes from Jewish legend.

5. Even the independent gay cinema usually treats the couple as unique, negotiating the only same-sex romance that has ever existed in all the history of the world. In *Get Real,* for instance, no one ever acknowledges the existence of gay youth groups, social clubs, pride festivals, churches, newspapers, magazines, or even gay bars. *Nico and Dani* and *Come Undone* go even further, refusing to use the g-word lest anyone realize that boys who fall in love with each other have a name.

6. Plummer, David. 2001. "The Quest for Modern Manhood: Masculine Stereotypes, Peer Culture and the Social Significance of Homophobia." *Journal of Adolescence 24*: 15-33; Human Rights Watch. 2001. *Hatred in the Hallways: Violence and Discrimination Against Lesbian, Gay, Bisexual and Transgender Students in U.S. Schools.* New York: Human Rights Watch. Hostile Hallways, a 2001 report by the American Association of University Women, notes that 73 percent of students surveyed would be upset if someone called them gay or lesbian, but adamantly refuses believe that any of the students might actually be gay or lesbian, or to address the conditions under which the terms are considered insults. The goal is to end the

accusations, not to suggest that maybe gay men and lesbians aren't the worst people in the world.

7. "Saved by the Bell," *E! True Hollywood Story*. Aired December 1, 2002.

8. Lisa does mention in one episode that her ancestors were slaves, so she must be aware that she is African American, but she never mentions any distinctive historical or cultural apparatus. A. C. (Albert Clifford) Slater was evidently written Anglo, but in the spin-off *Saved by the Bell: The College Years*, he acknowledges his Hispanic ancestry.

9. *Blossom, Boy Meets World, Breaker High, California Dreams, Clarissa Explains It All, City Guys, Clueless, Even Stevens, Hang Time, Hey Dude, Lizzie McGuire, Sabrina the Teenage Witch, Saved by the Bell: The New Class, Sister Sister, Smart Guy, Social Studies, Step by Step, Sweet Valley High, Teen Angel, U.S.A. High, Welcome Freshmen.*

10. Monson, Sarah. "Pop Opera Focuses on 'Bare' Emotions." *UCLA Daily Bruin* (October 11, 2000): 5.

11. Of course, it may be a directorial decision. "Dream Date" was directed by Gail Mancuso, who also directed gay-friendly episodes of *Ellen, Roseanne*, and *The Nanny* and probably knows that some straight people are not homophobic, while "Sabrina the Teenage Boy" was directed by Peter Baldwin, a veteran of forty years on TV who got his start on *The Andy Griffith Show*, who may have thought a horrified double-take the most likely response.

12. One can't imagine that they have much in common, but since they are the only two gay people in town, they must settle for what they can get.

13. Though she decides that she is really straight after all, the episode was nominated for a GLAAD award for its nonpredatory portrayal of the lesbian writer.

14. Alyssa Lee (2004). Review of *Dawson's Creek: The Complete Third Season* DVD. *Entertainment Weekly* 771/772 (June 25-July 4): 145.

15. 1985: Billy Zabka, Brian Bloom, Danny Nucci, Glenn Scarpelli, Jack Wagner, Joey Lawrence, John Candy, Ken Olandt, Marc Price, Michael J. Fox, Noah Hathaway, Ricky Schroeder, Rob Lowe. 1995: Brad Renfro, Chris O'Donnell, Devon Sawa, Elijah Wood, Joseph Mazzello, Joshua Jackson, Joshua Taylor Thomas, Keanu Reeves, Matthew Lawrence, Paul Sutura, Rider Strong, Thomas Ian Nicholas, Wil Horneff. When the over-thirty outliers, thirty-five-year-old John Candy and thirty-one-year-old Keanu Reeves, were removed, the average age dropped to 18.6 in 1985 and 15.7 in 1995.

16. When *American Pie* (1999) unexpectedly made $105 million and ranked number twenty at the box office, a new rash of older teen-themed movies appeared, but none of them did as well (except for *American Pie 2*). *Dude, Where's My Car* (2000) ranked number fifty-four, *The Skulls* (2000) number seventy-one, *Orange County* (2002) number sixty, *Clockstoppers* (2002) number seventy-three. Tobey Maguire plays a high school Spiderman in the top-grossing movie of 2002, but it hardly counts as teen-themed.

17. In one episode, he casually mentions that he has a date, but he doesn't specify with whom, and it is never mentioned again.

18. We are still waiting for a gay character named Doug or Steve.

Index

Order a copy of this book with this form or online at:
http://www.haworthpress.com/store/product.asp?sku=5484

QUEERING TEEN CULTURE
All-American Boys and Same-Sex Desire
in Film and Television

_____in hardbound at $34.95 (ISBN-13: 978-1-56023-348-0; ISBN-10: 1-56023-348-6)

_____in softbound at $16.95 (ISBN-13: 978-1-56023-349-7; ISBN-10: 1-56023-349-4)

Or order online and use special offer code HEC25 in the shopping cart.

COST OF BOOKS_____

POSTAGE & HANDLING_____
(US: $4.00 for first book & $1.50
for each additional book)
(Outside US: $5.00 for first book
& $2.00 for each additional book)

SUBTOTAL_____

IN CANADA: ADD 7% GST_____

STATE TAX_____
(NJ, NY, OH, MN, CA, IL, IN, PA, & SD
residents, *add appropriate local sales tax)*

FINAL TOTAL_____
(If paying in Canadian funds,
convert using the current
exchange rate, UNESCO
coupons welcome)

☐ **BILL ME LATER:** (Bill-me option is good on
US/Canada/Mexico orders only; not good to
jobbers, wholesalers, or subscription agencies.)
☐ Check here if billing address is different from
shipping address and attach purchase order and
billing address information.

Signature_____

☐ **PAYMENT ENCLOSED: $**_____

☐ **PLEASE CHARGE TO MY CREDIT CARD.**

☐ Visa ☐ MasterCard ☐ AmEx ☐ Discover
☐ Diner's Club ☐ Eurocard ☐ JCB

Account # _____

Exp. Date_____

Signature_____

Prices in US dollars and subject to change without notice.

NAME_____

INSTITUTION_____

ADDRESS_____

CITY_____

STATE/ZIP_____

COUNTRY_____ COUNTY (NY residents only)_____

TEL_____ FAX_____

E-MAIL_____

May we use your e-mail address for confirmations and other types of information? ☐ Yes ☐ No
We appreciate receiving your e-mail address and fax number. Haworth would like to e-mail or fax special
discount offers to you, as a preferred customer. **We will never share, rent, or exchange your e-mail address
or fax number.** We regard such actions as an invasion of your privacy.

Order From Your Local Bookstore or Directly From
The Haworth Press, Inc.
10 Alice Street, Binghamton, New York 13904-1580 • USA
TELEPHONE: 1-800-HAWORTH (1-800-429-6784) / Outside US/Canada: (607) 722-5857
FAX: 1-800-895-0582 / Outside US/Canada: (607) 771-0012
E-mail to: orders@haworthpress.com

For orders outside US and Canada, you may wish to order through your local
sales representative, distributor, or bookseller.
For information, see http://haworthpress.com/distributors

(Discounts are available for individual orders in US and Canada only, not booksellers/distributors.)
PLEASE PHOTOCOPY THIS FORM FOR YOUR PERSONAL USE.
http://www.HaworthPress.com   BOF06